THE
PICTURE BOOK
OF
ANNUALS

THE
PICTURE BOOK
OF
ANNUALS

ARNO AND IRENE NEHRLING

ARCO PUBLISHING COMPANY INC.
219 Park Avenue South, New York, N.Y. 10003

First Arco Printing, 1977

Published by Arco Publishing Company, Inc.
219 Park Avenue South, New York, N.Y. 10003
by arrangement with Hearthside Press, Inc.

Library of Congress Cataloging in Publication Data

Nehrling, Arno.
  The picture book of annuals.

  Includes index.
  1. Annuals (Plants) I. Nehrling, Irene, joint author.
II. Title.
SB422.N44 1977   635.9'31   76-45745
ISBN 0-668-04158-7

Printed in the United States of America

Dedicated to
Henry Nehrling (1853-1929)

IN APPRECIATION

We are grateful to the busy seedsmen who cooperated wholeheartedly in answering questions and supplying photographs for this book. Their recommendations—of most important (or least expendable) annuals, of little known but meritorious kinds, of those easiest to grow from seed, and of annuals most disease-free—were valuable and practical. Through their answers, we are able to present the annual story as it unfolds in the varied climates of our country. In addition, our thanks go to W. Ray Hastings, Executive Secretary-Treasurer, All-America Selections, for much helpful information.

The seed companies to whom we are indebted include: Asgrow Seed Co., George J. Ball Co., Bodger Seeds, W. Atlee Burpee Co., Ferry-Morse Seed Co., Herbst Bros. Seedsmen, Mandeville and King Co., Northrup, King and Co., Pan-American Seed Co., George W. Park Seed Co., Pearce Seed Co., Vaughan's Seed Co. and Waller Flowerseed Co.

Carlton B. Lees, Executive Secretary of the Massachusetts Horticultural Society and director of its publications, which include the magazine *Horticulture*, deserves special mention. The staff members of the magazine and of the society's library cooperated willingly and generously. Muriel C. Crossman, head librarian, and Elizabeth Higgins, research librarian, were especially helpful. A most heartfelt and warm "thank you" goes to Richard C. Hands, an assistant editor of *Horticulture*, for help in so many, many ways.

Professor Robert P. Meahl, Head of Ornamental Horticulture, Pennsylvania State University, was our advisor on the dictionary, the A to Z of annuals; and Ruth and Percy Merry, experienced and knowledgeable gardeners in our home town, read the material pertaining to the culture and care of annuals. Warren D. Whitcomb, recently retired professor of Entomology, University of Massachusetts, Waltham Field Station, offered his expert advice on controlling insect pests and fungus diseases. Dr. Christos C. Mpelkas, plant physiologist, read the section on seedlings grown under lights. Our good landscape friend of long standing, Harold D. Stevenson, Marshfield, Mass. drew some plans for the use of annuals to show how one puts garden ideas on paper. Dr. Richard A. Howard, Director of the Arnold Arboretum, Jamaica Plain, Mass., read the list of annuals that may be injurious.

Charlotte Bowden, who illustrated our other books, was unable to do the sketches for this one but we were fortunate to find Emma Crafts Earley of Beverly, Mass., an excellent illustrator. It was a pleasure to work with her. John Bodger, President of Bodger Seeds, Ltd., of El Monte, Calif., sent us many of the photographs used in Part I. Paul Genereux took many of the pictures used throughout. Betty Kelly Mellett typed the manuscript. To all of the above who helped us in the preparation of this book, our sincere thanks.

We are deeply indebted to Nedda Casson Anders, our editor, for her suggestions, ideas, encouragement, and enthusiastic support over the years.

                                        Arno and Irene Nehrling

Needham Heights
Massachusetts

CONTENTS

Why Grow Annuals

We begin our book with the story of the gardener who considered world conditions so bad that he would plant only annuals. Whether or not the story is apocryphal, the fact is that even the most pessimistic gardener can count on annuals to bloom quickly, even in the worst circumstances. For this asset alone, they would be a tremendously important group of plants, but annuals have many other virtues:

Maximum color. Many annuals produce masses of bloom and vivid color, while others such as torenia, nigella and Shirley poppies provide more subtle harmonies. Annuals come in every color imaginable and such favorites as zinnias, marigolds and petunias run a wide color gamut. When spring bulbs and June perennials have finished flowering, annuals supply the principal color in the summer border. Placed advantageously, one can see and enjoy their color to the fullest all summer long.

Variety and interest. Varied shapes, sizes and height of flowers and of the plant itself bring contrast even to the garden planted only with annuals. Zinnias are an excellent example of great variety within just one genus, in height, flower size, petal formation and color.

Ease of cultivation. No plants are easier to grow. They are fun and easy for the beginner but also useful to the experienced gardener since many rare and unusual species and varieties are available to try. Many annuals such as cleome, nigella, nicotiana, calendula and bachelor's button have a tendency to self-sow, which makes them practically perennial in some gardens.

Economy. An inexpensive seed packet with its quick and abundant returns is one of the least expensive investments a homeowner can make. Practically no expense except labor is involved.

Maximum bloom. Under favorable conditions no other ornamentals bloom so profusely. Unsurpassed for their length of flowering, they prolong the blooming period in the garden. Most favorite annuals are enjoyed for this purpose, but some of the less common ones which bloom long are arctotis, emilia, oxypetalum and xanthisma.

Quantities of cut flowers. One of the rewards of growing annuals is the abundant supply of good flowers for cutting. The more you cut the more prolific the supply! It's convenient and fun to be able to decorate indoors with flowers cut from one's own beloved garden.

Solving problems. Nothing will fill in bare spots, such as open spaces between shrubs, places where dead plants have been removed, and other bare corners more quickly than annuals. Their roots are usually shallow so they can be planted among deeper-rooted perennials and bulbs to carry the landscape through the months when bulb foliage may look brown and perennial flowers may be scarce.

Easily changed gardens. With annuals the garden may be easily changed with each succeeding year. By using new colors and shifting clumps, an entirely new pattern of both form and color is possible each season. Shrubs remain the same, except for growing larger and perennials also are constant, at least for a few years, but an endless series of changes can be had with annuals.

The small garden. It is much easier to avoid monotony with annuals than with any other ornamental if the area is small. The possibilities are endless for selection of varieties in the size and color scaled to even the smallest garden. Here is where annuals really shine.

Pot plants. Many annuals are forced yearly by florists in greenhouses for cut flowers and as pot subjects. With adequate facilities and the proper know-how, amateurs too can grow annuals in the cool greenhouse, the sun-heated pit, and the artificially lighted basement. Plants so grown may be used to decorate the home. In window boxes and other containers for the porch or terrace they are invaluable during the summer months. Easily grown pot plants, properly scheduled or planned, can supply successive flowers the year round.

Annuals produce in a hurry. Growth is rapid and the results are a lifesaver for the homeowner who moves into a new, unlandscaped place and wants quick, temporary effects, until more permanent plant material can take over. A few annuals will bloom from seed in as little as six weeks and if started with purchased young plants, even faster. This is especially helpful for young couples who live in a house for only a short while and then move elsewhere. Such notably quick bloomers as annual baby's breath, marigolds and sweet alyssum have redeemed many a barren site.

Annuals are adaptable. Plant explorer, hybridist and seedman have cooperated to provide an annual for every garden need. Through selection and hybirdization, colors and forms of annuals from the world's far corners have been improved. These ready-in-a-year plants fill not only the quick-color spots, but also those with the most exacting requirements for landscape design. Annuals such as portulaca, nicotiana, poppies and petunias make ideal ground covers for dry, waste areas. Some will quickly cover sunny slopes; planted in broad drifts, they will smother the ground. Others make excellent temporary occupants for bare spots in the garden. There are useful climbers that will form a screen until slower perennials become established. Some annuals are invaluable as bedding or border plants, and as bulb covers, when planned for gradation in height, for harmony or contrasts in color. Some are delightful in the rock garden. Shade lovers such as balsam, browallia, impatiens and sweet alyssum may be planted under trees or in the open woods. Some will self-sow under favorable conditions and become more or less permanent. Many annuals possess a pleasing and delightful fragrance, notably the sweet pea, stock and mignonette. What more could one ask of a group of plants! Their rapid growth, prolific blooming, abundance of color all summer long, and low cost make annuals a must on every gardener's list.

Part I

The A to Z of Annuals

The A to Z of Annuals

An annual is a plant that lives for only one growing season. It sprouts from seed, grows, blooms, sets seed and then dies, all in one year. For this reason annuals depend entirely on their seeds for survival.

Normally a biennial is sown one season and blooms the following year while perennials should live at least three years or more. Some perennials, however, are grown in gardens as annuals or biennials. Through constant selection for a profusion of bloom and a resulting depletion of food reserves, many deteriorate quickly after their second year from seed. New strains have been developed which do better grown as annuals or biennials. Actually, annual, biennial and perennial habits are not entirely inherited but depend to a large degree upon their environment.

The terms "annual," "biennial" and "perennial" are merely terms of convenience with little botanical (or even horticultural) validity. For example, wallflowers and verbenas are treated as annuals in the North, yet in the South often behave as perennials, at least short-lived ones. Also many perennials and most biennials will bloom the first year if sown early indoors. In many gardens self-sowing nicotiana will prove more enduring than a delphinium or chrysanthemum. A gaillardia could be called an annual, biennial or perennial depending on the parentage and location where it is grown.

Some biennials have been included in this alphabetical list of annuals since the culture is so similar. Several short-lived perennials, best grown as annuals or biennials, have also been included. After the alphabetical listing, in Part II, you will find more detailed information as to seed-sowing, spacing, soil and care in general.

ABRONIA UMBELLATA—Sand Verbena. Four O'Clock Family.

Treated as an annual in the colder sections of the United States, since it flowers freely from seed the first year, this prostrate perennial is native to the California seacoast. Except in mild climates, it rarely survives the winter. It is much grown for its showy, small, fragrant rosy-purple or pink flowers which are crowded in a close 10 to 15 flower cluster. Plants grow to 8 in. tall.

A good little plant for edging the border or use in the rock garden where its verbena-like flower heads provide a display of color throughout midsummer and early autumn. The flowers are good for cutting and last quite well. Its trailing habit makes it valuable for hanging baskets.

Half-hardy abronias prefer a light sandy soil in an open, sunny position, but like coolness such as they enjoy along the California seacoast. Space 6-12 in. apart. Seeds should either be soaked in water for 24 hours or the husk should be removed before sowing. Seeds are slow to germinate, requiring about 20 days. For early bloom sow indoors 6 to 8 weeks before outdoor planting is safe. Best sown in small pots because of difficulty in transplanting. *Grandiflora* is a variety with larger blooms.

ADONIS ANNUA (*A. aestivalis, A. autumnalis*)—Pheasant's Eye. Buttercup or Crowfoot Family.

This species of *Adonis* comes from Central Europe and is grown for its showy crimson buttercup-like flowers which measure ¾-1½ in. across and bloom freely in June and July. The feathery foliage is also attractive; its fine dark-green leaves are deeply cut into many divisions. Plants grow 18 in. high. When well grown they make useful border plants and are effective massed in broad, sweeping drifts on gentle slopes. Also useful in the rock garden and for cutting.

Hardy. Average garden soil and a not-too-exposed area will give best results. Plants do not like intense heat, will take full sun or part shade. Space 8-12 in. apart. Sow seed in fall or early spring. Germination takes place in about 10-14 days and flowering begins in about 14 weeks.

A. annua var. *citrina* has yellow flowers. It is not as attratcive as the type.

Abronia umbellata

Adonis annua

Ageratum houstonianum

AFRICAN DAISY—See *Arctotis, Dimorphotheca and Gazania.*

AGERATUM HOUSTONIANUM (A. *mexicanum*)—Ageratum, Floss Flower. Composite Family.

A tender annual from Mexico represented in cultivation today by many fine garden varieties of dwarf, compact habit as well as tall, upright kinds. Its blue flowers, fairly rare among annuals, is one of the reasons for its wide popularity. A profusion of dainty, fluffy heads ¼-½ in. in diameter, often delightfully fragrant, usually completely cover the plant from June or July until frost. Heights will vary from 6-24 in. depending upon the variety. Although the prevailing color is blue or lavender-blue, there is a pink and also a white. However, the white varieties are not as attractive as many other white annuals on the market.

It is a splendid plant for summer bedding and the dwarf, compact kinds are useful for edging; tall varieties are useful for cutting; also a good rock garden plant. They like a rather rich soil and plenty of water in full sun or partial shade and cannot stand a hot, dry location. Buy plants or sow seed indoors, 8-10 weeks before outdoor planting is safe, for an early start. Germination takes 5 days. Set seedlings outdoors after danger of frost is past. Pinch tips to encourage branching. Space dwarfer kinds for edging 6-8 in. apart, taller kinds 10-12 in. They will bloom 60-100 days from seed. Keep faded flowers picked, otherwise they will stop flowering. Can pot and bring indoors for winter bloom. With proper facilities cuttings may be taken from stock plants all through the winter and early spring for uniform carpet-bedding plants. However, such stock is subject to whitefly, also red spider.

Among the annual kinds most often grown are Blue Mink, 9-12 in. tall with large powder-blue flowers, usually very uniform; Blue Perfection, a rich blue, 12-14 in. high; Midget Blue, 3 in. high; and Fairy Pink, a salmon-pink, 6 in. tall. Blue Blazer (earlier than Blue Mink) is a new F_1 hybrid about 6 in. high, a soft clear blue, about the same as Midget Blue. Habit more uniform than other types. Blue Mist is another new F_1 hybrid with color a little deeper than Blue Blazer. Grows to 6 in. as does Blue Ball.

Eupatorium coelestinum or mistflower is a perennial known as hardy ageratum.

Alonsoa

ALONSOA—Maskflower. Figwort Family.
Showy, half-hardy perennial from tropical America, related to the snapdragon. They are grown almost entirely as annuals since under cultivation they are at their best the first year from seed. Excellent plants for the border or the rock garden. Their showy flowers are produced in great profusion during the summer and early autumn.

Seeds may be sown indoors in March for an early start or later in the open garden. Sunshine and good drainage are essential. Sensitive to the heat in the Middle West. If position is exposed staking will be necessary. Attractive and dainty as cut flowers for small vases, but do not last long cut. A good greenhouse plant.

A. acutifolia (*A. myrtifolia*). This bushy strong-growing plant which grows to a height of 18 in. or more comes from Peru and has broad, pointed, ovalish leaves which are sharply toothed along the margin. It has tiny deep-red flowers in terminal racemes; the lip of the flower is three or four times as long as the calyx. Flowers from June until frost.

A. acutifolia var. *candida* (*A. albiflora*). Has white flower with a yellow center.

A. warscewiczi (offered sometimes as *A.*

grandiflora, A. compacta and *A. mutissi*). Resembles *A. acutifolia* but is larger with bright scarlet flowers.

ALTHAEA ROSEA (*A. chinensis*)—Hollyhock. Mallow Family.
The common garden hollyhock is a short-lived perennial from China grown as a biennial or annual but is very likely to persist from self-sown seeds. This old-time flower, associated with the past, is a much loved and popular garden plant. It is tall and erect with spires 5-7 in. high. The flowers on the long, slender, terminal spikes bloom from the bottom upward, throughout July and August. Although the typical flower is single and rose-pink in color, horticultural forms in many shapes and colors are now listed.

Flowers may be double, semi-double or single with petals curled, frilly and fringed, but considerable instability is likely to be encountered. In a packet of annual hollyhock seed perhaps only 50 percent will come true. In ordering seed state color and whether you want single-flowered, double, curled, or fringed types.

Althaea rosea Indian Spring

Hollyhocks look well in groups at the back of a planting; their tall spikes of bloom are valuable as accents or background material and are effective used along a picket fence or against the wall of a house.

Seedsmen have developed annual strains that will flower the same year they are planted. For annual strains sow seed indoors in February or March. Germination takes about 12 days. Transplant seedlings to permanent location. They will do well in warm sun in fertile, well-drained soil. Space 1-2 ft. apart. These plants will bloom the first season but later than those sown the previous July or August and grown as biennials. In transplanting hollyhock seedlings see that their naturally downward-pointing roots are placed pointing downward. Avoid windy sites. If wind is a factor hollyhocks will need staking. Watch for Japanese beetles. Rust is a common disease on hollyhocks. Control by removing and destroying leaves on which it appears. Dust with sulphur or spray with zineb for rust control before infestation to be effective.

Indian Spring is a good annual pink hollyhock with ruffled flowers that will bloom from early August until frost if started early. Chater's Strain from England supplies uniform plants, almost all double flowered, and comes in single colors or a mixture, offered by most American seedsmen. Powderpuffs Double Mixture produces long spikes of fully double flowers in shades of yellow, white, pink, scarlet and salmon.

ALYSSUM, ANNUAL—See *Lobularia maritima.*

AMARANTH FEATHERS—See *Humea elegans.*

AMARANTHUS — Amaranth. Amaranth Family.
Strong-growing, rather coarse but showy annuals from the tropical and sub-tropical world, closely allied to the pigweeds and celosias. Their ornamental foliage, in many bright colors, makes these plants popular for summer bedding. They grow 3 to 5 ft. tall. The tall varieties are useful as background material, the dwarf varieties with variegated foliage are good bedding plants. Because they do not blend well with all flowers their garden value is limited but they thrive in the hottest, driest climates and can be useful for foliage effects when properly placed.

Half-hardy. Start seeds indoors for bedding varieties and in the open for the taller kinds, as soon as the soil is warm. Space or thin 12-18 in. apart. All need sunshine. Ordinary or even poor garden soil will do. Grown in rich soil the colors are not as brilliant. Sometimes called Summer Poinsettia or Rainbow Plant.

A. caudatus—Love-Lies-Bleeding, Tassel Flower. Has long, drooping spikes of bright red flowers resembling thick tassels or chenille which may be dried for winter bouquets. Sometimes leaves are also blood-red. Grows 3 ft. or taller, erect but spreading. Some horticultural forms have green, pink and yellow flower spikes. Various kinds do not come perfectly true from seed. Sometimes listed by seedsmen as *A. dussi, A. elegantissima, A. margaritae, A. superbus*, etc.

Amaranthus-tricolor splendens Molten Fire

A. hybridus hypochondriacus—Prince's Feather. Showy with reddish foliage and much branched with dense flower clusters, red or brownish red; grows 3-4 ft. tall.

A. tricolor (A. gangeticus) splendens—Joseph's Coat. Gets its name from its bronze-green leaves blotched with scarlet and yellow. Grows 1-4 ft. tall except in dwarf forms. Molten Fire has variegated deep red foliage.

AMETHYST FLOWER—See *Browallia speciosa.*

AMMOBIUM ALATUM—Winged Everlasting. Composite Family.
Hardy perennial from Australia easily grown as an annual in any ordinary or even sandy soil. A pretty little everlasting. The plant is erect, growing 2-3 ft. tall and is covered with silvery hairs. The stiff, branched stems are prominently winged bearing narrow, pale-green or silvery-white wooly leaves. The small yellow flowers are surrounded by attractive silvery-white bracts. Useful in the border or dried for winter bouquets.

Seed may be sown in the open in early fall, started early indoors or outdoors where they are to flower and thinned to 12 in. They like a sandy, well-drained soil.

Var. *grandiflorum* has larger flowers and is superior in every way to the type.

Anagallis linifolia Mixed

ANAGALLIS LINIFOLIA (*A. grandiflora*)—Pimpernel. Primrose Family.
A biennial or short-lived perennial from the Mediterranean region usually grown as an annual. It forms a soft, compact plant of fine-leafed foliage, to 18 in. tall, smothered during the summer with large clusters of deep blue flowers about ¾ in. in diameter. The flowers are deeper blue at the base and turn crimson with age. The blue kind is excellent, the best low blue annual available. Good for the rock garden or planted in generous drifts if a distinctive blue is wanted. Not a good cut flower. Attractive pot plant for winter flowering under glass, 60° to 65° temperature.

Grows best in the cool areas of California and in temperate northern or mountain states. Seeds are slow to start. Cover only lightly; they should sprout in 2 or 3 weeks.

There is a kind with oval leaves and another with red and rose-purple flowers.

Anagallis arvensis — Scarlet Pimpernel, Poor Man's Weatherglass. Has trailing stems and scarlet or white starlike flowers ¼ in. across. Var. *caerulea* has blue flowers. Useful in window boxes and hanging baskets.

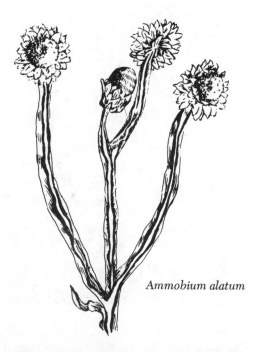

Ammobium alatum

ANCHUSA CAPENSIS—Cape or Summer Forget-Me-Not. Borage Family.

Most anchusas are biennials or perennials but *A. capensis* from South Africa is treated as a hardy annual. The popular variety Blue Bird is a compact, attractive plant about 18 in. in height with the bluest of all blue flowers. Most effective in the garden planted in large drifts. The flowers are too fragile for indoor arrangements and do not last when cut. Leaves are narrow and pointed, plants vase-shaped with many slender, upright branches. Var. *alba* has white flowers.

Sow seed indoors for early start, covering to a depth of ⅛ in., or sow outdoors as weather permits. Germination takes about 12 days. In setting out, space 12 in. apart. Thrive best in full sun or light shade and a rich, moist, well-drained soil. If flowers are cut as they fade plants will bloom over a long period of time. Shear back after first big show of bloom, feed and water, and plants will make a good come-back producing a good second bloom.

Anchusa capensis Blue Bird

Androsace lactiflora

ANDROSACE LACTIFLORA (*A. augusti-folia, A. coronopifolia*)—Rock Jasmine. Primrose Family.

This annual from Siberia blooms in June and July. It is an erect plant up to 12 in. in height. Small lance-linear leaves about 2 in. long are mostly in rosettes. Above these rise long slender stems terminating in ½ in. wide white flowers in rather loose clusters. Flowers resemble a miniature primrose and bloom from April to June. An attractive plant for the rock garden or for edging and excellent for the cold greenhouse.

Hardy. Seed should be sown in September or March where it is to flower. Thin young plants 4-5 in. apart. If left undisturbed will self-sow. Prefer a position in partial shade and a humous soil to ensure a high moisture content during the summer months. During dry weather frequent watering is necessary. Plants do not like wet feet either, so a well-drained soil is important.

ANGEL'S TRUMPET—See *Datura metel*.

APPLE-OF-PERU—See *Nicandra physalodes*.

Antigonon leptopus

ANTIGONON LEPTOPUS—Coral or Confederate Vine. Buckwheat or Rhubarb Family.

A showy Mexican vine widely grown as an ornamental in warm regions. Will quickly form a dense screen on a wall or fence. The good-sized, arrow- or heart-shaped leaves are 1-3 in. long and small bright pink or white flowers are borne in long drooping clusters. Grows 30 ft. tall or more and is used over porches, fences, walls and trellises. Must place support for vine so tendrils can reach it and take hold.

Plant anytime in the South. Greenhouse plant in North or grown as a tender summer annual. Of easy culture. Sow seed in any ordinary or even poor soil. Rich soil promotes leaves at the expense of flowers. Enjoys full sun. May also be propagated by cuttings taken in the fall.

ANTIRRHINUM HYBRIDS — Snapdragon. Figwort Family.

This popular perennial from the Mediterranean region is grown by home gardeners as an annual. Millions are forced each year by florists for use as cut flowers, since they last well cut. The buds continue to open from the bottom to the top of the spike. The hybrids have been greatly improved over the years by breeders who have worked toward more and larger flowers with a wider range of colors, as well as double-flowered varieties; more vigorous plants, resistant to disease, especially rust; and varieties that will take more heat than the older strains. They now come in all colors but blue. Some are delicate pink, or deep maroon and others come in yellows that look like giant flowers of Toadflax. In height they vary from 10-36 in. Excellent used in borders where a vertical form is needed for variety and interest. The taller types are stately and effective among other garden flowers and in small borders they make good accent plants. Dwarf types are good as edging plants and in raised beds.

Buy young plants or sow rustproof seed indoors, if early start is desired, 8 to 10 weeks before outdoor planting is safe. Seed is very fine so scarcely cover. Room in which they are started must not get over 55°. Seeds take about 2 weeks to germinate. Transplant seedlings and transfer to a cold frame about the middle of April to harden off. Protect if freezing night temperatures are likely. Move to the open garden around the middle of May, in full sun, in any good well-drained garden soil. Space 6-12 in. apart depending upon variety. Will bloom 120 to 136 days from seed. The earlier they can safely be put in a permanent position the better because they do not like intense heat. They will bloom with some shade. The tall kinds will need staking if planted in a windy area. Pinch out leaf-stem tips for bushy plants with shorter and more flower spikes or if you want fewer but taller and larger flower spikes do not pinch back. Cut flowers frequently and remove faded blooms for maximum blooming season. If plants seem to be bloomed-out cut them back, feed and water to revive them and get a new crop of flowers.

Watch for rust at about the time the flower spikes are developing—easily recognized by the dusty, dark brown spots that appear on the underside of the leaves and on the stems. If rust is prevalent in your area grow the rust-resistant varieties available. To prevent rust start dusting every 2 weeks early in the season with sulphur or spray with a fungicide. Avoid getting the leaves wet by watering at the base of the plants rather than from overhead.

Varieties, Strains or Races:

Standard (diploid). Available in a wide range of colors, mixtures and by named varieties. Plants grow 18 in. to 4 ft. high.

Tetraploid. This class was developed in the late '40s. The Tetra snaps are stockier than the diploids, have particularly heavy stems, richer green foliage, and big ruffled flowers 2½ in. across. They grow 2 ft. tall. Hybridists use the drug colchicine to increase the number of chromosomes in the cells from 2-4. Available in straight colors or mixed,

Super Tetras. Huskier plants than the Tetras with larger flowers. Well-branched from the base, they grow 2 ft. high.

F₁ Hybrids. Stronger and more vigorous with fuller, longer spikes than any other type. Height 2½-3 ft. Greater resistance to adverse weather. Rocket Series (All-America) comes in red, rose, orchid, bronze, gold, white, or in a color mixture; excellent outdoor snaps.

F₁ Hybrid nanum (semi-dwarf). Sprite series are 12-16 in., excellent for both bedding and cut flowers.

F₂ Class. Stronger and better than the old diploids but not quite as uniform as the F₁ hybrids. Available in straight colors or mixtures. Panorama and First Ladies are two good ones.

Extra Dwarf Snapdragons. Grow 6-8 in. tall. The newest, most desirable types are the Floral Carpet Series, all F₁ hybrids. Available in red, pink, rose, bronze, orchid, yellow, and white, plus a color mixture. Floral Carpet Rose was an All-America winner for 1965. Magic Carpet is a good color mixture. All ideal for low borders or as edgers.

Knee High. A new introduction of F₁ hybrids, 18-24 in. tall.

Antirrhinum F₁ hybrids, Rocket Series

Aquilegia Long-Spurred Hybrid

Arctotis stoechadifolia

AQUILEGIA HYBRIDS — Columbine. The Buttercup or Crowfoot Family.

Although a short-lived Eurasian perennial the Long-Spurred Hybrids make up a strain best raised from seed and can be grown in a wide range of colors including blues, pinks, yellows and white which come quite true from seed. Much grown for its handsome clusters of nodding, long-spurred flowers. Excellent for both the border and for cutting.

Like a good, well-drained sandy loam, slightly alkaline, and full sun or partial shade. Sow seed in September and keep in a cold frame until spring when the young seedlings may be planted out.

Choose only the Long-Spurred Hybrids to grow as annuals.

ARCTOTIS STOECHADIFOLIA (*A. grandis*)—African or Blue-Eyed Daisy. Composite Family.

The common name African Daisy is also applied to such other composites from South Africa as *Dimorphotheca, Gazania* and *Gerbera,* which clearly shows why common names do not always identify a specific plant. This annual from South Africa has lovely daisy-like flowers 2½-3 in. across, on good stems 10-18 in. long or more. The upper side of the flower petals is white and the reverse lilac-blue, with flower centers of steel-blue. The foliage is gray-green. The African Daisy is a splendid annual and makes a good showing planted in mass. It is excellent for cutting even though the flowers do close at night. The flowers will last for a week cut and many of the undeveloped buds will open in water.

Sow seed indoors 6 to 8 weeks before outdoor planting is safe for an early start or sow outdoors when weather permits. Seeds germinate in less than a week. Like full sun and a sandy soil with complete drainage. Space 12 in. apart. Will stand great heat and considerable drought but require full sun for success. Cut flowers freely to keep the plant blooming.

Improved forms are now on the market. Dwarf or low growing hybrids are offered in shades of cream, yellow, bronze and red; the center of the head is usually of a different color from the tips of the rays, the head appearing as if with an "eye" or halo.

ARGEMONE GRANDIFLORA — Mexican Poppy, Prickly Poppy. Poppy Family.

A perennial from Mexico but in northern states used as an annual. Smooth, white-veined, thistle-like leaves are faintly prickly on their toothed margins. Clusters of large, white, cup-shaped, poppy-like flowers, measuring up to 3 in. in diameter, with petals of a beautiful satiny lustre, attract immediate attention. The plants grow to a height of 2-3 ft. or more. The flowers are usually solitary or a few together, borne well above the finely cut foliage. Interesting to grow and handsome for the border. Flowers appear in early July and last until frost.

Sow seed thinly in mid-May where plants are to grow so it will not be necessary to move them as they are difficult to transplant, or sow indoors earlier in pots for easy transplanting. Seeds germinate in about 14 days (65-70°F.). Plants like a warm sunny location and a sandy loam. Thin to 2 to 3 ft. apart. This annual performs best in warm, dry regions and will not thrive in a wet or cool location. Stands up surprisingly well to high winds and heavy rains. Do not try to stake because the very succulent stems break readily.

A. *lutea* has yellow flowers and is more beautiful than the type.

Argemone grandiflora

Artemisia sacrorum viridis

ARTEMISIA SACRORUM VIRIDIS—Summer Fir. Composite Family.

Tall, slender and tree-like in habit, grown mostly as a bold foliage plant and treated like a hardy annual. Graceful and taller (9 ft.) than the type, it forms a dense pyramid of bright green, finely cut, lacy or feathery foliage which makes splendid plants for the back of the border, the foliage a perfect contrast for vividly colored annuals in front. Useful for planting in groups near trees. Flowers are very minute and unimportant. Native of Russia and Northeastern Asia.

Sow seed in fall or early spring where they are to grow. Germination requires 2 or 3 weeks. Thin young plants to 3 ft. apart. Will grow well on poor, dry soils. In sunny positions aromatic scent of leaves is intensified. Grown as pot plant in the greenhouse.

ASCLEPIAS CURRASSAVICA — Blood Flower. Milkweed Family.

A weed in tropical America but the showiest of all the milkweeds. Has long narrow leaves 3-5 in. in length. The flowers are in

Asclepias currassavica

Asperula orientalis

umbels—they all arise from a common point. Brilliant orange-red flowers are gayer in color than the common milkweed. Plants grow 2-4 ft. tall and may be used as hedges, screens, backgrounds or specimens in the garden. The cut branches with foliage blend well mixed with other cut flowers.

Sow seed indoors in February. Grow seedlings in pots, move outdoors after all danger of frost is past. Space 18 in. apart.

ASPERULA ORIENTALIS (*A. azurea-setosa*)—Woodruff. Madder Family.

A Eurasian hardy annual easily grown from seed. Not over 12 in. high. Small lavender-blue flowers are fragrant and narrow leaves are in whorls of 8. The slender-growing branching plant is useful for edging and also good for cutting. Along the banks of a small stream woodruff will form a dense blue carpet in late spring and early summer.

Broadcast seed in early spring where plants are to grow. Lightly rake in and germination should take place in 3 weeks. Little thinning is necessary. Prefers a moist, partially shaded area. Will flower about 12 weeks after sowing and bloom until around the end of July.

ASTER AMELLUS (*Amelius annuus*)—Italian Aster or Starwort. Composite Family.

Was first found in Italy along the River Mella. It grows 1-2 ft. high and has small narrow leaves with marginal teeth. Large purple daisy-like rays around a central yellow-disk measure about 1¼ in. across and are borne in great profusion in late summer and early fall. Attractive grown in small groups in the border. A good summer greenhouse plant.

Sow seed indoors 6 to 8 weeks before outdoor planting is safe. Germination takes 5 days at 60-65°F. temperature. Plant seedlings out in May spacing 4 in. apart. Prefer a light, well-drained soil in an open sunny location. May need staking. Flowering begins 3 months after sowing and continues for 5 weeks or more. If cut back after flowering you may get a second crop although not as good a display as the first one.

Var. *bessarabicus* has deeper purple rays. There are several named varieties that may be had in lavender and pink colors.

ASTER, ANNUAL OR CHINA—See *Callistephus chinensis* hybrids.

ATRIPLEX HORTENSIS — Sea Purslane. Goosefoot Family.

This native of Asia is an erect ornamental plant, growing 1-3 ft. or more, with dark red or purple-colored arrow-shaped leaves, the margins toothed or wavy. When young the leaves are covered with a glistening crystalline substance. Grown for its handsome foliage. Very decorative cut for indoor arrangement. Good bedding plants or attractive grouped in clumps in the border. Salt tolerant, so useful for seaside planting and used extensively along the coast of southern California. Excellent for hedges in the dry regions of the southwest.

Sow seed indoors 6 to 8 weeks before outdoor planting is possible or seed may be sown outdoors where plants are to grow later. Germination takes about 10 days at 50-55°F. Thin or space 12 in. apart. Prefers a rich, well-drained soil and a sunny location.

Var. *astrosanguinea* has dark crimson leaves, var. *cupreata* deep red leaves and violet stalks and var. *rosea* has red leaves with darker stems.

BABY BLUE EYES—See *Nemophila menziesi.*

BABY'S BREATH, ANNUAL—See *Gypsophila elegans.*

BACHELOR'S BUTTON—See *Centaurea cyanus.*

BALLOON VINE—See *Cardiospermum halicacabum.*

BALSAM APPLE—See *Momordica balsamina.*

BALSAM, GARDEN—See *Impatiens balsamina.*

BALSAM PEAR—See *Momordica charantia.*

BARTONIA—See *Mentzelia lindleyi.*

BASIL—See *Ocimum basilicum.*

BASKET FLOWER—See *Centaurea americana.*

BEARD TONGUE—See *Penstemon gloxinioides.*

Aster amellus

Artiplex hortensis

BEEFSTEAK PLANT—See *Perilla frutescens crispa*.

BEGONIA SEMPERFLORENS—Wax Begonia. Begonia Family.

The wax begonia, a native of Brazil, is included here because it is much used as a bedding plant and easily raised from seed. The seed is very tiny so must be sown thinly and just gently pressed in. Sow seed in pots in January and February (65°) and the young plants can be set out in the garden in June. They also make useful pot plants for the cool greenhouse.

They form compact bushy plants 9-15 in. tall and may be had in shades of white, pink and red. They remain in flower all summer and will take all kinds of weather. The glossy foliage is almost as decorative as the flowers. Improved strains and the introduction of F₁ hybrids are keeping this versatile plant in demand for the garden border, where it thrives in partially shaded areas. Thousand Wonders (Tausendschon) is an F₁ hybrid which may be had in rose, red, and white.

BELLIS PERENNIS—English Daisy. Composite Family.

From Europe and the British Isles, this little plant grows to a height of 6 in. or more and forms rosettes or basal tufts of somewhat oval-shaped leaves. Above these rise slender stiff stems terminating in white, yellow-centered flowers about 1-1½ in. across; the rays in some varieties are quilled. Although strictly a perennial they are usually grown as annuals or biennials for bedding plants. Excellent for edging borders or for carpeting the ground in shady places. Flowers are long lasting when cut. A good plant for the cool greenhouse.

Grown as an annual, sow seed outdoors in fall where they are to flower or indoors 6 to 8 weeks before outdoor planting is possible. Germination takes about 7 days. When planting out space 4 to 6 in. apart. They like a moist, rich soil and full sun or partial shade. Flower from May to July. Will not take much heat.

The type has given rise to many lovely varieties in pink, rose, red or white, some

Bellis perennis Giant Double

Begonia semperflorens

with fully double flowers. Var. *helichry-soides* has pink flowers, var. *alba* white, var. *lutea* cream-colored, var. *rosea* rose-pink and var. *monstrosa* is a large-flowered form. Longfellow has dark rose-colored flowers, Etna is a brilliant red, and Alice a delicate pink.

BELLS OF IRELAND—See *Molucella laevis*.

BLACK-EYED SUSAN VINE—See *Thunbergia alata*.

BLANKET FLOWER, ANNUAL—See *Gaillardia pulchella*.

BLAZING STAR—See *Mentzelia lindleyi*.

BLISTER CRESS—See *Erysimum murale*.

BLOOD FLOWER—See *Asclepias curassavica*.

BLUE DAISY, BLUE MARGUERITE—See *Felicia amelloides*.

BLUE-EYED DAISY—See *Arctotis stoechadifolia*.

BLUE LACE FLOWER—See *Trachymene caerulea*.

BLUE SAGE—See *Salvia patens*.

BLUE SUCCORY—See *Catananche caerulea*.

Borago officinalis

BORAGO OFFICINALIS—Borage. Borage Family.

Only this one annual species, a British native, is in cultivation. Much sought after by the bees. Usually found in the herb or kitchen garden but it is a very charming plant for the border. Its pointed, silvery-gray, downy, oblong or oval leaves provide a nice contrast for the more vivid summer-flowering annuals. The plant grows to a height of 1½-2 ft. or more and has large drooping sprays of blue-violet or purple flowers. Its aromatic young leaves and flowers may be used in salads or to flavor cool drinks.

Hardy. Sow seed outdoors in early spring where plants are to grow. Enjoy full sun and any ordinary garden soil. Does not transplant easily. Thin to 10 in. apart.

Var. *albiflora* has white flowers. Listed under herbs in seed catalogs.

BRACHYCOME IBERIDIFOLIA – Swan
River Daisy. Composite Family.
A long-season annual from Australia. Bush-
like plant with slender stems, about 10-15 in.
tall, bearing small, much-divided pale green
leaves and sweet-scented daisy-like flowers
in white, rose, pink, blue and lilac which
measure about 1 in. across. The cineraria-
like flower heads come in almost all colors
except yellow, are solitary and long-stalked.
Good greenhouse plant. Low enough to be
useful for edgings, producing as they develop
a profusion of bloom throughout the summer. Excellent low covering for any bare
places in the border. Useful cut in small bouquets.

Tender. Sow seed indoors 6 to 8 weeks
before outdoor planting is safe for an early
start or sow directly in open soil in May when
settled weather arrives. Transfer seedlings
outdoors in full sun in warm ordinary garden
soil or sandy loam. Space 6-9 in. apart, closer
if used for an edging. Will bloom 75 to 100
days from seed. Flowers last well and should
bloom 6 weeks or more if old blooms are cut
as they fade.

Best to order by color.

Browallia speciosa major

Brachycome iberidifolia

BROWALLIA SPECIOSA MAJOR—Browallia, Amethyst Flower. Potato or Nightshade
Family.
Half-hardy annual from Colombia grown for
its attractive steel-blue flowers. An excellent
free-flowering bedding plant, growing 12-15
in. tall. Excellent for pot culture or hanging
baskets and an excellent greenhouse plant.

Sow seed indoors 8 to 10 weeks before soil
has warmed in spring. Seeds germinate in 2
weeks. Transfer seedlings outdoors in ordinary, even poor garden soil in sun, but with
some protection from hot afternoon sun.
Space 8-10 in. apart. If bed is protected over
winter, plants often self-sow. Pinch for good
branching and more dwarf, compact plants.
Water and feed.

There are horticultural forms with violet,
also white flowers. The white variety is less
showy but desirable. Blue Bells, a deep sky-
blue, and Silver Bells, a glistening white, are
popular.

B. viscosa compacta. Sapphire is of compact growth, 10 in., with small light-eyed,
dark blue flowers.

I. Opposite   *Cleome is one of the "perennial annuals"—once you plant it
you will always have it, for this favorite self-sows freely. Often used as a
background plant, cleome continues to flower up the stem without the
picking which many other annuals require if they are to have a long blooming season. The foliage odor is not entirely pleasant, so the plant is best
kept away from the windows or outdoor living areas.*

BURNING BUSH—See *Kochia scoparia trichophila.*

BUSH MORNING-GLORY—See *Convolvulus tricolor.*

BUTTERFLY FLOWER—See *Schizanthus wisetonensis.*

CACALIA COCCINEA—See *Emilia sagittata.*

Calandrinia grandiflora

CALANDRINIA GRANDIFLORA — Rock Purslane. Purslane Family.
A showy Chilean perennial usually grown as an annual since it blooms from seed the first year. A more or less erect plant growing 12-24 in. in height. It has succulent reddish stems bearing long, somewhat oval, pointed leaves (5-7 in. long) and pale or light purple flowers that measure 2 in. or more in diameter. The flowers close at night, opening the next morning, and are produced in profusion during the summer months. Excellent for the rock garden or border and a good pot plant for the cool greenhouse.

Sow seed around mid-May in an open sunny position in a light sandy soil. Germination takes only 5 days but for a time the young plants grow very slowly. They begin to flower about 15 weeks after sowing. At their best in July and August. Plant thickly for the best effect, about 6 in. apart. In hot, dry summers they provide a dazzling display of color but are disappointing if the weather is dull and cool since the flowers open only in full sun. If ground is left undisturbed self-sown plants often make their appearance the following year. North of Philadelphia, for an early start, you may want to sow seed indoors 6 to 8 weeks before outdoor planting is safe.

CALENDULA OFFICINALIS — Pot Marigold. Composite Family.
Hardy annual. This all-time favorite from the Mediterranean region has showy daisy-like flowers characterized by shades of yellow, gold and orange; usually borne one to a stem, some types have small chrysanthemum-like flowers, others have petals rolled at the edge to make a quill. The plants are bushy, grow 1½-2 ft. tall. The scentless leaves are long, narrow and slightly sticky. Mass plantings are bright and cheerful. Picked in bud or near-bud, the flowers keep well cut. Florists often force them for winter use. For wealth of bloom the calendula is without a rival. The plants self-sow but will often revert to the smaller, single type so it is better to purchase new seed. '
Average, well-drained soil and full sun best meet their needs but calendulas will adapt to adverse soils although generous watering and good drainage is appreciated, and they will tolerate some shade. They bloom all summer in cool climates. Do not enjoy the heat of midsummer but often make their best showing late in the season. In case aphids attack the plants in hot weather spray with malathion or nicotine sulphate. For an early start, sow seed indoors 6 to 8 weeks before outdoor planting is possible or sow in open soil as soon as it can be worked. Space or thin to about 8-12 in. apart, depending

II. Opposite *Although many excellent strains of double hollyhocks have been developed, there is a special charm to the single types and they seem especially suited to old gardens. Often they have more of a perennial tendency than double forms, especially if grown on very well-drained soil, and if blooms are removed right after they fade.*

Calendula officinalis

CALIFORNIA POPPY — See *Eschscholzia californica.*

CALLIOPSIS — See *Coreopsis tinctoria.*

CALLIRHOE PEDATA — Poppy Mallow. Mallow Family.
An attractive hardy annual from the southern United States about 2-3 ft. tall, erect, bearing 5 to 7 deeply lobed leaves. It is pyramidal, with loosely branched flower clusters of cherry-red or purple-red flowers, each about 1 in. across, produced in stem axils. Useful in the border where its showy flowers are produced in great profusion through most of the summer. Plant seed early outdoors where they are to grow.

Plants prefer an open, sunny position and will grow well on poor, light soils. Will thrive in dry situations. Staking is necessary if in an exposed windy area.

Callirhoe pedata

upon the variety. Seedlings transplant readily. Will bloom 60 to 90 days from seed.

Fading flowers and seed heads must be removed promptly to insure continuous bloom. If larger flowers are desired pinch off all but the terminal one when in bud; but for good branching and more, smaller flowers, pinch back the main stem when the first flower head starts to form. In climates such as California the calendula is an outstanding winter bloomer and planted prior to Labor Day will bloom for Christmas and well into the spring.

There are many varieties on the market, although some are not always reliably named. The Pacific Beauty strain has been bred to withstand summer heat. The large well-formed flowers in clear tones of cream, apricot (Apricot Beauty), lemon (Lemon Beauty) and deep orange (Flame) on long stems are most attractive. Campfire (Sensation) is a bright orange, excellent for cutting, as is the buttercup-yellow Chrysantha. Orange Quills has 3 in. blooms and grows to 1½ ft. in height.

CALIFORNIA BLUEBELL — See *Phacelia campanularia.*

CALLISTEPHUS CHINENSIS HYBRIDS—
Annual or China Aster. Composite Family.
Half-hardy annual from China and Japan.
From a violet-colored daisy-like flower with
a yellow center the China aster has been
bred so it is now represented by a multitude
of forms and colors including many shades
of blue, lavender, purple, pink, crimson,
wine, rose, peach and pure white. The innumerable types and strains come with
showy flowers in a variety of shapes both
single and double, described as peony-flow-
ered, pompon and chrysanthemum flowered,
ostrich feather, etc. suggesting the shapes of
the flower head. A wonderful source of cut
flowers all summer long, the leggy 1-3 ft. tall
plants have long wiry stems which tend to
bend under the weight of the heavy flowers,
which measure 2-3 in. across. Perennial asters are known as Michaelmas daisies.

The annual China aster is effective used
in beds in straight colors or mixed. It is unexcelled for use as a cut flower, and is a
popular florist crop for this purpose. Asters
are the exception to the rule: "The more you
cut the more they bloom." After the first picking few are borne thereafter, so if you want
a lot of asters better plant succession crops
rather than depend on one planting.

Always buy seed which has been bred for
wilt resistance and sow indoors 8 weeks before outdoor planting is safe. Barely cover.
One ounce contains 10,000 to 12,000 seeds.
Keep in as cool, moist and airy a place as possible. Careful culture will prevent damping-
off. Transfer seedlings outdoors in full sun
in a rich sandy loam. Space taller kinds 15
in. apart, lower varieties more closely together. Best not to plant them two years in
the same place. Do not let plants dry out
during droughts. Keep growing well, for
checked growth will cause poor flowers. Dust
or spray the plants frequently with malathion. Aster yellows is a serious disease making
plants turn yellow and die. Control by good
housekeeping, protecting against sucking insects, carriers of the disease. If plants become
badly diseased burn them and stop growing
asters for a few years.

Queen of the Market is earliest to bloom,
grows about 20 in. tall with medium-sized
flowers. Super Giants and the older Giants
of California bear flowers 4½ in. across with
long curly petals from late summer until frost.
Crego has large, shaggy-petaled blooms on
plants about 2½ ft. tall. Early Beauty, American Branching, Royal and American Beauty
are other favorites. Princess asters are a
newer kind with a high crested center surrounded by several rows of petals, blooming
in late August. Another new type is Bouquet
with quilled flowers on upright plants 2 ft.
tall. They come early and a plant in bloom
gives the appearance of a whole bouquet.
Powderpuffs of the Bouquet type comes in
a good color range and is probably one of
the best double-flowered home garden asters
with upright, compact 2 ft. tall plants. Single
asters like California Sunshine and Rainbow
Mixture add diversity. Duchess has pure yellow globe-shaped flowers like a chrysanthemum.

Callistephus chinensis hybrid, Rainbow Single

Calonyction aculeatum

Campanula medium Mixed

CALONYCTION ACULEATUM — Moon-flower. Morning-Glory Family.

The moonflowers are perennial vines from Tropical America and southern Florida. Closely related to the morning-glories but bloom at night instead of in the sunshine. They bloom at sunset and fade in late morning or around noon. While perennials, they are grown from seed in the North as they will not take frost and bloom the first year from seed. Commonly grown throughout the United States for covering open trellis work, lattice fences and as porch climbers for their showy, sweet-scented, trumpet-shaped flowers. It is a milky-juiced vine with somewhat prickly stems and grows 10-20 ft. in length. Flowers are fragrant, white (sometimes green-banded) and pink, measuring 4-6 in. across and bloom from July to frost. *C. muricatum* is similar but smaller and has purplish flowers about one-half the size of the above.

Tender. The hard, small seeds are slow to germinate. Notch or soak overnight before planting. Spread on or just lightly bury them in wet sand, cover with plastic and with underheat from an electric bulb keep temperature 70-75° F. to hasten germination by several days. Seeds should germinate in 12 to 14 days. Plants prefer a moist, moderately rich loam but grow well in any good soil and require little attention. Grown in cool greenhouses to form a light shade for plants requiring protetcion from direct sun.

Var. *heterophyllum* has leaves divided into 3, 4 or 5 lobes; var. *variegatum* has variegated leaves and var. *grandiflorum* has larger flowers than those of the type. The seed packets listed as Giant White are popular and excellent planted where you sit outdoors in the evening since the flowers open at sunset and are luminous.

CAMPANULA MEDIUM—Canterbury Bells. Bellflower Family.

A beautiful biennial from Southern Europe planted each year in the same way as hardy annuals. Seeds must be sown each summer to provide bloom every season. A sturdy plant which grows from 2-4 ft. in height with large single or double bell-shaped flowers in colors of white, blue, lavender, violet, pink or rose, blooming in May and June. A popular border plant, the strong, heavily-flowered stems are also excellent for cutting.

If started from seed very early they will bloom the first summer, but produce far more profuse and handsome flowers the second year from summer sown seed. Sow seed in July. The leafy plants may be killed in open winters so it is safer to transplant seedlings to cold frame or nursery in September and carry through the winter with a light mulch. Transplant seedlings where wanted early in May. They prefer full sun and good garden soil; space them 15-20 in. apart. Water well during the growing and blooming season. Will reseed if conditions are favorable. Do not enjoy winter slush.

Available in Single, Double and Dwarf in straight colors or mixed. The variety *C. medium calycanthema* (Cup-and-Saucer Canterbury Bell or Bellflower) with the calyx colored and flattened below the flower in the shape of a saucer is available in all the colors or mixed.

C. isophylla—Ligurian Bellflower. A tender trailing plant useful for window boxes and hanging baskets with small, oval or heart-shaped leaves and shallow bell-shaped, starry, pale blue flowers about 1 in. wide. Var. *alba* is white. In cold regions winter over as a house plant.

CANDYTUFT, ANNUAL OR GLOBE—See *Iberis umbellata.*

CANTERBURY BELLS—See *Campanula medium.*

CAPE OR SUMMER FORGET-ME-NOT— See *Anchusa capensis.*

CAPE MARIGOLD—See *Dimorphotheca.*

CAPE STOCK—See *Heliophila leptophylla.*

CARDINAL CLIMBER—See *Quamoclit sloteri.*

CARDIOSPERMUM HALICACABUM — Balloon Vine. Soapberry Family.
A native of Bermuda, Texas and South Amer-

Cardiospermum halicacabum

ica, this is an attractive perennial vine in frost-free regions, grown in the North as an annual since it will bloom from seed the first year. An interesting addition to any collection of vines with its rapid growth to a height of 10 ft. or more. Used along fences, trellises and low buildings. May be used any place where vines are needed making a pleasant and ornamental screen. Its clusters of small white flowers are followed by spherical, papery pods that resemble tiny balloons about 1 in. in diameter. The leaves are oblong, pointed at the end and deeply toothed along the margins.

Sow seed outdoors in May. Germination takes about 3 weeks. Choose any ordinary light soil which will retain some moisture and place in full sun; thin 1-2 ft. apart. For earlier bloom plant indoors 6 to 8 weeks before outdoor planting is safe. Transfer seedlings outdoors when settled warm weather arrives. Will not take frost. Does best in warm situations in a sheltered sunny position. Needs moisture; also a trellis or wire for tendrils to cling to.

CARNATION, ANNUAL—See *Dianthus caryophyllus.*

CASTOR-BEAN PLANT—See *Ricinus communis.*

Catananche caerulea

CATANANCHE CAERULEA – Cupid's Dart, Blue Succory. Composite Family.
A southern European perennial resembling the cornflower, frequently grown as an annual because of its tendency to die out. A good everlasting. Not over 2 ft. high. Oblongish, hairy leaves with a few scattered teeth, mostly basal and narrow. Flower heads are nearly 2 in. wide with blue rays, which are white or white-margined in a horticultural variety. Useful in the border. May be dried for winter bouquets.

Sow seed outdoors in early spring in any ordinary garden or sandy soil and full sun. Thin to 9-12 in. apart.

Var. *alba* is white and var. *bicolor* is blue and white.

CATHEDRAL BELLS—See *Cobaea scandens.*

CELOSIA ARGENTEA—Cockscomb. Amaranth Family.
A half-hardy annual from the Tropics, which, if used with discretion, can be very effective and decorative in the landscape. There are two quite different forms of this old-fashioned plant. *C. argentea plumosa* has flowers in the plumed or feathered cockscomb. It is a large plant 1-3 ft. tall with many feathery bright flower clusters, which can be useful as background plants; if used wisely can be magnificent. Lovely dwarf forms make striking edging plants. *C. argentea cristata* has the crested or true cockscomb of velvety or plush-like flowers arranged in big fan-shaped clusters which can be effective massed in beds. Grow 6 in.-2 ft. tall. Crinkled heads are like great roosters' combs. Both types are extremely showy in either tall or dwarf kinds. The prevailing colors are reds and golds although improved kinds now extend the color range. They bloom through the summer and autumn. Are much used in dried arrangements.

For an early start sow seed indoors or broadcast or sow in rows outdoors in early spring where plants are to grow. Thin to 1-2 ft. apart. Must have full sun; will grow in any ordinary well-drained garden soil. Requires a reasonable amount of water. Will bloom 76 to 104 days from seed.

C. argentea cristata types. Toreador (All America) is crested with huge, deep-rich-red combs on 18-20 in. plants with light green foliage. Fireglow (also All-America) is a bright cardinal red, 20-24 in. tall. Royal Velvet is ruby red, about 2 ft. tall. Especially nice for cutting is Empress, 10 in. tall, with bronzy foliage and crimson-purple combs. Gilbert which is popular for drying is an improved strain with pastel tints, as well as the more usual colors.

C. argentea plumosa. Some of the feathered or plumed kinds include Golden Fleece with soft yellow grading into golds with plumes on 3 ft. plants with light green foliage; Forest Fire, a dazzling orange-scarlet with bronze-red leaves for bedding or background; Pampas Plume with well-formed, fleecy heads in bright colors. Dwarf plumed varieties are Fire Feather and Golden Feather.

Celosia argentea cristata Fireglow

CENTAUREA. Composite Family.
The annuals in this genus are best treated as hardy annuals and sown where wanted. They seem to flower better when somewhat crowded so they require little thinning.

C. americana—Basket Flower, Star Thistle. Gets its popular name from the odd fringed bracts that form a basket which envelops its bud. The thistle-like flower pushes through the basket's top and remains seated in a straw cup. The flowers are rosy-lavender. Plants grow 3 ft. tall. For use and culture see *C. cyanus.*

C. candidissima (*C. cineraria*) and *C. gymnocarpa*—Dusty Miller. Both known as dusty miller, are grown for their attractive, gray-green, silvery foliage. Used for bedding, as edgers and in window boxes. Can carry over the winter as cuttings, rooted in September, or start from fall-sown seeds or buy started plants. Set purchased plants in full sun in any sandy well-drained loam. Will not stand winter slush or water at its roots; not reliably hardy north of New York City.

C. candidissima is slow growing, so start it early. Whitish-gray leaves make it attractive for bedding. A 12-18 in. plant.

C. gymnocarpa is tall, 12-20 in., strong growing with fern-leaved, silvery-felty foliage.

C. cyanus—Bachelor's Button, Cornflower. From southern Europe, also called ragged robin and blue bottle. The national flower of Germany. Most familiar in its rich blue color but there are also purple, pink, rose, red, deep wine and white kinds. A popular annual easy to grow and dependable. They bloom in such profusion some inevitably go to seed and once you get them started you are sure to have seedlings coming up but they are often single and inferior in color and size. Plants range in height from the dwarfer types 12 in. tall to some that grow to 3 ft. Plants are inclined to sprawl. Their gray-green foliage is an asset, contrasting nicely with the gay flowers. However, the lower leaves can be unsightly so a sweet alyssum or annual candytuft edging may be advisable. Excellent for cutting and an ideal buttonhole flower.

Centaurea cyanus Mixed

across, come in delicate tints of white, pink, lavender and yellow, and have a musk-like fragrance, feathery and light in appearance. Plants are spreading with ascending branches growing to 2-3 ft. tall. Plants lack the substance for a good bedding plant, are best used in drifts among other plants. Slender stems are good for cutting during summer months.

Easy to grow. Broadcast seed in fall or early spring in ordinary garden soil and full sun. Plants grow rapidly. Thin to 9 in. apart. Cut generously so plants will not form seed, to prolong bloom. Pull plants out in late summer when bloomed out.

Giant Mixed seed is generally sold, providing large fringed flowers on 3 ft. plants. *C. imperialis* is a hybrid, thought to be derived from a variety of *C. moschata,* 2 to 4 ft. high with fragrant heads in a variety of colors including white, purple, lilac and pink.

CHAMOMILE, GERMAN, SWEET OR FALSE—See *Matricaria chamomilla.*

The plants enjoy ordinary garden soil, full sun or part shade. Broadcast seed which is good size and sprout quickly in October, lightly rake in, and cover lightly with leaves over winter. You should have flowers for Memorial Day and many more weeks of bloom. Sown in early spring will flower in midsummer, 8 weeks from seed. Keep dead flowers picked off for good blooming.

Double varieties are fuller, larger and more symmetrical and preferred by some. Jubilee Gem is especially good for edging, a 12 in. bushy plant with double, blue flowers, stems a bit too short for cutting. Taller kinds include Blue Boy, Red Boy, Pinkie, Rosie and Snowman. Tall Blue is a favorite tall double and comes in mixed colors, has long stems liked by arrangers.

C. moschata—Sweet Sultan. A popular, attractive hardy annual from the Orient related to the bachelor's button. The sweet-scented, silky, fringed, thistle-like flowers, to 2 in.

Cheiranthus cheiri

CHEIRANTHUS CHEIRI — Wallflower. Mustard Family.

A European species, quickly naturalized in Britain, where they do best on old walls. The erect plant is about 2 ft. high with narrow, lance-shaped, pointed leaves and showy terminal spikes of large yellow, orange, red or brown 1-in. flowers, sweetly scented. A perennial grown as a biennial since it deteriorates rapidly after the second year from seed. Widely used for spring bedding and cutting. Also a useful cool greenhouse pot plant. Effective grown in drifts in the border or used as an edging and a few should be planted where the scent will be carried into the house.

Sow seed thinly outdoors in April or May in a reserve border. Germination takes about 12 days. When large enough prick out and space 6 in. apart; break off the point of the tap root to induce a fibrous root system and sturdier plants. When 4-5 in. tall pinch out the growing points to encourage bushiness. Plant out in October where they are to flower, spacing them 12 in. apart. Do well in well-limed soil with good drainage, in full sun or partial shade. Bedding plants may be purchased in the fall for setting out.

Many garden varieties are listed in seed catalogs. There are double wallflowers, tall and dwarf. The Giant strain produces vigorous bushy plants with many handsome spikes of flowers in a wide range of colors. Early-flowering varieties are much improved and come into flower several weeks before the Giant kinds.

The Siberian wallflower has been known so long as *Cheiranthus allioni*, it is hard to think of it as *Erysimum asperum*, now its correct name. Its culture is similar to *C. cheiri* but it grows more rapidly, can be sown later in July in the open ground. Its beautiful orange-colored flower trusses bloom in May and June.

CHILEAN BELLFLOWER—See *Nolana atriplicifolia*.

CHINA ASTER—See *Callistephus chinensis* hybrids.

CHINA OR ANNUAL PINK—See *Dianthus chinensis*.

CHINESE FORGET-ME-NOT—See *Cynoglossum amabile*.

CHINESE LANTERN—See *Physalis alkekengi*.

CHRYSANTHEMUM, ANNUAL. Composite Family.

The hardy annual chrysanthemums are not to be confused with the perennial fall-blooming or greenhouse varieties. Although popular in England the annual chrysanthemum is not so much grown in this country even though they are valuable for summer gardening. They bloom profusely from early summer until frost and are easily grown from seed. When grown in masses or large beds their bright colors make a splendid show. The plants vary in height from 18-24 in. They are excellent for cutting.

Seed may be sown in September or started indoors 6 to 8 weeks before outdoor planting is possible for an early start, or sow directly

Chrysanthemum parthenium alba

in the open soil when weather permits. The double varieties are slower to germinate and get started than the singles. Space or thin seedlings to 1 ft. apart. They like a light, well-drained soil in full sun. Pinch for good branching. Will flower in 94 to 104 days from seed. Remove dead flowers to encourage more blooming. Staking may be necessary if position is exposed.

C. carinatum (C. tricolor)—Painted Daisy. A half hardy annual from Morocco, 2-3 ft. high, not much branched. Has flower heads about 2½ in. wide in white, red or yellow with a characteristic different-colored ring at the base of the rays and yellow at the center. Surprising tricolor blends. Rainbow Mixture offered in seed catalogs includes a collection of bright-hued tricolored blooms.

C. coronarium—Crown Daisy. A hardy annual from the Mediterranean region. Stout branched, 3-4 ft. tall, numerous flower heads about 1½ in. across, sometimes double, typically yellow. Seeds come in tall and double forms and mixed colors.

C. parthenium—Feverfew. Usually listed in seed catalogs as *Matricaria capensis* or *M. parthenioides*. A bushy perennial not permanently hardy in cold regions, frequently grown as an annual since it flowers readily from seed in one season. Grows 15-30 in. tall, has many white, button-like flower heads, scarcely ¼ in. wide, in July and August. Fine for cutting and valuable for borders or bedding, especially in semi-shade where they will do well, in ordinary garden soil. May be had in white and yellow, doubles, and Tom Thumb dwarf forms. Some good whites include Ball Double white, Snow Ball and White Stars. Golden Ball is a double golden yellow. Var. *aureum* has yellow foliage and grows 12 in. tall, good for edging.

C. segetum—Corn Marigold. A popular Eurasian annual with many named forms. Much branched, stems 1-2 ft. high, daisy-like flowers 1½-2½ in. across, white, cream and good clear yellows, solitary at the ends of the branches. Plants sparse of leaves which are notched but not deeply cut.

Varieties: Annual chrysanthemums may be purchased in Single Mixed, Double Mixed, straight colors, or Mixed Annual Varieties (including a choice assortment of all the popular annual Mum colors); also named varieties. There is a dwarf type for edging or small beds. Merry Mixture is offered by some seedsmen. Brilliant colors and easy to grow. Quite distinct from the autumn flowering chrysanthemums they come in attractive bright colors that range from bright scarlet through purple, orange, salmon, yellow and white. Large single blooms 2-3 in. across on 2 ft. plants.

CIGAR PLANT—See *Cuphea.*

CINERARIA—See *Senecio.*

CLADANTHUS ARABICUS *(C. proliferus).* Composite Family.
Sometimes listed as *Anthemis arabica.* A native of southern Spain and Morocco. Forms a nicely shaped, branching mound of finely dissected leaves which are strongly scented. Plant is covered with a profusion of daisy-like yellow flowers. As each flower opens, 4 or 5 branches appear immediately below it. These are terminated by flowers and the process continues, the number of flowers and the mound of foliage increasing steadily until

Cladanthus arabicus

the plant reaches a height of 2-3½ ft. An unusual plant for the border producing its flowers from June until Sept.

Hardy and of easy culture. Sow seed in early spring where plants are to grow. They like a fairly light, well-drained soil in a warm sunny position. Germination takes around 4 weeks. Thin plants to 12 in. apart. Flowering begins about 10 weeks after sowing and will continue until frost.

CLARKIA ELEGANS—Rocky Mountain Garland. Evening Primrose Family.
Hardy annual discovered in the Rocky Mountain area by members of the Lewis and Clark Expedition. In sections with hot summers the plant will fail to bloom and may even die. A free bloomer in cooler climates. The dainty rose-like flowers in many colors are borne along slender wiry stems, tucked in the axils of the leaves. Plants are 2-3 ft. tall and are prized for cutting as a single spray. Cut while still in bud—it will bloom for several days. The wild form has single, pink blooms but flowers are much doubled in most horticultural forms. Found in colors of white, cream, yellow, orange, pink, rose, lilac and salmon. Used for the border and for hanging baskets in the cooler regions of the United States as Denver, Seattle and the cool valleys of California. Inclined to be prostrate unless staked.

Effective in clumps among taller flowers as hollyhock or foxglove. Frequently forced in the greenhouse as pot subjects and cut flowers.

Sow seed in sandy, well-drained loam in sun or partial shade as soon as weather permits. Not too fussy about soil. Thin to 8-12 in. apart. Pinch out tips for bushy plants. Don't water unless wilting. Will bloom from July until frost. Flowers in 85 to 94 days from seed.

Varieties: *C. pulchella* is a low growing species about 1 ft. tall with reddish stems. Flowers in white, pink, rose and lilac but seed seldom listed in catalogs. Popular forms of *C. elegans* include May Blossom, a deep pink; Royal Bouquet, a fine English strain, bushy compact plants, many wonderful colors; Snowball; Purple Prince, etc. All the varieties are double-flowered. Can buy Double Mixed seed packets.

CLEOME SPINOSA—Spider Flower. Caper Family.
A tropical American annual cultivated for its showy, terminal, big, airy, rosy-pink and white flower clusters. The large shrub-like plants grow 3-5 ft. tall with a spread of about 3-4 ft. Although rather coarse, it is useful for planting in beds as a substitute for shrubs or where other bold masses of ornamentals

Clarkia elegans

Cleome spinosa

have failed. Plants are inclined to be leggy and leafless at the base so it is best to have something else planted in front of them. Attractive as a background against a fence or wall with lower plants set in front of them. A quick grower, cleome is useful for temporary effects and decorative in tubs for the terrace. If used in a small garden perhaps 3 plants will be sufficient. Unopen buds effective as a cut flower; will open for a week cut indoors, but the old flowers should be removed daily to look well.

Sow seed outdoors in spring in poor or rich soil. Seed germinates readily and does well almost anywhere, even in hot dry sites, and can take considerable shade. Thin to 20 in. apart, closer if among shrubs. Will flower from 60 to 74 days from seed. Keep plants on the dry side. Often self-sows with tendency to take over. From late June until frost each flower head opens a fresh crown of blossoms every afternoon. As the lower blossoms fade and go to seed their pods sprout out like spider legs along the lower stem. Seem to be insect and disease free.

Varieties: Var. *alba* has white flowers and *rosea* has bright rose-colored blooms. Popular named kinds are Pink Queen (All-America), a deep pink which blooms until late fall; Helen Campbell, a white one; and Purple Queen, a lilac purple.

CLOCK VINE—See *Thunbergia alata.*

COBAEA SCANDENS—Cup-and-Saucer Vine, Cathedral Bells. Phlox Family.
A vigorous tendril-bearing climber from Mexico, sometimes called Mexican Ivy. Although a woody perennial vine in the tropics and deep South, in the North it is much grown as an annual because of its quick growth and showy bloom. It is most attractive and unusually graceful for such a rampant climber. Freely produced flowers are large and cup or bell-shaped resting in a green saucer, and ranging in color from pink to purple followed by plum-shaped fruits. Useful wherever a mass of foliage and flowers are needed in a hurry to cover a trellis or wall. Will grow up to 20 ft.

Sow seed indoors, 5 to 6 weeks before outdoor planting is safe, one to a pot. Press

Cobaea scandens

seed into the soil edgewise as they are large and flat and germinate poorly placed broad side down. Require 10 to 14 days to sprout. When settled weather arrives move seedlings outdoors. Space 2-3 ft. apart. Like full sun or half-shade; a southern exposure is good. Any ordinary well-drained garden soil and a wire, string, fence or trellis support. When 6 in. high pinch back to make them bushier. Seeds may rot if soil is wet. Planting them in a slanting position helps avoid this. Plants are killed by frost.

Varieties: Var. *alba* has white flowers and runs fairly true from seed. Var. *variegata* has variegated foliage and must be propagated by cuttings to come true.

COCKLE or COW HERB—See *Saponaria vaccaria.*

COCKSCOMB—See *Celosia argentea.*

COLEUS BLUMEI—Coleus. Mint Family. A perennial foliage plant from tropical Java. Although much less grown than formerly it is still used as a bedding annual in northern climates and much grown as a house plant. One of the best for colored foliage. The varicolored leaves with fancy markings are richly colored and have toothed, often deeply cut leaves in shades of green, yellow, orange, red, purple and white. Grows 1-2 ft. or more in height but better if kept low and bushy. The whorls of small, dark blue, lilac or white flowers held in spikes are unimportant and should be kept picked off for greater profusion of foliage. Plant under trees or use in the border or as an edging plant. Striking in masses and decorative in window boxes or planters. A long season annual, attractive until frost. Very useful in arrangements.

No two plants grown from seed will be exactly alike. For exact reproduction use cuttings. For an early start sow seeds indoors in March. For quick germination bottom heat of 70° to 75° is helpful. Set seedlings outdoors after settled weather has arrived. Space 12-20 in. apart. Will do well in almost any good garden soil, well drained, in full sun or half-shade, but colors are more vivid when grown in partial shade. Pinch back the tips of the shoots now and then for compact, bushy and lower growing specimens. Water if dry weather makes it necessary. For winter pot plants make tip cuttings in September and bring indoors before cold weather arrives. Control aphids and mealy bugs (cottony white insects) with an insecticide such as lindane or malathion.

Varieties: Seeds come in many Rainbow strains. Rainbow Mixed is a mixture of various foliage colors; Rainbow White has a green edge; Rainbow Color Pride is bright amaranth-red, margined green, mottled with bronzy red; Rainbow Gold Dust is light green dusted golden yellow, very showy; Golden Rainbow, green flecked on gold; Pastel Rainbow is pale green on pink; and Scarlet Rainbow, scarlet on green. Candidum, green edged on ivory and Red Velvet are separate colored varieties. Rustic Splendor is a dwarf bushy coleus, scarlet-rust edged with amber, excellent for bedding use. Or seeds may be purchased in packets labeled Fringed Leaved; Croton-Leaved Mixture; Small-Leaved Types, Separate Colors and Mixtures; Large-Leaved Types, Separate Colors and Mixtures and Finest Mixed Hybrids.

Coleus blumei

Collinsia bicolor

COLLINSIA BICOLOR—Pagoda Collinsia. Figwort Family.

An attractive, hardy California annual grown from spring-sown seed but cannot take intense summer heat. Erect, slender stems 2 ft. in height bear clusters of large, showy flowers, 1 in. in length, produced in whorls and huddled at the leaf joints. The flowers are two-lipped, the upper lip is white, the lower lip violet or rose-purple. The oblong or lance-shaped leaves 1-2 in. long are toothed along the margin and arise from the stem in pairs or groups of three. Showy plants for the border or bedding out. Very fine for cutting. Good pot plant in the cool greenhouse.

May have to order seed from a California dealer. Sow in open in September for early flowers. Germination takes around 14 days. Thin in April or May as many young seedlings may be lost during the winter. Seed may also be sown in spring where they are to flower. Space or thin to 6 in. apart. Prefer a moist, well-drained soil and a little shade. Have rather weak stems so may require staking but make this as unobtrusive as possible since foliage is not abundant. By means of successive sowings one can have bloom from June until October unless summers are hot. Where summers are hot speed growth for blooms, as plants cannot take intense summer heat.

Varieties: Var. *alba* and var. *candidissima* have pure white flowers, var. *purpurea* deep purple and var. *multicolor* multicolored flowers—white, lilac, rose or violet predominating.

COLUMBINE—See *Aquilegia hybrids.*

CONEFLOWER, ANNUAL—See *Rudbeckia bicolor.*

CONVOLVULUS TRICOLOR (*C. minor*)— Dwarf or Bush Morning-Glory. Morning-Glory Family.

A beautiful annual from Southern Europe not often grown but gaining in popularity for a low trellis, at the top of a wall, hanging baskets, raised beds and container gardening. Excellent anywhere you want a low edging mass at the base of taller plants. The low-growing, trailing plants grow to 1 ft. high but spread 2 ft. or more. Constantly in bloom, the miniature flowers resemble the tall climbing morning-glories and are usually in 3 colors; the main part blue, pink or purple; the center yellow with a band of white between the center and the expanded part. Flowers are open all day in good weather.

Convolvulus tricolor

Seed coats are tough so nick with a file so moisture can enter. Sow seed outdoor where they are to grow after warm weather arrives, in full sun as they love sunshine and warmth. Grow well in sandy or even poorish soil. Thin to 10 in. apart. Not readily transplanted and they do not like humid regions where they will damp off in wet seasons. Keep plants on the dry side.

Varieties: Royal Ensign spreads 12-18 in. and has small, bright blue blossoms with a yellow throat and white markings. Japanese Imperial has large flowers in a variety of colors. Plants trail 3-4 ft.

CORAL or CONFEDERATE VINE—See *Antigonon leptopus.*

COREOPSIS TINCTORIA—Calliopsis, Annual or Golden Coreopsis. Composite Family. This best known and most popular of the hardy annual species is an old-time favorite from central United States, grown for its dependable and vivid profusion of bloom all summer long. Most seedsmen list the annual species under Calliopsis (or sometimes Leptosyne) and the perennial species under Coreopsis. For masses of color in the garden or for cutting it is hard to find anything more gay or easier to grow. Long stems are an asset in cutting. Flowers often have a band of contrasting color on the daisy-like single or semi-double flowers. Some have golden-yellow rays, reddish brown at the base, and brownish-purple centers; others are almost solid brown or mahogany. Foliage is very finely cut. Tall varieties reach 3 ft. in height and with their slender, loose, open growth habit are best used as background plants. Dwarf types which grow 8-12 in. tall make good edgings. They will, however, bloom themselves out and stop flowering in late summer.

In October or in the spring scatter seed outdoors where plants are to grow. Rake in lightly. Seeds are not bothered by the cold. Coreopsis needs full sun. Any ordinary well-drained garden soil will do; in fact, they can endure a rather hot, dry place and some neglect. Do not thin out as plants bloom best when crowded. Once started it usually self-sows. Cut flowers freely for an abundance of

Coreopsis tinctoria Semi-Double Golden Crown

bloom. Plants bloom 64 to 75 days from seed. If worms attack plants at the crown grow in another spot the next year.

Varieties: There are forms with all-crimson rays and with double flowers. Crimson King and Golden Sovereign are two good dwarf varieties for the front of the border, as is Tiger Star, crimson striped and mottled yellow. Golden Crown is a taller variety, 2 ft. high and yellow with a maroon center. *C. drummondi* (Golden Wave) is a tender annual species native to Texas sometimes grown.

CORNFLOWER—See *Centaurea cyanus.*

CORN MARIGOLD—See *Chrysanthemum segetum.*

COSMIDIUM—See *Thelesperma burridgeanum.*

COSMOS BIPINNATUS HYBRIDS—Cosmos. Composite Family.

A showy, half-hardy annual from Mexico. The big daisy-like blossoms are borne on long pliant stems and come in shades of white, pink, rose, lavender, purple and crimson (all colors but blue) with tufted yellow centers. The rays are always slightly toothed at the tip. A profusion of lacy leaves cut into threadlike segments gives a feathery, graceful effect. Plants grow 2½-5 ft. high supplying a fast-growing, graceful background. Excellent planted in mass against an evergreen or shrub border, along a fence or in a corner. There are many hybrids on the market. The old-fashioned cosmos bloomed so late in the season they are now bred for earlier bloom. Cosmos give big returns for very little care and no garden should be without a few plants. If dead flowers are picked off plants will bloom from July until fall. Tall kinds may need staking in a windy site. An excellent cut flower.

Sow seed of early-flowering strains outdoors in May where you want them to grow. They like a sunny location in any ordinary garden soil; even a quite poor soil will do. Rich soil promotes foliage instead of flowers. Thin to 18-20 in. apart. The more common pink, red and white forms transplant easily, the yellow and orange kinds must be handled carefully with plenty of soil around the roots. Will often self-sow. Pinch out terminal shoot when about 18 in. high for best bloom. Will flower 65 to 115 days from seed. Later blooming varieties should be sown indoors 6 to 8 weeks before outdoor planting is possible.

Varieties: In areas where summers are short the Sensation strain is desirable. They come into bloom 10 weeks after seed is sown, grow 5 ft. high and have 4-6 in. flowers with fluted petals in white, pink and crimson. Good for background planting. Sensation Mixed Colors may be purchased. Radiance (All-America) is a Sensation strain with rosy-red and crimson-shaded flowers on tall, robust plants. Pinkie is a clear pink and Purity a pure white.

The Klondyke strain are dwarfer, forming bushy 3-foot plants. Mandarin is a bright golden yellow with double flowers and long lasting. Fiesta is a novelty with gaily striped orange and scarlet petals, bushy habit, height 2½ ft. Double Crested has a fully double center surrounded by a flat row of petals; plants grow 2½ ft. high.

Cosmos bipinnatus hybrid, Sensation Radiance

Crepis rubra

COW HERB—See *Saponaria vaccaria.*

CREAM CUP—See *Platystemon californicus.*

CREEPING ZINNIA—See *Sanvitalia procumbens.*

CREPIS RUBRA—Hawk's Beard. Composite Family.
A native of Italy and Greece. Its dandelion-like leaves are mostly basal, above which rise slender stems bearing rose-purple flowers, about 1 in. wide, in small, solitary, long-stalked heads. Plants grow 24 in. tall and make good annuals for the border. May be used effectively to cover rough, waste places in the wild garden. Begin to flower in June and will continue for a month or more.
Hardy. Sow seed where wanted in the fall or spring where they are to flower. Germination takes about 2 weeks. Thin plants to 6 in. apart. Grow well on poor soils. Sets seed freely and if ground is left undisturbed a large number of new plants will appear the following year. Usually require staking. The flowers close in early afternoon.
Varieties: Var. *alba* has white flowers and var. *rosea* rose-pink flowers.

CROWN DAISY—See *Chrysanthemum coronarium.*

CRYOPHYTUM—See *Mesembryanthemum.*

CUP-AND-SAUCER VINE—See *Cobaea scandens.*

CUP FLOWER—See *Nierembergia rivularis.*

CUPHEA PLATYCENTRA (*C. ignea*)— Mexican Cigar Plant. Loosestrife Family.
An attractive little plant from Central and South America grown for its showy unusual-shaped rosy-scarlet flowers—narrow tubes with a dark ring at the base and a white mouth. The compact little plants grow only about 1 ft. tall. They have reddish stems bearing lance-shaped green leaves. Used as bedding plants throughout the U. S. and as cool greenhouse pot plants. Excellent for cutting.
Half-hardy. Easily grown from seed. Sow indoors 6 to 8 weeks before outdoor planting is safe. Germination takes about a week (70°-75°). When 4 in. tall pinch out the growing points to ensure a bushy compact plant. When danger of frost is past plant out, spacing 9 in. apart. Will bloom 16 to 18 weeks

Cuphea platycentra Firefly

from sowing. Likes a warm sheltered location and a rather rich, well-drained soil.

Varieties: Avalon hybrids are lavender, lilac, pink, rose-purple, crimson and vermilion. Firefly is a dark-red variety which grows 10 in. tall, useful for edging.

Cuphea llavea. A somewhat shrubby species with bright red flowers from July to September. Var. *alba* has white flowers, var. *compacta* is more compact than the type, 9-12 in. tall, and var. *miniata,* the Cigar Flower, has more hairy stems. The type and its taller varieties grow to 2 ft. or more and should be planted 12 in. apart.

Cupea miniata—C. *llavea* var. *miniata.*

Cynoglossum amabile

CUPID'S DART—*See Catananche caerulea.*

CYNOGLOSSUM AMABILE—Chinese Forget-Me-Not. Borage Family.
An eastern Asiatic biennial but grown as an annual since it blooms from seed in a single season. Much like a tall forget-me-not with long upright, branching stems of deep, clear-blue flowers, somewhat weedy with rather coarse foliage but effective grouped in masses. Plants grow 1½-2½ ft. tall. A splendid blue border plant and a fairly good cut flower even though it does not keep very long.

Broadcast or sow seed in rows outdoors in early spring where plants are to grow. Barely cover seed. Will not be harmed by cold soil. Seeds are sticky so you may find them almost anywhere. Thin seedlings to 12-18 in. apart. Will do well in sun or light shade, in ordinary or even poor garden soil. Often self-sows and some will live over the winter. Has tendency toward being a biennial and may become too plentiful unless controlled. No special culture required.

Varieties: Pink and white forms are available. Blue Bird with sky-blue flowers grows to 2 ft. Firmament is indigo-blue, a compact 15 in. plant which will do well even in poor soil. Pink Firmament and Snowbird are also good.

CYPRESS VINE—See *Quamoclit pennata.*

DAHLIA MERCKI—Bedding or Dwarf Dahlia. Composite Family.
Bedding dahlias, originally from Mexico, are grown in large numbers for use as bedding plants. Usually handled as annuals, the small, compact plants grow about 12-18 in. tall and are covered with flowers from midsummer until frost. Single, semi-double and double blossoms are held erect on long, slender stems and come in many rich and glowing colors. Flowers measure 2-3 in. in diameter. Excellent and long lasting flowers for cutting if cut just before blossoms are fully open. Seal ends of stems by plunging into boiling water.

For an early start sow indoors 6 to 8 weeks before planting outdoors is possible. In warmer regions sow seed directly in the open

Dahlia mercki

Datura metel Double

ground. Like an open sunny location with afternoon shade. Grow well in almost any good garden soil provided it is retentive of moisture. Rich soil tends to produce luxuriant foliage and restrict flower production. In hot, dry weather mulch and water freely. Pinch out the growing tips to encourage bushiness. Seeds germinate in about 9 days (60°-65°).

Varieties: Unwin's Dwarf has semi-double 3 in. flowers in a wide range of colors and is considered a good mixture. Coltness Hybrids have single flowers in many colors, some with fluted rays. Fall Festival has single and double flowers in shades of red with some apricot-yellow and purple, 2½ ft.

DATURA METEL—Angel's Trumpet. Potato or Nightshade Family.
A variable annual from India with a dangerously poisonous juice. Grown for its large trumpet-shaped yellowish-white flowers sparingly produced. Grows from 3-5 ft. in height, bearing large, oval to lance-shaped dark green leaves, strongly scented and handsome huge flowers about 8 in. long and 4 in. across the mouth. The outside petals are frequently washed with a purple color. A weedy, coarse-growing plant closely related to the Jimson-Weed. Children should be warned about the poisonous juice, which from wilted foliage is deadly.

Sow seed indoors 5 to 7 weeks before outdoor planting is safe. Germination takes about 10 to 12 days. Transfer seedlings outdoors in rich sandy loam, although most any soil will do. Place in full sun. Space 1½-2 ft. on all sides. Will flower in 14 weeks from seed and continue until September. Thrives best in great heat and drought. Will take high winds and heavy rains without staking.

Varieties: Some have double or even triple flowers. Var. *alba* has pure white flowers, var. *caerulea* deep blue ones and var. *huberiana* blue, yellow and red.

DELPHINIUM AJACIS—Annual or Rocket Larkspur. Buttercup Family.
For blue masses in the garden and for use when cut, this erect, branching, hardy annual from the Mediterranean region is much in demand. Plants may vary from 2-4 ft. in height and will bloom for about 2 months in late spring and early summer. The tall full spikes of spurred flowers 1-1½ in. across, in shades of blue, violet, dark purple, rose, light pink, scarlet and white may be single or double in form. In front of a tall fence, as a background flower or grouped for accent, the beautiful colors and airy spikes are effective and will provide bright, cheery masses of color from early in the summer on. Larkspur needs a lower planting in front of it to hide the foliage which becomes unattractive in many locations in early summer. The blooms are valuable as cut flowers since they are graceful, easy to arrange, long lasting and come in lovely colors. Clear colors are more readily obtained in the annual than in the perennial kinds. They have been greatly improved in color and fullness of spikes. Spikes

are easily dried for arrangements. They retain their colors very well.

Seed should be sown in the fall just before the ground freezes or in very early spring because plants must have a cool growing season. Thin to 10-12 in. apart. Very difficult to transplant. To do so successfully must keep ball of earth around the roots. Will bloom 88 to 110 days from seed. Plants often self-sow in which case they gradually become poorer and poorer each year, so it is better to buy new seed. If the weather turns very hot this will shorten the blooming season.

Varieties: Giant Imperial is an older strain offered in colors of blue, pink, rose, salmon, lilac and white. The Regal strain is an improvement with huge double flowers, closely set on long spikes, that come early and are excellent for cutting. Both may be bought in separate colors or mixed seed packets. Connecticut Yankees are shrub-like in appearance with the branching plants 2½-3 ft. tall. Colors from soft lavender to deepest blue and purple.

DIANTHUS—Pink. Pink Family.
The flowers of the annual pinks are less fragrant than the perennial kinds, and some are with no fragrance. Their leaves are also broader. The universally popular annual pinks are useful for flower beds and edgings, planted in drifts or masses, and excellent for cutting. Although not difficult to raise, all members of the pink family prefer cool, rather than hot, dry summers and need sun to bloom.

D. allwoodi (D. caryophyllus x D. plumaris)—Hybrid Pinks. Flowers of wonderful colorings, the petals smooth-edged or fringed, generally tufted, with narrow, bluish-green foliage. May vary from 4-20 in. in height. Var. Sweet Wivelsfield blooms freely and continuously from June until frost. Fancy-edged petals, contrasting color zones, fragrant flowers, larger than sweet william, and borne in trusses. Fine bedding plant. Good cut flower.

D. barbatus—Sweet William. A biennial, but in some horticultural forms grown as an annual since they will bloom from seed in a

Delphinium ajacis Regal Mixed

season if the growing season is long enough. The dwarf edging varieties, 8-10 in. tall, may be purchased in the spring, ready to be set out as soon as soil can be worked. Often persistent in the South from self-sown seeds. Flowers are only slightly fragrant, in rounded clusters, and may be had in white, pink, and red; foliage is a rich green; plants grow 1-2 ft. tall.

As an annual, sow seed indoors 6 to 8 weeks before planting outdoors is safe. Transfer seedlings to any ordinary garden soil in full sun. Space 8-10 in. Such plants will bloom by August.

Varieties: Giant White, Pink Beauty and Scarlet are attractive, the names self-explanatory. There is an annual sweet william, Summer Beauty, a hybrid strain producing scented flowers and including shades of pink and red, some with rich-colored zones on a white background; plants grow to 1 ft. tall. Wee Willie is an annual sweet william 3-4 in., and comes in a blend of colors (rich shades of red).

D. caryophyllus—Annual Carnation. Although it blooms from seed in a single season it is not hardy outdoors in regions of severe frosts or north of Washington, D.C. so it is best treated as an annual. South of this line they may be biennials or perennials and should persist. Similar to the florist's carnation, the flowers are smaller in size but more spicily fragrant. All have wandlike stems, bluish-gray leaves and much-doubled flowers. A constant delight both for the garden and for cutting. They come in a wide color range including red, scarlet, white, pink, purple and yellow and grow 12-18 in. tall.

Plant seed indoors 6-8 weeks before outdoor planting is safe for certainty of bloom. Transfer seedlings outdoors when trees leaf out. Space 8-10 in. apart in full sun in any ordinary garden soil except an acid one. If soil is acid add 1 teaspoon of lime for each plant thoroughly mixed with soil. For large flowers take off all flower buds leaving only one to a plant. But for bushy specimens and an abundance of smaller blooms pinch out center of young plants. Do best in a cool climate.

Varieties: Some are striped, others have petals edged with a contrasting color. Chabaud hybrids are a fine strain for outdoor bedding and to use cut. Come in wide range of colors. Dwarf Fragrance has large double flowers in a full range of colors and compact, upright plants, 12-14 in. Very fragrant and earlier than Chabaud, with about the same degree of doubleness.

D. chinensis (D. sinensis, D. seguieri)— China or Annual Pink. Originally an Asiatic short-lived perennial but through hybridizing now the source of several annual pinks of various colors. Although less fragrant than the perennial pink they form nice bushy plants with gray-green, grass-like leaves about 12-18 in. tall. Stiff erect stems bear slightly fragrant flowers in white, rose, pink or lilac, solitary or in sparse clusters, 1-2 in. wide. Bloom in early summer. Effective planted in drifts. A good cut flower.

Grows quickly from seed which may be sown in late fall or early spring. Barely cover since seed is very small. Thin plants 6-8 in. apart. Give plants full sun and a rich, well-drained soil (sweet rather than acid). Pinch to produce branching plants. Will bloom 88 to 106 days from seed. Cut back after first crop of flowers to encourage plants to bloom again. They often will live over the winter. A light covering in severe climates will help

Dianthus caryophyllus Dwarf Fragrance

Digitalis purpurea

carry them over. Really more than annuals, since if protected during the winter they may bloom the second year, but cannot be depended upon.

Varieties: Single- and double-flowered varieties are available. Heddensis, a tetraploid hybrid, is 1½ ft. tall with single blooms in mixed colors; Bravo (All-America) is excellent for edging flower beds and has deep scarlet-red single blossoms, 1½ in. wide on 8 in. plants; Carnation-flowered types have fully double flowers like miniature carnations in white, pink and red and grow 1½ ft. high.

D. heddewigi (*D. allwoodi* x *D. barbatus*). Both single and double. Baby Doll is an outstanding extra dwarf dianthus, with well-rounded large flowers 2-2½ in. across, in a brilliant range of true dianthus colors.

DIGITALIS PURPUREA (*D. tomentosa*)—Foxglove. Figwort Family.

Although a biennial from western Europe and sometimes a perennial, this charming, old-fashioned flower is treated much the same as an annual. Generally speaking biennials bloom earlier in the year than most annuals and are at their peak in spring and early summer. Foxgloves reseed themselves so readily you have a new supply of plants each year, although individual plants are not long lived. The long, tapering spires, 2-4 ft. tall, encircled with speckle-throated purple, white, yellow, salmon or rose-colored flowers bloom in early summer with early lilies and the Canterbury bells. They contrast nicely with daisy-shaped flowers and are excellent at the rear of a border or make striking accent plants in the landscape. A clump combines nicely with shrubs. One of the showiest of plants when grown in favorable locations.

Does much better along the New England coast and in coastal Washington and Oregon areas than in hotter, drier regions. May start seed indoors in early spring or sow seed in boxes or pots outdoors in late August or early September. Winter over in the cold frame or some other protected area with no heat. In spring transfer seedlings to permanent site spacing 1-1½ ft. apart in a partially shaded, cool, moist but not wet location, protected from wind if possible. Soil must be well-drained. Where winters are severe a light cover of evergreen branches is a good protection. The soil should be rich in humus but not acid.

Varieties: The Shirley Hybrids have large bell-shaped blooms in shades of soft pink to deep rose, spotted with brown, maroon and crimson. Newer is the Excelsior Strain with large flowers better distributed all around the stalk in colors of white, pink, rose, purple, cream and yellow.

DIMORPHOTHECA AURANTIACA — Cape Marigold, African Daisy. Composite Family.

A South African perennial but best treated here as an annual. Will supply a mass of color all summer in the garden. Has bright orange flowers with black centers but forms are offered with flowers in shades of buff, cream, yellow, salmon and orange which are carried on thin, wiry stems. Plants are rather dwarf, only 12-15 in. tall, spreading into solid mounds useful for edgings along walks, for massed effects in flower beds and in rock gardens. Like other daisies these flowers are excellent cut although they do close at night.

Sow seed indoors for an early start or sow outdoors when weather permits where they are to grow. Barely cover with soil. Thin to 8-10 in. apart. Will bloom in 6 weeks from sowing. Flower when quite young so planting indoors is of little advantage. Like a warm sunny location with good drainage. They do not like shade or a heavy soil. A showy plant for hot, dry climates.

DOLICHOS LABLAB—Hyacinth Bean. Pea Family.

An interesting climber from the Old World tropics where it is a perennial and grown as such in the South but killed by our frosts in the North, where it is grown as a half-hardy annual. This rapid-growing twining climber reaches a height of 10 ft. or more and flowers freely from July to October. Long spikes of pea-like purple or white flowers are followed by purple seed pods. The green leaves are each divided into three large, broad, shapely-pointed leaflets. May be used any

Dimorphotheca aurantiaca

Dolichos lablab

place where a rapid-growing vine is needed. An attractive climber for the cool greenhouse. Grown here as an ornamental but of considerable economic importance in native habitat as food and forage.

For early bloom sow seed indoors, in pots, 6 to 8 weeks before outdoor planting is safe or sow seed outdoors when weather permits where vines are to grow. Germination takes about 2 weeks. Does not transplant easily. Thin or space 1-3 ft. apart. Will bloom 4 months after sowing and continue to bloom until cut down by frost. Provide string, trellis or some support for climber to twine around or it will sprawl. Will bloom first year from seed if started early enough and weather is warm; requires heat and is not suited to short growing season and cool nights. Enjoys a warm, sheltered position and a rich, moist soil. Not bothered by pests.

Varieties: There are several brightly colored varieties listed in the seed catalogs.

DOWNINGIA. Lobelia Family.
Low-growing, half-hardy annual from the Pacific Coast. Good small plant for edging. Resembles a large-flowered lobelia in appearance and may be used similarly for hanging baskets or window boxes. Blooms from June to September.

For an early start sow seed indoors 6 to 8 weeks before outdoor planting is safe. Germinate most readily at 55° to 60° F. Plant seedlings outdoors in May or sow seed in April where they are to flower. Thin or space plants 6 in. apart. Like a good well-drained garden soil and will grow equally well in full sun or partial shade.

D. elegans. This California annual rarely exceeds 7 in. in height; has oblong or lance-shaped leaves and a profusion of sky-blue, white-throated, yellow or green spotted flowers, stamens long and protruding.

D. pulchella. Also from California and similar to *D. elegans* but is only 4-6 in. tall; has smaller, narrower leaves and deep blue flowers. The lower lip of the flower is marked with a bright yellow, white-fringed blotch. The throat is streaked with yellow and purple stamens scarcely protruding. More loose in habit than *D. elegans.*

DUSTY MILLER—See *Centaurea candidissima* and *Senecio cineraria.*

ECCREMOCARPUS SCABER. Trumpet-Creeper Family.
A tall climbing vine from Chile with slender

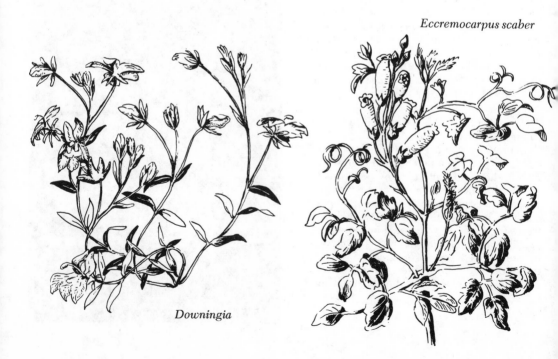

Eccremocarpus scaber

Downningia

reddish stems bearing attractive dark green leaves but grown for its very handsome blooms. Long, slender, terminal spikes or racemes of orange-red, yellow-tipped tubular flowers about 1 in. in length flower throughout the summer. The leaves are divided into oval-pointed leaflets which are entire, occasionally toothed along the margin. Hardy in the South but in the North treated as a tender annual. Grows up to 10 ft. or more and its pleasant green foliage with brilliant sprays of tubular flowers make it a showy climber for screening a garden shed or wall. Flowers are charming for cutting.

Start seed indoors 6 to 8 weeks before outdoor planting is safe. Germination takes about 2 weeks (65°-70° F). Plant out in May spacing 12 in. apart where wanted. Likes a light, well-drained soil and a sunny position. Will start to flower 4 months after sowing and continue to bloom for 10 weeks or so. May also be grown as a biennial.

Varieties: Var. *aureus* has bright golden-yellow flowers, var. *coccineus* scarlet flowers, var. *ruber* deep red and var. *carmineus* rich carmine-red blooms.

ECHINOCYSTIS LOBATA—Wild or Mock Cucumber. Cucumber Family.

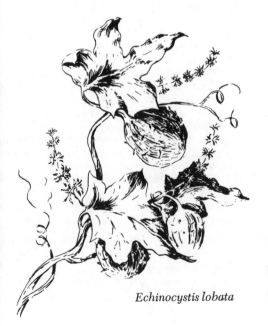

Echinocystis lobata

Echium plantagineum

One of our fastest growing South and North American tendril-bearing vines, often reaching a height of 20 ft. It has light green, oval-ish-heart-shaped leaves 3-5 in. long, 3 to 7 lobed, the lobes with a minute soft prickle. The small white flowers in branched racemes appear during July and August followed by an abundance of 2 in. long, spiny seed pods, puffy and rather papery. Useful for a quick covering. Grow on trellises or for covering unsightly objects or fences. Usually described under the heading of gourds.

Seed should be nicked and soaked in warm water before sowing to hasten germination. Will grow in any soil.

Varieties: Sometimes offered as *Micrampelis.*

ECHIUM PLANTAGINEUM—Viper's Bugloss. Borage Family.
A native British species, quite hardy. Produces branching spikes with clusters of flowers which start pink and turn pale-purple or blue. The plants grow 3 ft. tall and are covered with stiff, bristly gray hairs. A good plant for the border, its showy flowers are produced in abundance from June until September.

Seed may be sown outdoors in the fall or

early in the spring where they are to flower. Germination takes 3 to 4 weeks. Thin to 18 in. Plants thrive in light, dry soils in an open sunny location. Flowering begins about 12-14 weeks after sowing and continues for about 2 months.

Varieties: Var. *excelsum* is very handsome, superior in every way to the type. Dwarf varieties are also now available.

EMILIA SAGITTATA (E. *flammea*)—Tassel Flower. Composite Family.

Cataloged also as *Cacalia coccinea*. A native of the Old World tropics, worthy of a place in any garden. It forms dense clusters of oval, pointed, coarsely-toothed, gray-green leaves above which rise a profusion of long, wiry stems terminating in sprays of brilliant red or scarlet tassel-like flowers. These provide a dash of noticeable color even though the plant is not large—about 18 in. tall. Blooms from June until frost. Best when crowded. Interplant among more robust annuals. Good rockery subject and useful cut.

Of easy culture. Treated as a half-hardy annual. Sow seed outdoors early in the spring in sun and a moderately light soil. Germination takes 5 days (60°-65°). Thin seedlings 4-5 inches apart. Flowering begins about 12 weeks after sowing and plants will continue to bloom for 10 weeks or more.

Varieties: Var. *lutea* has golden-yellow flowers.

Emilia sagittata

Erysimum murale

ENGLISH DAISY—See *Bellis perennis.*

ERYSIMUM MURALE (E. *perofskianum*) —Fairy Wallflower, Blister Cress. Mustard Family.

A dwarf, compact biennial from Europe about 9 in. tall bearing short narrow leaves and dense spikes of golden-yellow flowers. Closely related to the wallflower, Cheiranthus. Especially attractive in late summer when some other subjects are beginning to wane. Excellent plant for edging the border, splendid for rockeries, and a good subject for the cold greenhouse. Sweet-scented flowers are excellent for cutting.

May be treated as an annual. Sow seed in September or early spring where they are to flower. Or treat as a biennial and sow seed in June, then transplant in September where they are to flower. Thin or plant 6 in. apart. Germination takes about 2 weeks. Plants prefer a deep, rich, well-drained, alkaline loam and an open sunny position. Self-sow and naturalize themselves on gravelly slopes.

E. *asperum*—Siberian Wallflower, often sold as *Cheiranthus allioni*. A North American perennial best treated as a biennial and often confused with E. *murale.*

ESCHSCHOLZIA CALIFORNICA — California Poppy. Poppy Family.

The state flower of California and the very essence of California sunshine. Its silky, golden-yellow blossoms are borne in great profusion. A perennial, usually grown as an annual. Hybridizers have greatly improved the plant until now we have both singles and doubles in a great range of satiny-sheen colors in creamy-white, scarlet, pink, orange and yellow. Some forms have delicately-fluted or frilled petals. Although it does spread over the ground it grows about 12-15 in. tall and has lacy, blue-gray-green foliage which adds much to the simple beauty of the flowers and produces a light, airy effect. Flowers appear profusely from June until frost. Readily naturalized in dry spots, useful planted in masses or drifts in beds or borders, along drives or in hard to cultivate places; their bright orange-gold will brighten any area. Scatter seed on ground around spring-flowering bulbs for color when bulbs are gone. If cut in the bud, before quite open, the flowers may be used in arrangements and will keep for several days. In the garden the golden and lemon varieties combine nicely with cornflowers, blue lupine and larkspur. Blossoms close at night and when they fade drop off the plant.

Broadcast seed in the fall or early spring where plants are to grow, in full sun, as soon as the soil can be worked. They like a hot, dry spot in loose, well-drained soil. Will tolerate some shade and will grow in quite dry and otherwise adverse places. Thin to 8 in. apart. Do not attempt to transplant as plants do not move readily. The old plants will self-sow if protected in the fall. Plants bloom 45-60 days from seed. Do not let go to seed if you want bloom to continue.

Varieties: Usually seed is sold in a mixture but separate colors are also available as Honolulu (orange), Carmine King, Dazzler (scarlet), Gloaming (coral) and Golden West. Mission Bells mixture includes double and semi-double flowers in yellow, pink, scarlet and deep red and may have bicolored flowers or frilled petals.

EUPHORBIA HETEROPHYLLA—Annual Poinsettia, Mexican Fire Plant, Fire-on-the-Mountain. Spurge Family.

Grown as a tender annual and native to Central America. It is not as showy as its close relative, the florist's poinsettia, but this outdoor annual makes a neat, compact bush of dark green foliage until about the middle of the summer when the leaves turn a vivid

Eschscholzia californica

Euphorbia heterophylla

scarlet, either all over or merely at the base. Actually the leaves are first green, toward the base of the stem, gradually turning white and finally red. It grows 2-3 ft. in height. The flowers are inconspicuous and unimportant. When grown well the plants become much branched and are quite handsome. Useful in the border where their oddly colored leaves attract attention.

Sow seed in open ground when warm weather arrives and danger of frost is passed, in full sun, in any ordinary garden soil. Will grow in rather poor soil but likes heat and full sunshine. Sow 3 or 4 seeds in one place and when the seedlings appear pull out all but the best one. Need space to develop, at least 12-18 in.

No varieties. Frequently offered as *Poinsettia heterophylla* in seed catalogs.

E. marginata (E. variegata) — Snow-on-the-Mountain. This species grows wild in central United States from the Dakotas to Texas and eastward. Its common name comes from the appearance of the white-edged, light green foliage and flower bracts. Flowers are inconspicuous. A vigorous, strong-growing well-branched plant, it grows from 2-2½ ft. tall. Its green and white leaves are very showy, best used to blend colors or tone down intense ones in the border. Begin to develop the characteristic white-edged leaves when only half grown. Branches at height of about 1½ ft. so that when it should be at its best it is often bare at the base. Plan to use plants around 18-24 in. tall in front to hide this bareness. Foliage may be cut for arrangements. Sear stem ends to congeal the milky juice by dipping in boiling water. Juice irritates some skins so handle with care.

Easy to grow. Sow seed where plants are to grow in early spring in full sun or partial shade in any, even poor, garden soil. Thin to 10-14 in. apart. Plants grow rapidly but are hard to transplant. Self-sows readily and in favorable locations comes up each spring behaving like a perennial and may become a weed.

EVENING PRIMROSE—See *Oenothera drummondi.*

FAIRY WALLFLOWER—See *Erysimum murale.*

FALSE CHAMOMILE—See *Matricaria chamomilla.*

FELICIA AFFINIS. Composite Family.
A half-hardy annual from South Africa with showy, blue, daisy-like, rich-yellow-centered flowers about ¾ in. in diameter, borne on long stalks well above the foliage. The dark-green hairy leaves are oblong or somewhat oval in shape and taper toward the base. Plants grow to a height of 12 in. Lovely for the border or for bedding out. Also charming plants for the cool greenhouse.

Sow seed indoors 6 to 8 weeks before outdoor planting is safe. Germination takes place in about a week (60°-65° F.). Plant out in May spacing 6 in. apart. Plants can stand a few degrees of frost. Prefer a warm, sheltered, sunny position and any good, ordinary, well-drained garden soil. Will flower about 15 weeks after sowing and will continue to flower for about 10 weeks. By cutting the plants back after the first flowering it is possible to secure a second crop.

F. amelloides (Agathaea coelestis)—Blue Daisy, Blue Marguerite. Grows 1-3 ft. tall and provides a mass of blue flowers from July to October. Plants may then be lifted, potted and brought into the greenhouse to continue flowering through the winter. It is a cool greenhouse pot plant. Var. *monstrosa* has much larger flowers than those of the type, often measuring up to 3 in. in diameter. When grown in the open, plant out 9 in. apart.

F. bergeriana — Kingfisher Daisy. This small dwarf-growing species is 6 in. in height and will flower through the summer in a warm, sunny location. Plant out 6 in. apart. Flowers may close in dull weather. Excellent for the rock garden or as an edger. Useful in window boxes or as pot plants in the cool greenhouse.

FEVERFEW—See *Chrysanthemum parthenium.*

Felicia amelloides

FIG-MARIGOLD — See *Mesembryanthemum.*

FIRE-ON-THE-MOUNTAIN—See *Euphorbia heterophylla.*

FLAX, ANNUAL or FLOWERING—See *Linum grandiflorum.*

FLOSS FLOWER—See *Ageratum houstonianum.*

FORGET-ME-NOT, ANNUAL—See *Myosotis sylvatica.*

FORGET-ME-NOT, CAPE OR SUMMER —See *Anchusa capensis.*

FORGET-ME-NOT, CHINESE—See *Cynoglossum amabile.*

FOUR O'CLOCK—See *Mirabilis jalapa.*

FOXGLOVE—See *Digitalis purpurea.*

FUCHSIA HYBRIDA—Lady's Ear Drops. Evening Primrose or Fuchsia Family.
There are hundreds of varieties in both upright and hanging types. *F. magellanica* var. *riccartoni* is the hardiest of all and will take frost up to New York if in a sheltered site. This fuchsia reaches a height of 6 to 9 feet in California and lines the roadsides in parts of Ireland. As grown in the North by florists and amateurs in a cool greenhouse, fuchsias are propagated from 3-inch cuttings taken from tender spring growth. They are included here because of their popular use as summer bedding plants, as tree or standard forms, and for decoration as used in hanging baskets, window boxes and pots.

Unless you have a cool greenhouse, pit or cold frame to winter over stock plants and make cuttings in the spring, buy young plants to set out when danger of frost is over. They do best under cool, humid conditions as found along the coastal areas and are especially popular in California. They bloom well in partial shade, where they are free from winds, in rich soil (slightly on the acid

Fuchsia hybrida

warm shades of red, yellow and gold and are carried on long, rather weak stems during the summer months, providing a wealth of long-stemmed flowers for cutting. Especially valued when other flowers in the garden have been cut down by frost.

Plant seed indoors for an early start or where plants are to grow, in full sun, in any well-drained soil. Thin or space 12 in. apart. Will bloom 75 to 107 days from seed. Cut flowers freely for continuous bloom.

Varieties: Come single, double and quilled and in colors from red through orange, copper, yellow and white. Picta comes in single and double forms, with large heads and many fine colors. Tetra Fiesta is red, tipped yellow. Indian Chief is a rich bronzy red, large single, daisy type. Lorenziana has double flowers as does Sunshine. Gaiety Mixed contains many bright and warm shaded doubles.

There is the Lillipop Series with 2½-in. ball-shaped double flowers and compact 10-in. plant mounds which includes Raspberry Red, Butterscotch Bronze, and Lemon Delight.

side) and require good drainage. For summer bedding, plant pot and all directly into the bed, up to the rim. In the fall, lift the pot, (repot if necessary) and take back into the house for decoration or store in a cool room at 45 to 50 degrees to keep them dormant through the winter, watering just enough to keep the wood from shriveling. A covering of peatmoss over the roots is helpful.

GAILLARDIA PULCHELLA *(G. drummondi, G. bicolor)*—Annual Blanket Flower. Composite Family.

A very showy, hardy annual found wild from North Carolina to Florida and westward. Its bright, sunset colors are an asset to any garden. Generally the perennial forms of *G. aristata grandiflora* are yellow and the annuals are red with tubular florets, although now they come in many fine horticultural forms. An easy to grow border or bedding plant, 1½-2 ft. tall, its flower heads come in

GARDEN BALSAM—See *Impatiens balsamina.*

Gaillardia pulchella Lorenziana Mixed

Gazania longiscapa

Sow seeds indoors 7-9 weeks before outdoor planting is safe. Transfer seedlings outdoors, in full sun, in a sandy loam and space 6-10 in. apart. Will stand hot, dry weather and will flower first year from seed from an early sowing but needs warmth to develop; not suited to sections with short growing season and cool nights.

Varieties: Hybrids Mixed, Cream and Pink Shades; Red and Orange Shades are listed in seed catalogs. *Splendens grandiflora* Mixed grows 8 in. high and comes in shades of yellow, orange, light and dark brown, salmon, red and ruby zoned.

GERANIUM—See *Pelargonium*.

GILIA CAPITATA—Blue or Globe Gilia. Phlox Family.
A very graceful annual from the Pacific Coast area sometimes known as the Thimble Flower. It has finely cut foliage and long-stemmed, dense, spherical, clover-like heads of small, funnel-shaped pale blue flowers 1 in. across. Plants are erect, growing to a height of 1½-2 ft. Useful for the border or rock garden. Smother themselves during the summer with small but showy flowers. Ex-

Gilia capitata

GAZANIA LONGISCAPA—African Daisy. Composite Family.
A handsome South African annual 8-10 in. in height with mostly basal leaves, white-felty beneath, and more or less deeply cut, feather-fashion. The flowers are short-stalked, solitary, with golden-yellow daisy-like heads with a dark eye. Flowers may measure 2-3 in. in diameter and are day-blooming, closing at night. A fine summer blooming plant, best treated as a tender annual. Many of the hybrids are beautifully spotted with black, green and white around the discs. Excellent for potting.

cellent for cutting and a good pot plant for the cool greenhouse.

As soon as warm weather arrives sow seed in an open, sunny position in a light, well-drained soil, moderately rich. Germination takes 16 to 18 days. Thin to 10 in. apart. Quite hardy. Only the taller varieties will require staking; very slender twigs may be used and will be hidden by the foliage.

Varieties: Var. *alba* has white flowers, var. *major* larger flowers than those of the type.

GLOBE AMARANTH—See *Gomphrena globosa.*

GLORIOSA DAISY—See *Rudbeckia hirta* selections.

GODETIA GRANDIFLORA—Satin Flower. Evening Primrose Family.
A beautiful native annual of California and the West Coast; compact and bushy, the

Godetia grandiflora

plant grows about 24 in. tall, with some of the dwarfer strains only 18 in. The showy satiny-petaled flowers, both single and double, open wide and furnish masses of bloom throughout the summer and fall if you live in a cool, moist climate. Flowers measure 3-5 in. in diameter. Always attractive in the garden and noticeable because of the interesting texture of the bloom. Excellent cut for arrangements.

Sowing seed indoors early in pots will hasten the bloom, or scatter seed where wanted outdoors as soon as warm weather arrives. Plants resent transplanting. A cool, moist climate is necessary for the satin flower. It simply cannot take hot weather. Likes full sun or partial shade and a sandy loam, or even poor soil will do. Rich soil produces leaves instead of flowers. Space or thin to 6-12 in. apart. Will bloom 104 to 115 days from seed. If too crowded becomes leggy, yet bloom is more profuse if reasonably crowded. In very hot weather bloom will be reduced and plants may die. In warm climates will self-sow.

Varieties: Seed is available in separate colors or mixed including rose, scarlet, dark crimson, lavender and pure white. Usually a deeper color is found near the center of the flower. Some strains are double-flowered. Varieties include var. *carminea* with carmine-red flowers and var. *lilacina* with lilac-colored ones, both well worth growing. Var. *azaleaflora* is a small, very compact form with rose-colored flowers.

GOLDEN CUP—See *Hunnemannia fumariaefolia.*

GOMPHRENA GLOBOSA—Globe Amaranth. Amaranth Family.
An erect, bushy, branched plant from the Old World tropics. A deservedly popular garden annual, 12-24 in. tall, much grown for its pink, red, magenta, purple, white and orange clover-like flower heads about ¾ in. across, usually solitary or in sparse clusters. It is an excellent plant for hot summer areas and is good cut either fresh or dried. One of the everlastings, its flowers dry quickly retaining color and shape.

III. Opposite   *This attractive entrance to the garden of George Taloumis, Salem, Massachusetts, demonstrates the effectiveness of pot plants, placed at such important and strategic locations as in front of fences and near gateways. The bright and familiar red of geraniums and the well-designed simple containers provide a welcome note.*

Gomphrena globosa

Gourds, Ornamental—Assorted Varieties

Seeds germinate slowly so soak them in hot water before sowing. For early start sow indoors 6 to 8 weeks before outdoor planting is safe. Transfer seedlings outdoors when trees leaf out spacing 1 ft. apart, in full sunlight, in ordinary garden soil that is not too rich. When flowers are thoroughly developed (around mid-August) cut and dry for winter decoration.

Varieties: Seed packets come in straight colors or mixed. Cissy is a new dwarf, pure white; Dwarf Purple Buddy is a neat compact plant only 9 in. tall with rich purple miniature flowers. Rubra, 18 in., is reddish purple. Dwarfs are good for edging but not practical for cutting.

GOURDS, ORNAMENTAL. Cucumber Family.

The ornamental gourds are tendril-bearing vines, mostly tropical, and grown chiefly for their showy fruits. Most are included in the following genera: *Abobra, Cucumis, Cucurbita, Lagenaria, Luffa,* and *Trichosanthes.* Some of them have grotesque fruits while others are extremely decorative and are grown to cover fences and porches which they do in a very short time. Their fruits make handsome table decorations.

Treat as tender annuals. They do not like transplanting so are best sown where wanted, after danger of frost is over. If grown in an open bed, a trellis or some sort of rough-barked twiggy support must be provided. They like heat, moisture and a rich sandy loam.

GRASSES, ORNAMENTAL. Grass Family.

Many are very ornamental when in flower and they can add charm to a garden with their grace and beauty of form. Some are plumy and waving, some tall and majestic; others are silvery and slender, or dainty and tufted. Easily raised from seed sown where they are to flower. Useful as decorative areas in the mixed border, some make good pot plants, excellent in the cutting garden. Many can be dried for winter decoration.

Annual grasses should be sown where wanted and handled just as any other tender annuals are sown and cared for. Some of the more interesting genera include:

Agrostis nebulosa—Cloud Grass and *A. pulchella*—Hair Grass.

Anthoxanthum gracilis—Dwarf ornamental grass useful for edgings.

Avena sterilis—Animated Oats.

Briza maxima—Quaking Grass, and *B. minor (B. gracilis).*

IV. Opposite   *This summer border shows purple and pink petunias, phlox and hollyhocks, and blue pansies and delphinium contrasted with yellow perennial anthemis. Annuals and perennials, skillfully grouped to give a continuous display of color, soften the lines of the house.*

Grass, Ornamental—*Setaria italica*

Bromus briziformis—Rattle Brome.

Coix lacryma-jobi—Job's Tears.

Cortaderia selloana (C. argentea)—Pampas Grass.

Eragrotis—Love Grass (*E. suaveolens, E. abyssinica, E. interrupta*).

Hordeum jubatum—Squirreltail Grass.

Lagurus ovatus—Hare's- or Rabbit's Tail Grass.

Pennisetum alopecuroides—Feather Top. *P. rueppeli*—Fountain Grass.

Setaria italica—Foxtail Millet.

Zea mays japonica—Ornamental Maize, Rainbow Corn. The most valuable of all corn varieties as an ornamental. A handsome grass with narrow green leaves striped up and down with yellow, creamy white, and occasionally pink. Var. *japonica variegata* is an excellent variegated form. *Quadricolor* has foliage striped with cream, rose and purple as well as green and white. Grows 3-4 ft. in height. Grown in the garden for their interest and can be used effectively for their decorative foliage; also useful indoors as cut fresh foliage or dried.

Sow seed indoors for an early start or in the open when danger of frost is over.

GROUNDSEL, PURPLE—See *Senecio elegans*.

GYPSOPHILA ELEGANS—Annual Baby's Breath. Pink Family.
A hardy annual from the Caucasus bearing one of the smallest, daintiest flowers of the garden. The frothy, light, much-branched flower sprays are excellent fillers for both the garden and in arrangements, with a softening and blending effect on bolder neighbors. Light and graceful, Baby's Breath was a favorite in most of our grandmothers' bouquets. Plants grow rapidly 1-2 ft. in height and can be used to good advantage planted at intervals in front of and among other annuals such as larkspur, lupines or poppies; a good carpet for summer-flowering bulbs. They always create a misty, airy appearance

Gypsophila elegans

wherever planted. Start blooming in June.

Excellent for use where you may want to clean up old bulb beds or any unused corner or a niche in the garden. Scatter seed, rake in just lightly, firm with board, as seeds sprout faster when pressed into firm contact with soil, which must not be soggy, heavy or hard. Flowers bloom in 6 weeks from sowing. Some of the seeds dropped by the first crop of blossoms will often flower during the season. Thin to stand 8-12 in. apart.

Plants prefer a limestone soil and will thrive in full sun, in any well-drained, non-acid garden soil. They enjoy only a short blooming season lasting 5 to 6 weeks. For a steady supply sow seed every 2 or 3 weeks.

Varieties: *G. elegans* comes in small-flowered, large-flowered, pink and crimson forms. Covent Garden and London Market are popular strains which have masses of pure white flowers on long stems. There is also a trailing kind excellent for use in rock gardens and in wall plantings. The perennial kinds are *G. repens* and *G. paniculata*.

HAWK'S BEARD—See *Crepis rubra*.

HELIANTHUS ANNUUS—Sunflower. Composite Family.

A giant sunflower, vigorous and quick growing, 7-8 ft. tall. Native from Minnesota to California, grown for its huge flower heads. Enormous daisy-like, single or double flowers in gold, red, bronze or brown, usually solitary and terminal, turning with the sun. Petals are often twisted or frilled. Tall, large kinds make attractive hedges in the distance and will screen poultry yards where seeds as they drop are usually eaten by the chickens. Valuable for background use, for screens and as seeds for the birds. They become quite shabby in the garden after mid-August.

Easy to grow and tolerate great heat. Great fun for children to grow. Sow seed outdoors in early spring where wanted. Need full sun and plenty of water and just ordinary soil. Space 3-4 ft. apart, space shorter ones closer.

Varieties: Russian Mammoth is tall growing, 8-12 ft., with single yellow blossoms 8-14 in. across. Sun Gold and Chrysanthe-

mum-Flowered are 6-8 ft. high in golden-yellow and double forms. Stella is yellow and single with a black center. Excelsior Hybrids are wine-red, brown and gold and 3-4 ft. tall. Teddy Bear is 3 ft., and Dwarf Sungold 15 inches. Miniature types are now readily available.

HELICHRYSUM BRACTEATUM—Strawflower. Composite Family.

A hardy Australian annual, one of the best everlastings, with colorful papery petal-like bracts in yellow, orange, pink, red, purple and white and glistening, 2½ in. wide yellow pompon-like showy flower heads or centers much prized for dried arrangements. Also useful for cut fresh flowers. Sturdy plants grow 2-3 ft. high. One of the largest and showiest of the everlastings. To dry, cut flowers just as they reach their peak of bloom. Strip off leaves, tie flowers in bunches and hang in warm, dark place with good air circulation.

Easy to grow. Sow seeds indoors 6 to 8 weeks before outdoor planting is safe or sow seed outdoors in spring when trees leaf out, in full sun, in most any kind of garden soil;

Helianthus annuus Miniature

Helichrysum bracteatum

Heliophila leptophylla

will take dryness and will take heat. Space 8-12 in. apart.

Varieties: Now available in a dwarf strain which is earlier blooming than taller types. Good color mixtures available and straight colors may also be purchased.

HELIOPHILA LEPTOPHYLLA — Cape Stock. Mustard Family.
Half-hardy annual from South Africa. A neat, compact, bushy plant with narrow, thread-like, bluish-green hairy leaves and sky-blue, yellow-throated, starlike flowers. Somewhat like a flax but with flowers in long clusters or racemes. Plants grow about 9-18 in. tall. Attractive for the border as an edger or growing in rock gardens. Useful for cutting.

Successive plantings will ensure flowering plants from June to September. For first sowing, sow seed indoors 6 to 8 weeks before outdoor planting is possible. Transfer seedlings outdoors in May and space 6 in. apart or sow later where they are to flower. They

prefer a deep, well-drained soil in a sunny position.

H. linearifolia is a tall bushy plant, 1-3 ft in height, with narrow, pointed leaves and long spikes of Wedgwood blue, yellow-centered flowers. Petals close at night.

HELIOTROPIUM ARBORESCENS (*H. peruvianum*)—Common Heliotrope. Borage Family.
A perennial from Peru but usually grown as a tender annual or greenhouse plant. Should not be confused with *Valeriana officinalis*, the perennial garden heliotrope. Clusters of small rich-purple flowers with their delightful fragrance are associated with this old-fashioned favorite. Greenhouse-grown plants are even more fragrant than those grown outdoors. Sometimes used as a formal bedding plant. Grow 12-20 in. tall.

Start seeds indoors in February. Transfer seedlings or buy plants from the florist to plant outdoors when danger of frost is over.

Space 1-2 ft. apart. Like plenty of heat; full, warm sun; and a rich, deep soil. If young shoots or stems are pegged down they will root. Grown indoors they must have plenty of moist air and sun. For winter pot-plants take cuttings from outdoor specimens in September. Should be carried through the winter indoors with a cool night temperature of 50° to 55°. Plant outdoors again the following spring. Without the proper wintering facilities it is easier to buy new plants each May.

Varieties: Seed packets come in mixed or straight colors, giant-flowered, dwarf and compact strains. Blue Bonnet is a deep lavender-blue with large flowers and Marine, deep violet. First Snow has fragrant snow-white flowers and Mme. Bruant has dark violet-blue flowers with a white eye. Pacific Hybrids have very fragrant large flower heads in rich shades of lavender, violet and purple. Dwarf Regale Mixture, up to 15 in., is richly fragrant with large lavender-violet flower heads.

HELIPTERUM MANGLESI—Swan River Everlasting. Composite Family.

A dainty, graceful, but not showy Australian annual sometimes cataloged as *Acroclinium* or *Rhodanthe*. Grown for its everlasting flowers and ashy foliage. About 12 in. tall with oval, pointed leaves it has solitary, bell-shaped, white, pink or rose-colored flowers on slender stems. Flowering is best from July to September. Good border plant and frequently dried for winter arrangements. The flowers should be cut before they are fully expanded, tied together and hung heads down to dry in an airy, dry place.

Lovers of hot weather. Tender. Sow seed indoors 8 weeks before you can sow outdoors safely. Germination takes place in about 1 week if night temperature is 55°-60° and flowering begins about 12-14 weeks after sowing. Transfer seedling outdoors only when soil and air are warm, in full sun, in light somewhat sandy soil. Grow well on poor dry soils but like open sunny position. Space to 6 in. apart. Transplant carefully

Heliotropium arborescens

Helipterum manglesi

keeping ball of soil around the roots. They
do not like root disturbance and are easily
damaged. For later bloom sow seed directly
outdoors. Stake if straight stems are wanted,
but if planted in dense drifts the plants will
tend to support each other, requiring little
attention.

Varieties: Var. *album* has white bracts,
var. *roseum* rose and var. *atrosanguinea* dark
red bracts. In var. *maculatum* the bracts are
spotted and flecked with red at the base.

HESPERIS MATRONALIS—Sweet Rocket.
Mustard Family.
A native British species easily raised from
seed, grown for its sweet-scented flowers.
Although a perennial it quickly deteriorates
after the second year from seed so it is usually grown as a biennial. An erect plant 2-3
ft. in height with lance-shaped or oval pointed, finely-toothed leaves and long spikes of
showy, white or lilac flowers, ¾ in. in diameter. Provide a colorful display from June
to September, massed in drifts or grown as
edging plants. Attractive for cutting or as
pot plants for the cool greenhouse. Excellent
for the wild garden.

Hibiscus manihot

Hesperis matronalis

Seed sown in May or June for flowering
the following year. Plant out in September
where plants are to flower spacing 6-18 in.
apart, according to variety. May be grown as
hardy annual from seed sown in September
or March but plants are never as good as
those sown earlier in the year as biennials.
Grow well on any good well-drained garden
soil, located in the sun.

Varieties: Several fine varieties have both
double and single flowers. Vars. *lapsanifolia*
and *purpurea* have large deep-mauve flowers
and vars. *alba* and *nana candidissima* have
pure white flowers. Var. *pumila* is a dwarf
form and var. *sibirica* differs from the type
in its entire petals. Both the type and the
taller varieties should be thinned to 18 in.
apart, dwarf forms 6 in. apart.

H. tristis. A useful plant for the wild garden and naturalizing. Very fragrant at night.
Plant grows to 1½ ft. in height and has yel-
lowish-green, rose-veined, sweet-scented
flowers.

HIBISCUS MANIHOT—Sunset Hibiscus. Mallow Family.

A beautiful short-lived perennial species from eastern Asia, usually grown as a half-hardy annual since it flowers freely the first year from seed. A bushy plant about 4-8 ft. tall having large, dark green leaves and soft-yellow or white flowers with purplish-maroon blotch in center, 4-9 in. in diameter. The divided leaves, character of the seed vessels and even the flowers remind one of okra. Excellent for large beds or background for other less tall annuals. Flowers do not last more than a day and for this reason are of no value for cutting.

Sow seed indoors 6 to 8 weeks before outdoor planting is safe. Sow seed in individual pots as they resent transplanting. Germination takes about 1 week (65°-70° F.). Must have a deep, rich, moist soil in a sheltered, sunny position. Thin to 12 in. apart. When frost comes too early the seeds do not ripen.

Variety Golden Bowl available.

HOLLYHOCK—See *Althaea rosea.*

HONESTY—See *Lunaria annua.*

HOP VINE, JAPANESE—See *Humulus japonicus.*

HUMEA ELEGANS—Amaranth Feathers. Composite Family.

An unusual and graceful biennial from Australia. Named for Lady Hume. Erect stems 5-6 ft. in height bear large oval or oblong, sharply pointed, sweet-scented leaves and long, loose, delicate sprays of small, pink, crimson or reddish-brown flowers in profusion from July to October. Useful for the open border; excellent as a cut flower or a charming plant for the cool greenhouse. Pot plants are very decorative for the patio or porch.

Grow as a biennial, sowing the seed in July or August. Germinate in a coldframe. Plant out the following June spacing 3 ft. apart.

Varieties: Var. *alba* or *albida* has whitish flowers and is not as attractive as the type, var. *purpurea* has dark, purple-brown flow-

Humea elegans

ers and var. *gigantea* is a very large variety.

HUMULUS JAPONICUS—Japanese Hop Vine. Hemp Family.

A rapid, vigorous climber from China and Japan attaining a height of 12-20 ft. Much prettier than the common hop, *H. lupulus.* It has slender, twining stems. The leaves are divided into several lobes and toothed along the margins. Flowers are not ornamental. Its luxuriant foliage makes a dense ornamental covering for fences, unsightly buildings, verandas or trellis-work arbors.

For early start sow indoors 6 to 8 weeks before outdoor planting is possible. Sow outdoors in light, rich garden soil at the base of the support on which the vine is to climb. Space 18 in. apart. Germination outdoors takes about 4 weeks, indoors at 60°-65° F. takes about 10 days. Not bothered by insects, and heat or drought do not affect the plants.

Varieties: A variegated form, *H. japonica*

Humulus japonicus

Hunnemannia fumariaefolia Sunlite

variegatus, is available and has leaves splashed with white. Var. *lutescens* has leaves bronzed or golden.

HUNNEMANNIA FUMARIAEFOLIA — Mexican Tulip Poppy, Golden Cup. Poppy Family.

A perennial from Mexico with beautiful, single, yellow, tulip-like flowers grown as a perennial in warm regions but in the North as an annual since it flowers freely the first year from seed. The sturdy upright plant is nice for midsummer bloom in the border, growing from 18-24 in. tall. Its cupped yellow flowers are especially attractive. The petals are more crinkled and of greater substance than those of the California poppy. Leaves are bluish-green, glaucous and thick but finely cut into narrow segments. A handsome garden subject and also a good keeper when cut in the bud, lasting a week. Flowers do not close at night.

Soak seed before sowing to soften hard coat. Sow seed outdoors where plants are to grow when settled weather has arrived. Like all poppies they are difficult to transplant so if seed is started indoors for early start use pots for easy transfer to sandy loam and place in full sun. Do not injure or hurt the roots which are brittle. Thin or space to 9-12 in. apart.

Varieties: Sunlite is a good semi-double, canary-yellow.

HYACINTH BEAN—See *Dolichos lablab.*

IBERIS UMBELLATA—Globe or Annual Candytuft. Mustard or Cress Family.

A hardy annual from the Mediterranean region grown for its mass of snow-white bloom in late spring and early summer. Plants grow 12-15 in. tall. Planted as a ground cover, in masses or drifts, as edgings or in the border they create a delightful effect with a profusion of somewhat fragrant, neat, close clusters of flowers in shades of white, pink, rose, lilac and purple. Attractive with spring-flowering bulbs in the garden or useful cut for indoor arrangements. *I. sempervirens* is the perennial candytuft.

Broadcast seed in late fall or early spring, as early as possible, where plants are to grow. Will adapt to most climates but prefers cool site to hot, dry places. Needs full sun or only slight shade to flower well. Will bloom 62 to 74 days from seed. Sow seed for continuous bloom every 10 days or so from mid-April to mid-July, if you want flowers throughout the summer. Thin to 8 in. apart. Immediately after the plants bloom cut back to make them bushy and flower again. Water during droughts. Fairy Mixed is early, with dwarf compact plants, 8 in.

I. amara—Rocket or Hyacinth-flowered Candytuft. A species much grown by florists as well as in the garden. More or less erect, about 10-15 in. tall with fragrant white flowers in long finger-shaped clusters, three or more on each plant. Known in many forms; some are dwarf.

Iberis umbellata

ICE PLANT—See *Mesembryanthemum crystallinum.*

IMMORTELLE—See *Xeranthemum annuum.*

IMPATIENS. Balsam Family.
This genus includes three species grown as annuals in the garden. *I. balsamina* is an annual usually called Balsam and *I. holsti* and *I. sultani* are listed as Impatiens in seed catalogs.

I. balsamina—Garden Balsam. A beautiful, tender annual from sub-tropical India and China related to the wild touch-me-not and like it has the characteristic seed pods, which burst open suddenly when touched. An old-fashioned favorite which is again coming into its own. This neat sturdy little plant 8-24 in. tall has double flowers like miniature camellias produced close to the stem, packed tightly all along the stalk and almost hidden among the leaves. Flowers last for days on the plant and drop off when they begin to brown. Not good cut. Colors range from soft pink to rose pink, salmon, lilac, red and white. Some flowers are variegated. Balsam is good for planting in masses, grouped in the border or used as a low hedge. The new dwarfer forms, more top flowering, are useful as edging plants. Bush-Flowered types have flowers more evenly spaced on top of plant as well as along stems. Often grown in pots to decorate the terrace or patio. Remove a few leaves to better disclose the blossoms.

Sow fat seeds outdoors after danger of frost. Will sprout in 4 to 5 days and quickly grow into flowering plants. Space 10-12 in. apart. They like a warm, rich, fairly moist soil and do best in full sun unless summers are long and hot; then protect from afternoon sun. Water and feed to keep glossy, dark-green foliage attractive. Easily transplanted even when in bloom. With proper care plants should bloom until frost.

Varieties: Camellia-Flowered, Mixed; Double Bush-Flowering, Mixed; Red Shades, Pure White, Purple, Rose, Scarlet Salmon and Mixed Colors are a few listings in catalogs. Color Parade (Tom Thumb) is a

Impatiens balsamina Camellia-Flowered, Mixed

group definitely more dwarf and more top flowering, a bush type, 12 in. high, containing many new gay colors in good double forms. Tom Thumb was the first dwarf balsam.

I. holsti—Impatience. A perennial from tropical Africa frequently grown as a tender annual in the North since it flowers freely the first year from seed. Hybrids with red-striped stems and flowers varying from white, shades of pink, salmon and scarlet make excellent summer border subjects, fine for shady areas; also grown as greenhouse and house plants. Not a good cut flower.

Will grow to 1 ft. in height; a more vigorous grower, with larger leaves and flowers than *I. sultani.*

Varieties: New hybrids of *I. holsti* come in lilac, salmon, orange-scarlet and scarlet shades and make up the tall varieties of Impatiens.

I. sultani—Sultan, Patience. Although usually propagated from cuttings this perennial from Zanzibar, Eastern Africa, is easily grown as an annual and used as a tender bedding plant. It forms a good bushy growth, about 15 in. high, with an abundance of bloom. A good greenhouse subject, it has long been a favorite house plant. Both *I. holsti* and *I. sultani* have brittle, translucent stems and glossy foliage and their spurred, waxy blossoms come in jewel-like colors of scarlet, crimson, rose, pink, orange and white, borne in clusters held well above the foliage. Excellent if you need color in a partly shaded location. Not a good cut flower.

For both of these half-hardy perennial species start seed indoors 10 to 12 weeks before warm weather. Use bottom heat of 65° to 75°. Plants are tender and will not tolerate frost. They grow best in half-shade as they do not like full sun. Arrange plants in groups under trees or in half-shaded spots in the border or set three plants in a large pot to decorate the terrace or patio. Need frequent watering. In the fall take cuttings, root in sand, vermiculite or water and grow indoors as house plants.

Varieties: *I. sultani nana* comes in dwarf, compact, free-flowering kinds in straight colors as deep rose, bright carmine, orange, bright coral-pink, scarlet, royal purple and white or is available in a mixture. Many F_1 hybrids are available and generally are preferred because of their faster growth rate and larger flowers. Jewel Series are among the F_1 hybrids and come in a wide color range—orange, pink, red purple and salmon. The Imp Series is new and more dwarf, in red, carmine and white. Snowflake, a white, is a bit more difficult to germinate than other Impatiens.

I. holsti and *I. sultani* are both also known as Patience Plant and Patient Lucy.

IPOMOEA PURPUREA (*I. major*)—Morning-Glory. Morning-Glory Family.
A beautiful, quick-growing, tropical North American vine, unsurpassed, providing good kinds are chosen. Free-flowering with showy, funnel- or trumpet-shaped flowers 3-5 in. wide that come in all colors, blue being particularly popular. Flowers stay open on cloudy days but soon wilt if the sun strikes them, but another day and there's a full new crop. May be used on trellises, arbors, verandas or to screen out any unsightly object. Stems twine readily around any handy support, a string or a wire. The attractive foliage is dense enough to give privacy.

Those with heart-shaped leaves climb readily, the spade-shaped types not so well. Can be used in arrangements. Pick with flowers and buds in different stages of development. Vines grow to 15-20 ft. and bloom from midsummer until frost.

Tender. The seed cover is hard so to hasten germination nick the corner with a file and soak overnight in warm water. For an early start sow seed indoors. When the soil is warm plant outdoors. Any ordinary soil will do. Place in full sun or light shade. Thin to 18 in. apart or place where needed beside supports. Do not fertilize. Rich soil will produce leaves in place of flowers. Do not let plants self-sow as the results are smaller-flowering vines with poor colors.

Varieties: Morning-glories come in straight colors or mixed. Specify whether you want a large- or small-flowered mixture. Heavenly Blue is the favorite, a deep blue shading to cream in the center. Pearly Gates (All-America) is pure white. Flying Saucers come in clear blue and white in mottled and striped patterns. Scarlett O'Hara is crimson-scarlet and Darling is rose colored with a white throat.

JOSEPH'S COAT—See *Amaranthus tricolor.*

KOCHIA SCOPARIA (*K. childsi*)—Summer Cypress, Burning Bush. Goosefoot Family. A half-hardy foliage plant from southern Europe. Plants grow quickly and make an up-

Ipomoea purpurea   *Kochia scoparia*

right, compact growth, reminding one of a small ornamental evergreen. Grown close together may be used as a hedge or for a screen, or as specimens for their rounded 2-3 ft. tall columnar, billowy or feathery form. Branches are densely covered with handsomely colored green foliage. Flowers are inconspicuous. Early in the season plants make a rapid growing hedge, producing quick results. Can be sheared for formal hedges. Good for the new home owner for temporary and quick effects. The foliage is a pleasant green during the summer, turning to a brilliant or rich russet-crimson in the fall, but in some cases to a not too desirable purplish-red.

Soak seed in warm water for a day before sowing. If plants are wanted early, sow seed indoors for 6 weeks before outdoor planting is safe, although outdoor sowing is usually practiced. Space or thin to 15-20 in. in full sunlight. Will not develop well in semishade. Plants prefer a moderately rich garden soil. See that they do not dry out. Plants often self-sow and can become troublesome weeds unless cut down to the soil before they turn color and shed their seeds.

Varieties: Var. *tricophila* is one commonly grown and cataloged. It is more oval and less dense than the pyramidal *K. scorpia* (*K. childsi*).

LANTANA CAMARA — Lantana. Verbena Family.

This tropical American plant is a tender, rather weak-stemmed shrub, widely grown as a greenhouse subject and excellent as a summer bedding plant. Bedding plants are 18-30 in. tall. The rough, ovalish or heart-shaped leaves are 2-6 in. long and the flowers are in flattish clusters, changing from brilliant yellow through orange to red, blooming from July until frost.

Easily raised from seed or cuttings. Hardy outdoors throughout the year from South Carolina south, along the gulf coast to California and northward to coastal Oregon and Washington. Tender in the North. Likes a rather poor soil and a sunny location. Space 12-18 in. apart. For winter indoor culture take softwood cuttings to root, before frost, or dig up plants and pot, keeping at a cool temperature of 55° to 65°. Plants will not thrive in dry heat.

L. montevidensis is trailing in habit. Attractive for use in hanging baskets with its cascading green foliage and countless heads of lavender blossoms.

LARKSPUR, ANNUAL or ROCKET — See *Delphinium ajacis*.

Lantana camara

Lathyrus odoratus

LATHYRUS ODORATUS—Sweet Pea. Pea Family.

The familiar sweet pea is a Sicilian annual loved for its delicate beauty. Now found in many varieties some of which have lost the fragrance of the originals. Vine-like, they grow 4-7 ft. in length and need some type of brush, twine or chicken wire support to which they can attach their tendrils. Free standing supports allowing plenty of air space are desirable. Flowers are usually at least four to a cluster, all long-stalked, and they come in all colors except yellow, blooming in great profusion during the spring and early summer. Must have cool, moist soil and cool weather for best results. Sweet peas are grown for cutting and the florists in past years found them a good crop for winter cultivation in their greenhouses. They are not grown nearly as much today as in bygone years.

To raise sweet peas in the home garden you must know how and when to plant and although the blooming period is short they do bring unequalled joy while in flower. Beds should be well prepared, 18 in. in depth, weeks in advance before sowing seed and then allowed to settle. Soil should be well-drained, rich in nutrients and humus. Start seed indoors in bands or paper pots 6 to 8 weeks before outdoor planting is possible. All except the white-seeded should be soaked overnight or 24 hours in water before planting. The white-seeded so treated are likely to rot rather than sprout. Those that do not swell should be nicked with a file on the side, away from the "eye." Plant seeds 1-2 in. apart and 1 in. deep. They will germinate in 5 to 10 days and speed is essential if blooms are not to wither on the plants and die in summer heat. Transplant in paper pots and never let the soil dry out. Space 6 in. apart in a sunny location protected from strong winds. Success is most likely in the coastal regions of New England and the Pacific Northwest, all but impossible in regions of great summer heat. Cheesecloth shading is a help where summers are hot. Regular weekly watering is important. Green lice on the stems must be sprayed with a solution of nicotine, malathion or lindane. Keep flowers cut to keep them blooming. During active growth a dressing high in potash and phosphate, low in nitrogen, will prove helpful.

Varieties: Giant Spencer sweet peas were developed for their huge, frilled flowers but newer strains stand warm weather better. Cuthbertson kinds, richly fragrant and in all colors, bloom early and were bred to resist heat. Cuthbertson Floribunda, an improvement, has five or more flowers on a stem. Zvolanek Multiflora, with many blooms to a stem, is fragrant and vigorous. Early-flowering kinds are for indoor winter culture or for planting in the fall in warm areas. Little Sweetheart is a bush form, 8 in. high, requiring no staking. Bijou Mixed (new), 10-12 in., are bushy plants requiring no support. The large, fragrant, ruffled flowers produced early and over a long season, in all colors, are more adaptable to a place in a bed or border than any other sweet pea. Hardy sweet peas make a good bank cover blooming from July to September but they are not fragrant.

Lavatera trimestris splendens

LAVATERA TRIMESTRIS SPLENDENS—
Annual or Tree Mallow. Mallow Family.
A widely grown annual from the Mediterranean region. It forms an erect, bushy plant about 3-4 ft. high with solitary, red or rose-colored flowers often 2½-4 in. wide; the petals are blunt or notched. All mallows bear showy flowers that resemble the hollyhocks. Pale green leaves are rounded or angled and coarsely toothed. As border subjects they are handsome. Although short lived, flowers are lovely for cutting. Plants produce flowers freely from July until frost if later sowings are made.

Sow seeds in fall or early spring where plants are to grow. Prefer a light, moist, well-drained soil, full sun and plenty of water. Germination takes place in about 18 days. For succession of bloom repeat sowings until nights get really hot. In hot places bloom is poor and plants may die; prefer cooler, moister climate. Do not like to be transplanted. Thin plants to 15-24 in. apart. Should have about 2 square feet in which to develop. Rarely require staking.

Varieties: White flowered varieties are attractive. Var. *alba* has white flowers, var. *grandiflora* very large rose-pink ones. Var. *splendens* or *rosea splendens* is similar to var. *grandiflora*.

LAYIA ELEGANS — Tidy Tips. Composite Family.
A California daisy-like annual with 2 in. wide, bright-yellow flowers, the ray often white-tipped, the disk-flowers a dark yellow. Plants grow about 12-18 in. tall. Entire or divided, soft hairy leaves are pleasantly scented, and gray-green in color. Excellent as a garden subject or as a cut flower. Good plants for covering dry, sunny slopes; in the rock garden; or for sowing in drifts in the border. Bloom from June until frost.

Like full sun and a light, well-drained, sandy loam although they will grow well on moist soils. Sow seed in open soil in early spring where they are to flower. Germination takes about 16 to 18 days, flowering about 14 weeks after sowing. Thin plants to about 9 in. apart.

Varieties: Var. *alba* has pure white flowers.

LIMNANTHES DOUGLASI — Meadow Foam, Marsh Flower. False Mermaid Family.
A quick low-growing annual from the western United States with clusters or white, yellow-centered flowers 1 in. in diameter. The plant has shiny green, deeply cut leaves and leafy stems about 6-12 in. in height. Free flowering, fragrant and beloved by

Layia elegans

Limnanthes douglasi

bees. Useful as edgings or planted in the
rock garden. It forms a low carpet of finely
cut foliage completely covered during the
summer with a profusion of flowers. A good
greenhouse plant.

Hardy. May be sown in the open in September where plants are to flower or sown
in early spring for later bloom. Germination requires about 3 weeks. Prefers an
open, sunny position but likes a cool, moist
situation for its roots. Thin plants to 4 in.
apart. Sets seed freely during the summer
and if ground is left undisturbed self-sown
plants will make their appearance in large
numbers.

Varieties: Var. *alba* has white flowers, var.
sulphurea pale yellow flowers and var. *grandiflora* larger flowers than those of the type.
Var. *rosea* has white, pink-veined flowers
which turn pale rose as they age.

LIMONIUM (*Statice*) SINUATUM – Sea
Lavender. Plumbago Family.
A half-hardy annual often listed in seed catalogs as *Statice*. An erect showy plant from
the Mediterranean region, probably the most
popular of the species. Two foot high, with
wiry stems which rise from a dense clump of
basal leaves. Flowers are borne in open clusters in late summer and provide colors in
blue, rose, lavender, purple and yellow; the
tiny petals are creamy white. For those who
like dried flowers this is an excellent source;
lends grace to bouquets as does baby's
breath.

Sow seed in full sun where plants are to
grow in almost any soil but clay. Do not
transplant readily because of their long tap-
roots. Do best when kept on dry side, requiring good drainage. Plants do not thrive
where seasons are rainy for they are then
subject to root rot.

Varieties: Single colors are available from
specialty seed houses. Mixed colors are also
available. There is much confusion in the
Latin names of these plants. *Statice* is also
frequently used for thrift (*Armeria*). The
arrangement of the flower clusters, *Armeria*
with a dense globe-shaped head of flowers
and *Limonium* with flower cluster open and
branching, is the chief difference between

Limonium (statice) sinuatum

the two. *Armeria* or thrift long known as
Statice is still listed this way by many seedsmen. Both *Limonium tataricum* and *Armeria
tatarica* are frequently offered as *Statice
tatarica*. All belong to the Plumbago Family.
L. latifolium is a hardy perennial.

LINARIA MAROCCANA—Annual Linaria,
Toadflax. Figwort Family.
This dainty, attractive, hardy annual from
Morocco is not over 8-15 in. tall and well
suited to the rock garden. It is also called
baby snapdragon because of the shape of its
flowers which it somewhat resembles. Borne
on thin stems and free-flowering, the soft
colors in white, blue, lavender, violet, pur-

ple, pink, red or yellow, blotched with another color on the lip, practically cover the
foliage. Best planted thickly in drifts, to
cover and color up fading bulb foliage in
bulb-beds or to brighten up meadows. Could
be used to advantage much more than it is,
for it is fast blooming. Its tiny-flowered
spikes are useful for cutting in miniature arrangements or as fillers among larger flowers.

Sow seeds outdoors in fall or very early
spring where they are to bloom. Thin to 6-12
in. apart. Like full sun or slight shade and a
light, well-drained soil. Should bloom in
about 8 weeks after sowing. A cool weather
plant so will not stay in bloom past July ex-

cept in cool areas such as the coastal and
mountain regions. Seed often will sow itself.
Pull up new plants if they appear where
they are not wanted.

Varieties: Fairy Bouquet (All-America)
makes a dwarf mound about 10 in. high and
is a mixture of pastel shades. Northern Lights
is taller, 12-15 in., and comes in mixed colors
only.

LINUM GRANDIFLORUM — Annual or
Flowering Flax. Flax Family.
A showy plant from North Africa and the
finest of all the Linum species. It makes a
continuous mass of color in the garden from

Linaria maroccana Northern Lights

Linum grandiflorum rubrum

Lobelia erinus

June on. Pink or red solitary flowers nearly 1½ in. wide drop their petals after only a day but are promptly replaced by others. Plants grow about 12-15 in. tall. Worthy of a place in the rock garden or as an edger. Grouped in clumps in the border the pleasant, slender plants are a delight of gracefulness.

Hardy. Seed may be sown outdoors where they are to grow in early spring. Give plants full sun and a light well-drained soil. Thin to 6-10 in. apart. For succession of bloom sow seed several times during the summer. They will bloom 108 to 114 days from sowing. Cut back as they finish flowering to encourage thick new growth.

Varieties: Var. *rubrum* has single, bright-red flowers, an attractive border plant; var. *coccineum* has scarlet flowers and var. *roseum* rosy-pink.

The common blue flax is a perennial, *L. perenne*.

LOBELIA ERINUS — Edging Lobelia. Lobelia Family.

Half-hardy annual from the Cape of Good Hope, South Africa. Enjoyed for its clear blues; flowers borne all summer long. One of the most popular of edging plants. Low and compact or trailing, depending upon the variety. It has small ovalish leaves with a profusion of tiny, two-lipped flowers in clear pale to deep blue.

The dwarf, compact types provide the best blue annuals for edging beds of any flowers, or for use as a ground cover. Also useful for rock gardens. The trailing kinds are graceful and attractive in hanging baskets and window boxes, spilling down over the sides.

Seed is very fine and a little slow to reach maturity. Plants flower in 72 to 100 days from sowing. Sow seeds indoors about 8 weeks before planting outdoors is safe or buy young plants. Keep seedlings moderately cool, not over 60° until warm weather arrives. Set young plants in ordinary garden soil when very small. For edging place about 6 in. apart. Thrives best in the cooler regions where the summers are not too hot. The 4-6 in. plant spreads easily making a compact mound in either full sun or light shade. After the first main blooming period, shear back lightly and feed to maintain good blooming throughout the summer. Slips taken in the fall will give flowering plants for the winter window garden.

Varieties: Cambridge Blue has clear light blue flowers with green foliage; Crystal Palace Compacta has masses of dark blue flowers with bronzy foliage; Mrs. Clibran has dark blue flowers with white eye, dark foliage; Rosamond, carmine-red flowers with white eye, medium-green foliage; White Lady, pure white flowers; and Sapphire, deep azure blue flowers with white eye, pendula or trailing type.

LOBULARIA MARITIMA — Annual Sweet Alyssum. Mustard or Cress Family.

Although a perennial in the warm climate of the Mediterranean region we grow this beloved white edging plant as a hardy annual and it is hard to beat. Flowers are very small but showy because they are so numerous in profuse clusters. They develop quickly, from seed blooming in 42 to 70 days from sowing, a boon for the gardener who wants something in a hurry. Some are dwarf, tufted plants, others are more trailing. Admirably adapted to rock gardens, especially while permanent plants are becoming established; they also fill in effectively around the base of shrubs or may be used as a border around other flowers. This charming little plant is effective for sowing in the crevices of stone paths, very attractive as a carpeting in a bed of spring blooming bulbs and later will hide the drying bulb foliage; adapted to old-fashioned gardens, pots and hanging baskets. Sweet alyssum combines well with other flowers in the garden and the fragrant tiny

blooms are attractive in miniature bouquets used with dainty forget-me-nots, English daisies or tiny roses.

Sweet alyssum likes full sun, and a light, well-drained soil. Broadcast seed where it is to grow, raking it in very lightly. You will get better coverage by mixing the tiny seed with some sand. If sown thinly, little transplanting will be necessary. For earlier bloom sow seed indoors 6 weeks before planting outdoors is possible, then transfer seedlings outdoors, spacing them 5-8 in. apart depending upon the variety. When plants become straggly in the middle of the summer cut them back, fertilize and water to induce branching and a constant display of blooms until frost.

Lobularia maritima

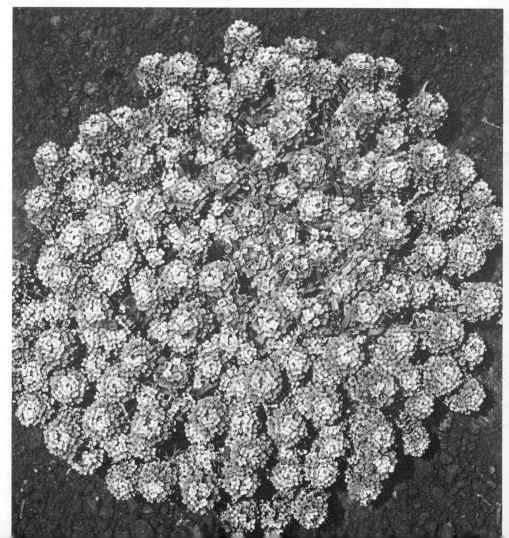

The old-fashioned sweet alyssum was white, growing 8-10 in. high, but newer named forms, more compact and low growing, are now more popular. Still popular older white varieties include Little Gem, 5-6 in. tall, and Carpet of Snow, 3-5 in. high. Pink, rose, violet and purple forms include Pink Heather and Violet Queen which make attractive masses of bloom; Rosie O'Day (All-America), soft, deep rose; and Royal Carpet (All-America), rich purple, deepening in cool weather. Seed packets with a mixture of violet and white are available if you wish to mix the two colors. A double sweet alyssum, widely used by commercial florists, is propagated from cuttings as it produces no seed. The perennial type alyssum is *A. saxatile*.

LOVE-IN-A-MIST—See *Nigella damascena*.

LOVE-LIES-BLEEDING—See *Amaranthus caudatus*.

LUNARIA ANNUA—Honesty. Mustard or Cress Family.
One of the old-fashioned everlastings. A quick growing biennial from Europe with branching stems about 2 ft. or more in height. Leaves are heart-shaped and coarsely toothed. Flowers are pink or purple and sweet-scented, not very showy, borne in a loose sparse cluster, followed by thin, silvery-white, round, silky, parchment-like seed pods about 1½ in. in diameter, in July and August. Plant resembles a weed but seed pods are interesting and used for winter decoration. Attractive sweet-scented flowers are excellent for cutting fresh.

Hardy. Sow seeds in open ground where plants are to grow in fall or early spring, early enough to allow time for seed pods to mature. Any ordinary sandy garden soil (not rich) will do. Partial shade is best. Plants do not like transplanting. Thin to 9-12 in. apart. If sown in fall cover young seedlings during first winter. Will bloom and set seeds during first season if sown early enough but spring sown plants are never as fine as those grown as biennials. Once established will perpetuate self by self-sown seeds. No staking is necessary.

Lunaria annua

For dried winter arrangements, if the outer covering has not been shed when seed pods are thoroughly ripe strip it away and the skin-like partition through which the seeds may be seen will then be disclosed. The transparency of the partitions has given the plant its name, honesty or honest pocketbook. May need bleaching to remove any spots caused by a fungus. Lay them in a bath containing a solution of 2 quarts of water, ½ ounce of soda and 1 ounce of chloride of lime. Cover, leave in a moderate temperature for 4 or 5 days. Pour off fluid and replace with a fresh solution of chloride of lime without soda. When pods are clear, dry in a dry, airy room.

Varieties: Var. *corcyrensis* has blue flowers, var. *alba* white ones, var. *atrococcinea* deep purple or crimson and var. *variegata* has variegated foliage.

LUPINUS HYBRIDS—Annual Lupine. Pea Family.
All of the many annual horticultural varieties are perhaps derived mostly from *L. hartwegi*,

Lupinus hartwegi hybrid

them from going to seed and to encourage other buds to form.

Varieties: Prevailing colors in blue, violet, white or rose. Mixed Annual Lupine seed packets most frequently cataloged. The Texas Bluebonnet grows 12 in. high and has purplish and white flowers.

LYCHNIS COELI-ROSA—Rose of Heaven. Pink Family.

Also offered under the incorrect names of *Agrostemma* and *Viscaria*. There are several perennials but this is a delightful hardy annual from the Mediterranean region with erect slender stems about 18 in. tall bearing narrow, sharp-pointed leaves and a solitary rose-red (with white center) five-petaled flower, slightly notched, to each stalk. The blossoms are about 1 in. wide. Plants are loosely branched and covered with a profusion of bloom. Useful for the rock garden, wild garden or at the front of a border where tiny, modest, free-flowering plants are needed. Flowers are choice for cutting.

Although cultivated extensively in England this annual is not very well known here.

Lychnis coronaria

a Mexican annual. Resemble the perennial lupines perhaps derived from *L. polyphyllus* but are lower and not so showy, although the annual is an attractive plant. It bears pealike flowers in whorls, upon long graceful stately spikes, in practically all colors. With flower spires and attractive soft green foliage they make handsome plants 12-24 in. or more in height, and are interesting border plants as well as lovely in arrangements for indoor decoration.

Sow seeds indoors in pots for an early start or in the open border as early as possible, where they are to grow, in full sun or partial shade, in well-drained, light, sandy loam. These plants resent transplanting so start in pots or handle so roots will have undisturbed ball of earth around them. Will bloom in 8 weeks from seed. Thin to 8-10 in. apart. If soil is rich plants will grow to 3 ft. and perhaps require staking. In cool regions a succession of sowings will provide bloom until frost. They do not do well in high summer temperatures. Should be watered in dry weather. Remove faded flowers to prevent

Sow seed where they are to bloom in early spring. Germination requires about 20 days. Plants like an open sunny position and grow well on any light, moderately rich soil. Thin seedlings to 6 in. apart. Flower soon after sowing. Does not like hot summers, thrives best in cool sites. Usually requires careful staking because of slender stems.

Varieties: Many lovely varieties are listed. Var. *alba* has pure white flowers, var. *fimbriata* fringed petals, var. *kermesina* deep red flowers and var. *oculata* showy saucer-shaped blooms, each with a deep purple center. Blue Bouquet is beautiful and makes a good pot plant for blooming in the cool greenhouse.

L. coronaria (Mullein Pink). A perennial that will bloom from seed the first season, in midsummer, if seeds are sown where wanted in mid-May. White-woolly foliage, height 15-24 in., crimson but a white variety is available, also a white-red bicolor.

MACHAERANTHERA TANACETIFOLIA
—Tahoka Daisy. Composite Family.

A splendid hardy annual closely related to the aster and named for the town of Tahoka, Texas. It is native from South Dakota to Montana and south to Mexico and California. An erect plant 1-2 ft. tall or more, it has deeply divided leaves 3-4 in. long. The pale lilac-blue flower heads are about 2 in. across, the blue rays slender and pointed with the disk flowers or center yellow to bright orange. Blooms continuously through summer and fall. An attractive plant for the border, for edging or for sowing in dense drifts among taller plants. Splendid for cutting and a good pot plant.

Keep seed in the refrigerator for 2 weeks (not in the deep freeze) before sowing. Sow in fall or early spring where plants are to grow. Thin to 6 in. apart. Plants prefer a moderately heavy soil and grow well in almost any location. Like the sun and will stand extreme heat. Staking is rarely necessary.

MADAGASCAR PERIWINKLE—See *Vinca rosea*.

Machaeranthera tanacetifolia

MAIZE, ORNAMENTAL—See *Grasses, Ornamental*.

MAJORANA HORTENSIS—Sweet or Annual Marjoram. Mint Family.

While a perennial in warm regions this plant from Europe is grown in the North as a long growing-season annual. Familiar in old-fashioned and herb gardens it is grown mostly for its aromatic and spicy foliage. Do not confuse it with *Origanum vulgare*, the Pot Marjoram, which is a true perennial and grown as such. Sweet marjoram has small stalked leaves only ½ in. long and its flowers are small, crowded in dense white or purplish clusters, grouped in spikes. Plants grow 1-2 ft. high.

Sow seed indoors for an early start since plants require a long growing season. Set seedlings outdoors in full sun when trees leaf out, in ordinary garden soil. Space 10-18 in. apart. Often grown in rows in herb gardens for seasoning.

Varieties: None. Sometimes incorrectly cataloged as *Origanum majoranum*.

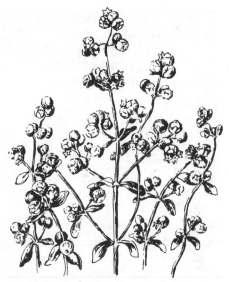

Majorana hortensis

Malcomia maritima Dwarf

Malope trifida

MALCOMIA MARITIMA—Virginian Stock. Mustard Family.

Showy little annual from the Mediterranean region, an old favorite of our grandmother's gardens. Plants of spreading habit and grow 6-12 in. tall. Four-petaled lilac, red or white flowers in a loose cluster at the end of the branches resemble those of ordinary stock. Excellent for the rock garden, for masses in a border, may be used as an edging plant, or for naturalizing in the woods.

Hardy. The seed may be sown in the fall where plants are to grow, in which case the plants will bloom in early spring. An early spring sowing is satisfactory too; plants will then bloom in early summer. Thin to 3-6 in. apart. Will self-sow for years.

Varieties: Listed in seed catalogs under Virginian Stock in straight colors and mixed. Also as Dwarf, 6 in. in height. Var. *alba* has white flowers; *M. kermesina* has carmine flowers and *M. lutea* has yellow blooms.

MALLOW, POPPY—See *Callirhoe pedata*.

MALOPE TRIFIDA—Malope. Mallow Family.

A beautiful annual from Spain and North Africa about 2-3 ft. tall with erect, branching stems bearing pale green leaves with 3 pointed lobes, toothed along the margins, and clusters of large trumpet-shaped rose-purple flowers about 3 in. across. Good plants for the border with a profusion of bloom from June to September. Flowers are attractive for cutting and last well.

Plants prefer a light, moderately rich soil in an open, sunny location. Sow seed in early spring where plants are to flower. Germination takes about 20 days. Thin seedlings to 9 in. apart.

Varieties: Var. *grandiflora* has large, deep rosy-red flowers, var. *alba* pure white flowers and var. *nana* is a smaller, more compact plant than the type.

MARGUERITE—See *Felicia amelloides.*

MARIGOLD, AFRICAN — See *Tagetes erecta.*

MARIGOLD, FRENCH—See *Tagetes patula.*

MARSH FLOWER—See *Limnanthes douglasi.*

MASK FLOWER—See *Alonsoa.*

MATHIOLA INCANA ANNUA—Common or Ten-Weeks Stock. Mustard or Cress Family.

A perennial from South Europe, not winter hardy here where it is grown as a cool season annual. The new kinds most commonly grown have been derived from *M. incana* and are greatly improved over earlier kinds. The delightful spicy fragrance, is one of its chief charms. In addition, it is a fine garden flower and its tall, blossom-packed spikes are excellent for cutting. Florists force them by the millions for sale as cut flowers. The rosette-shaped flowers come in shades of pink, rose, darker hues of red, blue, purple, yellow and white and there are dwarf and tall varieties.

For garden use it is essential to get early-blooming strains for if buds are not formed before hot weather sets in the plants are not likely to bloom. There should be no check in their development to obtain well-grown profuse-blooming specimens. It is safer to

Mathiola incana annua Giant Imperial, Canary Yellow

Matricaria chamomilla

buy young plants. Set them out in May in rich, well-drained soil, in full sun or light shade, and a cool location if possible. Stock needs moisture but stems will rot if water is allowed to collect at the base of the plants. Space about 1 ft. apart. Pinch off side shoots as they appear if you want a tall, large terminal spike of flowers. If a branching spike is preferred the center should be pinched once when the plants are 4-6 in. tall and the side shoots allowed to develop. Will flower magnificently in cool, moist places. Does not like a dry, hot location. May live through the winter but usually decays. When grown well, stock is very much worthwhile and admired but can be a disappointment if conditions are not favorable.

If you are venturesome sow seed indoors 6 to 8 weeks before outdoor planting is safe. Prick out seedlings when 4 to 6 leaves develop and pot up in paper pots. Do not let the temperature get above 65°. Transfer seedlings outdoors when trees leaf out. Will bloom 80 to 86 days from seed.

Varieties: Trysomic Seven Weeks type stock is the earliest blooming; branching, bushy plants 12-15 in. tall, available in mixed colors only. Ten Weeks is an older attempt to get plants into bloom early, grows 15-18 in. high, may be had in separate or mixed colors. In both types many are double, all are fragrant and should bloom until early July. The Giant Imperial (Bismarck) grows 2½ ft. tall and has long-stemmed double flowers. The Giant Imperial and Column types are excellent cut, available in straight colors and mixtures.

M. bicornis — Night- or Evening-Scented Stock. An extraordinarily night-fragrant annual from Eurasia, otherwise undistinguished with rather small, scattered, purplish-white flowers opening only at sundown. Low growing, 3-9 in. tall.

MATRICARIA CAPENSIS — See *Chrysanthemum parthenium.*

MATRICARIA CHAMOMILLA — German, Sweet, or False Chamomile. Composite Family.
A highly aromatic, rather weedy annual from parts of Europe, South Africa and the Far East. Resemble small single chrysanthemums to which they are closely allied. A branching plant 1-2 ft. in height, with finely cut leaves 1-2 in. long and attractive daisy-like flowers which bloom from early summer until September. The numerous flower heads are about ½-1 in. in diameter, with 10 to 20 ray flowers. Not particularly showy, the rays are white, the disk flowers yellow. Sometimes can escape from garden to roadsides in Eastern United States.

Sow seeds indoors 6 to 8 weeks ahead of outdoor planting for early start. Transfer seedlings outdoors as weather permits, in full sun, in a light, moist loam although plants do well in most garden soils. Seeds may be sown where they are to flower but will get a late start. Thin or space to 12-15 in. apart.

Varieties: None. Do not confuse this with the true chamomile *Anthemis nobilis* a perennial.

Maurandia barclaiana

Meconopsis heterophylla

Mentzelia lindleyi

MAURANDIA BARCLAIANA—Maurandia. Figwort, Snapdragon or Foxglove Family.
A vigorous, showy or trailing plant from Mexico usually grown as an annual, with large, gloxinia-type, deep purple flowers which measure about 3 in. in length, and are covered with soft, downy hairs on the outside. Leaves are smooth and sharply pointed. Will quickly form a dense 2-3 ft. screen of attractive soft green foliage covered in late summer with showy flowers. Good in planters or hanging baskets. Excellent plant for the cool greenhouse.

They prefer a deep, moist, moderately rich soil and a sheltered sunny position. Start seed indoors in late winter or early spring. Germination takes about 2 weeks (65°-70°). Put young seedlings in 3 in. pots. Plant out in May, spacing 12 in. apart. Will begin to flower 22 weeks after sowing and continue to flower until frost. Water in dry weather.

Varieties: Var. *alba* has white flowers, var. *rosea* rose colored and var. *atropurpurea* has deep purple flowers.

MEADOW FOAM—See *Limnanthes douglasi.*

MECONOPSIS (*Stylomecon*) **HETEROPHYLLA**—Wind Poppy. Poppy Family.
Hardy annual from western North Africa. A beautiful free-flowering plant with clusters of deeply cut leaves, above which rise slender branching stems 2 ft. or more, bearing long-stalked brick-red 2 in. flowers with satin-textured petals, surrounding a large cluster of golden-yellow stamens. At the base each petal is marked with a maroon blotch.

Excellent plants for the wild garden or border and splendid for naturalizing in somewhat shaded areas.

Sow seed early where plants are to flower. Resents transplanting and its succulent leaves break readily. Thin to 6 in. apart. Prefers a light, well-drained soil and a sunny location or partial shade.

Varieties: Var. *crassifolia* is a smaller, more branching plant than the type.

MENTZELIA LINDLEYI (*Bartonia aurea*) —Blazing Star, Bartonia. Loasaceae Family.
A showy annual from California. Its straggling growth hurts its popularity. It has succulent stems, 12-18 in. in height which bear narrow, coarsely toothed leaves and clusters

of glistening, poppy-like ornamental bright golden-yellow flowers with bundles of feathery stamens, each flower about 2½ in. across. Flowers are fragrant at night. Plants grow 1-4 ft. tall. Foliage is gray, hairy and deeply lobed. Useful in the rock garden. Well adapted to hot, dry places. They are good for cutting. Although each flower lasts only a short time in water new buds continue to replace the faded ones.

Sow seed outdoors where they are to grow after danger of frost. Germination takes about 3 weeks. Resent transplanting. Prefer a light, well-drained soil and a sunny position. Thin to 9 in. apart. Flowering begins about 10 weeks after sowing and will continue for 12 weeks or more.

MESEMBRYANTHEMUM — Fig-Marigold. Carpet-Weed Family.
We have listed the cultivated species below under the old genus *Mesembryanthemum*, long familiar to gardeners, although *Cryophytum* is the correct term today.

Splendid low-growing, succulent plants from South Africa grown for their showy, daisy-like flowers. Good for edging borders, for bedding out or for rock garden use. All are good pot plants for summer flowering in the cool greenhouse. The flowers close on dull days but when the weather is warm and sunny they make a gorgeous carpet of color.

They like an open sunny position and

poor, rather dry soil. For an early start sow seed indoors 6 to 8 weeks before outdoor planting is safe. Germination takes about a week at a temperature of 60° to 65° F. Plant seedlings out in May spacing them 6 in. apart. Flowering begins about 3 months after sowing and continues for 6 weeks or more. With successive sowings, until the end of May, they may be had in flower from June to September. Require little watering. Need a long, hot summer to bloom freely in the East.

M. crystallinum — Ice Plant. Also found under the genus *Cryophytum*. A curious and interesting annual from South Africa, California and the Mediterranean region grown in warm regions as a perennial but in the North as an annual. Runs wild on the seaside cliffs in California. On sunny days their pale green leaves glisten as though covered with minute chips of ice. The thick, fleshy, succulent leaves are covered with glistening white ice-like dots or globules. The plants are trailing or spreading, only about 6 in. in height, with small, solitary, white or rose-colored daisy-like flowers, nearly stalkless. Bloom freely from June to September. Attractive for edging borders or paths. Do well in the rock garden. Useful where the soil is dry and the sun very hot. Of no value for cutting. Attractive trailing pot plants for the cool greenhouse.

M. criniflorum. Also found listed as *Dorotheanthus bellidiformis*. With little or no stem, its prostrate branches form a low, dense mat of narrow succulent leaves thickly studded with 1 in. daisy-like flowers in pink, red, apricot, buff, orange, crimson or white.

M. lineare. Also found listed as *Dorotheanthus gramineus.* An even more attractive plant than the one described above. It forms dense tufts of narrow, cylindrical leaves covered with large, white, pink, red or rose-colored, daisy-like flowers about 1½ in. in diameter. In many of the cultivated forms the center of the flower is red or blue in color and surrounded by a broad white zone. It grows well in the hottest, driest positions in the garden. A showy pot plant for the cool greenhouse.

Mesembryanthemum (Cryophytum)

MEXICAN CIGAR PLANT — See *Cuphea platycentra.*

MEXICAN FIRE PLANT—See *Euphorbia heterophylla.*

MEXICAN POPPY—See *Argemone grandiflora.*

MEXICAN SUNFLOWER—See *Tithonia rotundifolia.*

MEXICAN TULIP POPPY—See *Hunnemannia fumariaefolia.*

MIGNONETTE—See *Reseda odorata.*

MIRABILIS JALAPA—Four O'Clock. Four O'Clock Family.
This showy species from tropical America was a favorite with our grandmothers. In the South it is frequently a persistent perennial but northward is grown as an annual, usually from self-sown seed, persisting from year to year. South of Washington, D. C., it is often weedy and invasive. This quick strong-growing plant with its dense dark green foliage reaches a height of 15-30 in. and as much in diameter, forming a bushy, shrub-like mass of growth which makes it valuable as a low hedge, screen or a temporary foundation planting. They will quickly fill in little-used areas or any bare spaces. Attractive in beds by themselves. Fragrant, trumpet-shaped, single flowers in red, yellow, pink, salmon, lavender and white are freely produced from July until frost. They remain closed until late afternoon but are open all day if dark and cloudy. Bloom late in the season, usually late October.

For early flowers start seed indoors 6 to 8 weeks before outdoor planting is safe or sow the large seeds thinly in the open ground in early spring. Seeds germinate in around 10 days. Plants bloom 60 to 74 days from seed. Plants should be 12-20 in. apart. They form large fleshy roots that can be dug up in the autumn, stored over winter in a frost proof place and planted out again in the spring. Four o'clocks like full sun or slight shade

Mirabilis jalapa

but almost any soil will do. They are useful in urban areas because they tolerate dust, fumes and soot or smoky environments. Just give them a washing occasionally. Seldom do they come perfectly true from seed. Watch out for Japanese beetles. Ward off with DDT or lead arsenate.

Varieties: Available only in mixed colors. Some flowers are striped with contrasting colors.

MOCK or WILD CUCUMBER—See *Echinocystis lobata.*

MOLUCELLA LAEVIS — Bells of Ireland, Shell Flower. Mint Family.
A half-hardy annual from Syria. This all-green novelty has many whorls of soft apple-green bell-like flowers which line the stem. Actually the whorls or bells are the calyx of the flower; the tiny, fragrant, white, mint-like flowers tucked in the center of the whorl are inconspicuous. The plant branches quite low with gracefully curving flower stems and grows 2-3 ft. tall. In favorable spots they will self-sow. Popular in old gardens, it has re-

Molucella laevis

cently become in vogue again because of its value cut, in both fresh and dried arrangements, by themselves or combined with other annuals. To dry the flower spikes cut them in their prime. Remove the foliage, tie spikes together and hang upside down in a well ventilated, dry place until they are cured. They may be sprayed for special effects.

Sow seed outdoors when ground has warmed, where they are to grow. They transplant readily as long as the plants are moved young and taproot is replaced straight downward. Thin to 12 in. apart. Water as necessary.

MOMORDICA BALSAMINA—Balsam Apple. Cucumber Family.
A remarkably handsome and ornamental quick-growing vine from tropical Africa, Asia and Australia. Grows to 6 ft. or more in length with slender stems bearing attractive, beautiful, dark green, lobed foliage. The solitary yellow, black-centered flowers are about 1 in. in diameter, followed by warty, orange, egg-shaped fruit. When ripe the pod opens,

displaying a carmine interior. Has prominent tendrils like its relative the cucumber. Excellent screen for covering rock work, stumps, walls, fences or trellises. A good climber for the cool greenhouse.

Sow seed indoors 6 to 8 weeks before outdoor planting is safe. Germination takes place in around 18 to 20 days (70°-75°F.). When settled weather arrives transfer seedlings outdoors at the base of the support upon which the vines are to climb spacing 1 ft. apart. Prefer a warm, sheltered location in a sunny position and moderately rich soil. When well established plants will flower and fruit freely from June to September. Will flower about 16 weeks from sowing and bloom for 5 weeks or more.

M. charantia—Balsam Pear, Bitter Gourd. Interesting climber from tropical Africa which grows 12 ft. or more in length. Has bright yellow flowers followed by pear-shaped, bright orange-yellow fruits covered with warty projections and at maturity they split into 3 segments disclosing a brilliant scarlet lining. Taller growing, with fruit larger and more showy than *M. balsamina*, but culture is the same.

Momordica charantia

Myosotis sylvatica

MOONFLOWER – See *Calonyction aculeatum.*

MORNING-GLORY – See *Ipomoea purpurea.*

MORNING-GLORY, DWARF OR BUSH– See *Convolvulus tricolor.*

MULLEIN–See *Verbascum.*

MYOSOTIS SYLVATICA – Annual Forget-Me-Not. Borage Family.
Hardy. Often cataloged under the incorrect name of *M. alpestris.* This British biennial, although sometimes flowering from seed in a single season and called annual forget-me-not, is usually best treated as a biennial. This low, free-blooming, familiar, spring-time plant is charming as a ground cover under daffodils, tulips and other spring-blooming bulbs and perennials, also useful in woodland areas and rockeries. Not over 9 in. high. The prevailing color is blue but there are

also pink and white forms.
Those in seed packets labeled annual can be sown in early spring. Grown as a biennial. Sow seed in July. In September or October transplant seedlings to cold frame or nursery bed if south of Philadelphia. In early spring transfer seedlings to place where wanted, in full sun or partial shade, in rich well-drained garden loam. Place 5-7 in. apart. Although the type itself is found in the dry woods, cultivated varieties grow best in moist, well-drained soil. It flowers best when weather is still cool, from May until August. For continuous bloom do not let seed form; keep dead blossoms cut. Plants often persist from self-sown seeds.
Varieties: Available in straight colors or mixed. Var. *alba* is white; var. *fischeri* has pink flowers; var. *Rosea* rose-colored blossoms and var. *atrocoerula* intensely blue ones. Var. *compacta* is dwarf and compact while var. *grandiflora* has larger flowers than the others. Royal Blue and Victoria are annual varieties, excellent for use in the rock garden. Others are Blue Basket, indigo blue, 14 in.; Blue Ball, rich sky-blue, 6 in.; Indigo Blue, deep indigo blue, 12 in.; Ultramarine, dwarf type of indigo blue; and Carmine King, a rosy carmine, 12 in. tall.

M. scorpioides, often cataloged under the incorrect name of *M. palustris,* is the perennial.

NASTURTIUM–See *Tropaeolum hybrids.*

NEMESIA STRUMOSA–Nemesia. Figwort Family.
From tropical Africa and unrivalled among annuals for creating a brilliant show outdoors in late spring and summer or for flowering in the greenhouse during the winter and early spring. A small bushy plant, 8-15 in. tall with small orchid-like flowers borne in terminal clusters in shades of pink, rose, scarlet, yellow, orange, blue, purple and white, deeply marked in contrasting colors. Effective and best massed in drifts in the border where it provides a bed of showy color; also useful in the rock garden. Most attractive interplanted in pots or containers

Nemesia strumosa

for the terrace. Good for cutting for miniature bouquets. Unexcelled in cool climates but does not do well in central and southern United States. Suitable for areas where late spring and early summer are cool.

Half-hardy. Sow seed indoors 8 to 10 weeks before outdoor planting is safe and grow on the cool side. Transfer seedling outdoors as soon as possible as they do not like the summer heat. Space 6-8 in. apart. When plants are 6 in. tall pinch off the tips to get bushy plants. Unless started early indoors in January or February and then cut back and set into the garden where they will harden off and take hold, summers may prove too hot and dry. A little protection from the hot afternoon sun will extend the life of the flowers. Keep soil moist but not wet, and fertilize.

Varieties: There are tall, dwarf and large-flowered forms. Sutton's of Reading, England, list several which come fairly true from seed. Sutton's Large-Flowered in separate colors; also in a Special Mixture; Sutton's Hybrid, a dwarf strain for edgings and pot

culture. Carnival and Triumph are both good blends of mixed rich colors. Aurora is a carmine and white bicolor, Blue Gem a medium blue, Fireking scarlet, and Orange Prince a golden orange.

NEMOPHILA MENZIESI (*N. insignis*) — Baby Blue Eyes. Waterleaf Family.
Hardy annual native to California. Dainty with attractive, pale green, deeply cut foliage, clear blue, bell-shaped flowers, 1 in. across, with white centers. Flowers are borne on short, fragile stems which rise above a spreading fine-leaved plant only 6-10 in. tall. Effective planted among tall daffodils. Little plants excellent for edging or used in drifts in the rock garden. Plants trail gracefully when used in hanging baskets or window boxes. Attractive cut and used with scillas and daffodils. Related to the *Phacelias*, California bluebells.

Scatter seed of this quick-blooming annual thickly, either in the fall or early spring, where plants are to grow. Prefer moist, ordi-

Nemophila menziesi (N. insignis)

Nicandra physalodes

nary garden soil and sun; however, shade from the bright afternoon sun will prolong the blooms. Space 6 in. apart. Intolerant of heat. Do best in cooler regions where they enjoy a long season of bloom.

NICANDRA PHYSALODES — Apple-of-Peru. Potato Family.
A half-hardy plant from Peru grown for its handsome foliage and showy bell-shaped flowers. A spreading plant about 3-4 ft. in height, it has smooth, oval leaves, wavy-toothed along the margins. Bell-shaped flowers are pale blue and white-throated, about 1 in. in diameter. Not often seen in cultivation. The flowers are not freely produced and open for only a few hours in the middle of the day. Each flower is followed by a round, hard fruit enclosed in a highly ornamental green and purple inflated calyx. Branches bearing these may be dried and used for winter decoration.

Seed should be sown indoors 6 to 8 weeks before outdoor planting is safe. Germination takes about 12 days (60°-65° F.). Plant out in May, spacing 12 in. apart. They begin to bloom about 14 weeks from sowing and continue to flower for 12 weeks or more. Like a deep, moderately rich soil and an open, sunny location. Seed may also be sown at the end of April where plants are to flower and thinned to 12 in. for later bloom.

NICOTIANA ALATA—Flowering, Jasmine, or Ornamental Tobacco. Potato or Nightshade Family.
An attractive, stout perennial from southern South America. Its fragrance is most delightful; one of the most night-fragrant of flowers. Here it is grown as a long-season annual. The tube or trumpet-shaped flowers are borne in great profusion in ample loose clusters upon flower stems 2-3 ft. tall. Colors are white, lavender, mauve, crimson and maroon. Abundant, large, coarse, velvety, hairy leaves form a cluster about the base of the plant. The blossoms usually close in sunshine but open toward evening or on cloudy days. Juice of leaves is poisonous. Plants grow to 4 ft. tall. Use groups of these flowers where

Nicotiana alata grandiflora Sensation

haps the most fragrant. Newer varieties that open during daylight hours, even in bright sunshine, are replacing *N. alata grandiflora;* also new, low growing, more compact forms, 1½-2 ft. tall, more suitable for the small garden. Sensation Hybrids Mixed are vigorous plants about 2 ft. tall with strong flower stems, color range from white, through mauve to chartreuse, wine, deep red and chocolate. Daylight is a pure large-flowered white form of the Sensation Hybrids that remains open all day and grows 1½-2 ft. tall. Crimson Bedder and White Bedder are compact bushy plants, 12-18 in. tall, long-tubed, with star-shaped flowers that bloom all summer long.

NIEREMBERGIA — Cup Flower.   Potato Family.
Tropical American perennials grown for their attractive tubular flowers. Can be brought into bloom in one season from seed sown early indoors. Best treated as tender annuals. Inclined to sprawl or creep. In the North dig them up and winter over in a cold frame. May be grown in a cool greenhouse.

N. caerulea. The hardiest of the cut-flowers. Grows 6-9 in. high with numerous blue, yellow-throated flowers about 1 in. wide, during August and September. Purple Robe

the evening breezes will blow their fragrance toward the patio or terrace. White forms are luminous at night and most attractive. Planted in groups of 3 or 5 they make excellent upright accents with lower growing plants. Cut flowers last well. Cut whole stems in full bloom, then remove faded blossoms each day; new ones open daily.

Plants grow slowly under cold conditions, so it is wise to start microscopic seeds indoors 8 to 10 weeks before outdoor planting is safe. Do not cover seeds; merely press them in lightly with a board. Once seeds have germinated, plants develop rapidly and are easy to grow. Transfer seedlings outdoors in full sun or partial shade in a rich, well-drained garden soil. Will tolerate considerable heat if given some shade. In cooler areas can take full sun or semi-shade. Water during dry spells. Space 2-3 ft. apart. Will bloom 50 to 80 days from seed, from midsummer on. Stake if site is windy. May self-sow so they practically become perennials.

Varieties: *Grandiflora* is an older variety and long-time favorite with large flowers, the tube being more open; the white form is per-

Nierembergia caerulea Purple Robe

V. Opposite   *An early summer border showing a wide variety of annuals and perennials grouped to create a pleasing picture. Delphinium and Paul's Scarlet climbing roses make a dramatic background and annual sweet alyssum is effective as edging.*

s a violet-blue, deeper than the original; plants are more dwarf and compact and do not fade under hot sun. A fine bedding plant.

N. frutescens. More erect than sprawling, often 1-3 ft. tall, flowers white, or lilac or blue tinted. Purple forms are offered, some forms with larger flowers.

N. rivularis (N. repens)—Whitecup. A perennial in its native Argentina and in warm regions but treated as an annual in the North since it blooms from seed the first year. It makes a creeping, mat-forming mound 10 in. in diameter and about 6 in. tall, rooting at the joints with needle-fine foliage. Cream-white, sometimes rose or blue-tinged cup-shaped flowers, 1 in. across, bloom over a long season, one to a stem. The small neat plant is useful in the rock garden, as an edger, in low borders and in window boxes.

It takes 4 months for the plants to bloom from seed so either buy young plants or sow seed indoors 6 to 8 weeks before outdoor planting is safe. Transfer seedlings outdoors when trees leaf out. Give them good, well-drained, sandy loam, full sun or light shade, and space 6 in. apart. Not hardy north of New York. May take cuttings in the fall or divisions of the rooting stems and winter over in a cool greenhouse. Purple Robe (All America) is an excellent bedding or edging plant, with deep violet-blue flowers.

NIGELLA DAMASCENA—Love-in-a-Mist. Buttercup Family.

From the Mediterranean or southern European region. Its common name reflects the fact that the handsome single or double sky-blue or white flowers are nestled in a misty mass of lacy, bright green, fernlike foliage. Of easy culture and much branched; the airy grace lent by these flowers is delightful in the garden. Plants grow up to 18 in. tall. Arrangers are using the dried seed capsules, 1 in. in diameter. They are shaped like a small egg and horned or covered with bristles and branched spines, hence another common name, Devil-in-the-Bush. Plants look best massed in a border among other taller, more solid-appearing neighbors. Not spectacular but the dainty flowers on 12 in. stems

are easily arranged and long lasting when cut; they mix well with other flowers. Bloom from July till fall. Watering as necessary will prolong blooming season.

Hardy. Sow seeds in fall or early spring in any good garden soil where the plants are to bloom, in full sun. Thin to 5-9 in. apart. Plants bloom when quite small. Do not transplant readily. Seeds germinate in about 10 days, and bloom in 70 to 85 days from sowing. If you are saving seed keep only seeds from the double flowers which are preferable to the singles.

Varieties: Miss Jekyll with cornflower-blue flowers is one of the most popular. There is also a white form.

Nigella damascena Miss Jekyll

VI. Opposite *This seaside garden brings to mind that flower colors seem brighter near the sea. Pinkish ageratum, left front, and red petunias at the right, supply bright contrast for the gray gate and wall.*

NIGHT- or EVENING-SCENTED STOCK
—See *Mathiola bicornis.*

NOLANA ATRIPLICIFOLIA (*N. para-doxa*)—Chilean Bellflower. Nolanaceae Family.

An attractive plant from Chile with low spreading stems, seldom exceeding 6 in. in height. Although a perennial it flowers freely the first year from seed and since it is not entirely hardy is usually grown as an annual. Its 2 in. blue flower with a white or yellow throat reminds one of a morning-glory. The broad, oval-pointed, or spatula-shaped leaves are 2-3 in. long. The prostrate plants have a fleshy taproot. They are excellent in rock gardens and for edging borders or garden paths or to cover a bare bank. Also used as pot plants for the porch or for softening steps.

Sow seeds outdoors as early as possible where they are to grow, after danger of frost is past. Germination takes about 1 week. Difficult to transplant. Plants thrive in poor, dry soil, in almost pure sand near beaches. They like full sun, and hot, dry situations. Thin plants to 6 in. apart.

Varieties: Var. *violacea* has violet flowers and var. *alba* pure white ones.

N. lanceolata. Whole plant covered with white hairs. Flowers deep blue, with throat spotted creamy-white, 2 in. across. Leaves lance-shaped, 4-6 in. long.

Ocimum basilicum Dark Opal

OCIMUM BASILICUM—Basil. Mint Family.

From the tropical Old World and the Pacific Islands. Listed under herbs. Widely grown in European countries for its ability to keep away mosquitoes and flies. A much-branched annual 1-2 ft. high with purplish oval leaves and insignificant, small, white or purplish-tinged flowers. As an herb, fresh or dried, it is used for flavoring. Dark Opal, an ornamental basil, was the first foliage plant to merit an All-America Selection (1962). Grown for its ornamental foliage and popular with arrangers.

OENOTHERA DRUMMONDI — Evening Primrose. Evening Primrose Family.

A showy, hardy annual from Texas. The cream-colored or bright yellow four-petaled flowers about 2 in. in diameter open in the evening. The plant grows 1-2 ft. tall. The soft, hairy, oblong- or lance-shaped leaves are frequently toothed. Good plants for the border or for edging paths in the wild garden. Also effective sown in drifts in the rock garden. Flower from July to September. Do not last well as cut flowers.

Sow seed outdoors early where plants are to grow. Germination takes about 20 days. Like a fairly light, well-drained soil in a

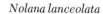

Nolana lanceolata

sunny, open location. Prefer sun but will take some shade. Thin to 12 in. apart. Sets seed freely and if the ground is left undisturbed self-sown plants come up in large numbers.

Varieties: Var. *nana* is smaller and more compact than the type.

O. lamarckiana is a biennial with large yellow flowers, in long spikes, with crinkled leaves and red-dotted stems.

OXYPETALUM CAERULEUM – Southern Star. Milkweed Family.
A tender plant from Argentina with changeable 5-lobed flowers about 1 in. across, pale silvery-blue when they first open, then purplish, and when withered, lilac. Flowers are in 3-4 flower clusters. The wide arching sprays are in bloom from June until the end of October, from direct sowing in open ground in April. Can have even longer bloom if sown indoors for early start. Rather slow to bloom from seed.

A good winter-blooming pot plant, very fine for pot container gardening. The seed pods are useful dried, perhaps a little smaller in size than the butterfly weed seed pod. A good bloomer even when not kept cut.

Like most members of the milkweed family it will take poor soil very well, perhaps even prefers it. Can be carried over indoors as a window or greenhouse plant.

Oxypetalum caeruleum

PAINTED TONGUE—See *Salpiglossis sinuata.*

PANSY—See *Viola tricolor hortensis.*

PAPAVER ALPINUM – Alpine Poppy. Poppy Family.
Although a perennial from the Alps, often treated as an annual. Most satisfactory rock garden poppy. Flowers on stems a few inches high, above gray cut foliage, are white, orange and in shades of pink. Modern varieties are exceptionally good. Likes good drainage and light, gritty soil. Seeds freely.
For culture see *P. rhoeas.*

P. nudicaule – Iceland Poppy. Strictly a short-lived perennial from the Arctic regions but usually and best grown as a biennial or annual. The plant has basal clusters of deeply lobed or cut leaves, above which rise slender

Oenothera lamarckiana

stems to a height of 12 in. or more, bearing sweet-scented, white or yellow flowers, measuring 1-2 in. across, both single and double. Valuable in the rock garden or for edging borders. Make charming pot plants for the cool greenhouse. Good for cutting when picked in bud. Easy to grow. For culture see *P. rhoeas.*

Varieties: May purchase seed in straight or mixed colors. Kelmscott Strain has graceful cupped flowers in many soft tints. Gartford Giant Art Shades include many fine pastel tints. Yellow Wonder is good for cutting.

P. rhoeas—Annual or Shirley Poppy. Hardy annual. This is the common corn poppy so abundant in cornfields in Europe—the poppy immortalized in Flanders during World War I. The brilliant, popular Shirley poppies are all greatly improved forms of this species. They bear their flowers on slender wiry stems 2 ft. high in late spring and early summer, flowering later in the year than the Iceland poppies. Their pink, scarlet, crimson, salmon and white flowers are both single and double. A delight to watch as they open day by day from their tight buds, pouring forth a great mass of petalage like crinkled silk of the sheerest texture. Plants grow 2½-3 ft. tall and are free branching. Unsurpassed for display with wide range of brilliant color, when massed in beds by themselves or sown in border where some other flower has failed.

Papaver alpinum

Sow seed in early fall unless winters are exceptionally severe; if so, in very early spring. Seeds germinate best in cool soil. Mix a little sand with the very fine seed and scatter sparingly where plants are to grow. Like sun and well-drained ordinary garden soil, light, not heavy. Thin short kinds 10-12 in. apart, taller ones 18 in. Will bloom 56 to 74 days from seed. Will flower over a longer period of time if plants are not crowded too close together and if dead flowers are kept picked off. They reseed readily and come up again the next year; are extremely hardy and easily grown. Will bloom for only a short time if seed pods are allowed to develop. Pepper-box seed capsules are small but filled with seed.

Varieties: You can buy them in single or double mixtures. Named varieties include Sweet Briar, a double, deep rose-pink; American Legion, a large single, orange-scarlet with black cross inside cup; Flanders Field is a single scarlet; and Peony, Double Flowered Mixed, has double flowers resembling a peony.

PATIENCE PLANT or PATIENT LUCY— See *Impatiens sultani.*

PELARGONIUM — Geranium. Geranium Family.
Although not annuals, they are used as such for bedding purposes and may be grown either from seed sown indoors in January or from purchased young plants. *P. hortorum,* the Zonal type, is the easiest to keep healthy for bedding purposes or to use as pot plants indoors in winter, or outdoors on the terrace in the summer, or for use in window boxes. It is one of the best for continuous bloom from early summer to late fall.

Start seed indoors in January and when danger of frost is past set plants outdoors in ordinary garden soil, not too rich, in the sun. Keep on the dry side. Or set out purchased plants. Keep pruned to desired shape and size; use trimmings as cuttings to start new plants. In the fall for winter bloom, take indoors the new young plants grown from cuttings started in the summer. Keep the

Pelargonium hortorum hybrid   *Penstemon gloxinioides* Mixed

buds picked off until the plants are brought indoors.

Nittany Lion Red is a bright red, true color from seed. Mixed packets also available.

P. *peltatum,* the ivy-leaved group, is vine-like in habit and popular for use in hanging baskets and window boxes.

PENSTEMON GLOXINIOIDES — Beard Tongue. Foxglove Family.
Penstemons are mostly perennials from North America but plants of P. *gloxinioides* (P. *hartwegi* x P. *cobaea*) are not always hardy and are therefore treated as summer annuals, blooming the first year from seed. Plants grow 2-3 ft. tall and bear brilliant flowers much like miniature foxgloves. The colors range from white to deepest crimson with various tints of pink and lavender predominating. Usually the throats are white and contrast nicely with the bright petals. Handsome flowers are excellent for the border. Look best planted in groups as they are

sometimes ungainly requiring staking. The tubular flowers, hanging like bells on slender stems, are nice to cut for arrangements indoors.

Sow seed in January if greenhouse is available. Otherwise sow in a sunny window or hotbed in March. Seeds germinate in 20 days. Transplant to open, well-drained, not-too-rich soil, in sun or a little shade, when danger of frost is past. Space 1 ft. apart. Water as necessary. Cut flowers off promptly as they fade, for continued bloom. In milder sections of the United States and in favorable years plants may live through the winter if protected. May be lifted in the fall and planted in cold frames for the winter. Florists propagate by cuttings taken in the fall. The young plants are wintered in a cool house. These plants will bloom in early summer.

Varieties: There are some lovely hybrids. Sensation is one of the best named strains with large tubular blooms from white to crimson.

PERILLA FRUTESCENS—Perilla. Mint Family.

A coarse-growing annual from Asia grown for its ornamental foliage. It was a favorite foliage plant years ago. Grows 2-4 ft. in height bearing broad, oval, deeply-toothed leaves and short spikes of small white or reddish flowers. Used for masses of bright foliage in the border. Makes attractive low hedges even though somewhat weedy. Some of the smaller varieties make good pot plants for decoration during the summer months.

Sow seed indoors 6 to 8 weeks before outdoor planting is safe. Germination takes about 8 days (65°-70°F.). Plant out in May, spacing 12 in. apart. Prefer a deep, moderately rich soil but will thrive in poor dry soil in a sunny open position. Requires little attention. Plants are decorative all summer long.

Varieties: Var. *crispa* (sometimes listed as *P. nankinensis*), called the beefsteak plant, is a handsome plant with dark red-dish-purple leaves and spikes of rather attractive pale violet flowers. The margins of the leaves are wavy and deeply toothed and the surface has a metallic, bronzy sheen. Plant somewhat resembles coleus. Var. *laciniata* has wavy, very deeply cut and crisped leaves, var. *macrophylla* has large, wavy-edged leaves, var. *variegata* white spotted foliage, var. *microphylla* has small leaves and var. *elatior* is a form similar to *microphylla* but with somewhat taller stems.

PERIWINKLE, MADAGASCAR — See *Vinca rosea*.

PETUNIA HYBRIDS—Petunia. Potato or Nightshade Family.

The modern day petunias have been derived mostly from crossing two native species from Argentina. They have been so improved it is now one of the most profuse flowering of all annuals. Colors have been developed to such an extent, the funnel-shaped blooms now come in deep rich purples and violets; superb light dainty pinks to the deepest velvety reds; showy whites; some striped and other novelty kinds; and some with starlike centers. The best yellow to date is a deep cream color. They come single, double, fringed, ruffled and frilled—marvels of the breeder's art. No wonder this versatile annual is now a widely used landscape favorite. Except for tall kinds, most suitable at the back of the border, they can be used almost anywhere.

The most compact varieties are unexcelled in beds by themselves or as wide edgings for other plantings. Steep banks, difficult to mow, may be planted with petunias producing striking, colorful effects. A smart intermixing of the larger and smaller kinds can be interesting and effective. The trailing kinds are incomparable for hanging baskets, window boxes, raised beds, and containers of all types. Excellent in arrangements; the singles keep better than the doubles when cut.

Half-hardy. For an early start buy plants or sow seed indoors 8 to 10 weeks before outdoor planting is safe. Seeds are very fine, so sow with care. Sowing petunias on a

Perilla frutescens laciniata

ground of sphagnum moss can be most effective. Germination takes 10 to 12 days. The slowest, smallest seedlings are apt to be doubles. The better kinds are well worth the extra cost in seeds. Transfer seedlings outdoors in full sun, or they will bloom in light shade, and in almost any soil although a light, well-drained one is preferred. Space 8-12 in. apart. When about 6 in. high pinch back to promote branching.

Of easy culture almost everywhere, petunias are quite adaptable, but they must have sun to bloom. They can endure a dry summer better than most plants. They thrive near the sea. Southward they are likely to persist from self-sown seed but since few come true it is better to start with fresh seed each year. They bloom in 90 to 130 days from sowing. Once established, petunias require little care but the dead flowers should be kept picked off, both for tidy appearance and better flower production. If they seem bloomed out in midsummer cut them back,

fertilize and water; in a short time they will revive and be producing flowers again. Petunias are seldom bothered by pests.

Varieties: Choose the right variety or type for the purpose it is intended to fill: the erect forms for bedding; the balcony and cascade types which are weak-stemmed and sprawling for raised beds, window boxes and other containers; and the dwarf kinds for edging plants. There are many new varieties each year so look over the new seed catalogs to keep up to date.

Dwarf, compact kinds growing up to 12 in. in height come in straight colors, bicolors and special mixtures, useful as edging plants.

F_1 hybrid petunias are the offspring of two selected inbred parents, which have been cross-pollinated by hand. This procedure involves far more labor and time than required to develop the ordinary open-pollinated kinds and consequently makes them more expensive. There will be less seed in their packets so use care in sowing and do not

Petunia multiflora F_1 hybrid, Small-Flowered Single

Appleblossom

up to date by visiting gardens, garden centers, and reading current articles and seed catalogs.

Multifloras. Multiflora means many or profusely flowered. The Multifloras are not as large flowered as the Grandifloras, but are more prolific bloomers. The plants grow to the same height and spread as the Grandifloras, but the smaller flowers measure only about 2¾ in. across. Their profuse bloom makes them highly desirable for a mass display of color.

F_1 *Singles.* These Multifloras have small single flowers, usually smooth-edged. Comanche, a brilliant scarlet-red and Coral Satin, a coral-rose are examples of two All-America selections in this group. Red Satin, a bright red, is similar to Comanche except the plant is slightly more dwarf and compact. Moon Glow is a rich creamy yellow and Paleface a pure white with small creamy eyes. Two bicolors include Glitters, with a distinct white strip on a rich red back-

unnecessarily waste seed. F_1 hybrid petunias have greater vigor than the old open-pollinated varieties and will reward you with earlier and more profuse bloom, stronger growth and more uniform compact plants. They are available in a great variety of colors and bicolors, flower textures and degrees of compactness. They are showy as bedding plants from early summer until frost and do well under almost all conditions except heavy shade. Seed should not be saved from these hybrids as it will not come true.

F_2 hybrid petunias are intermediates between F_1 hybrids and the inbred or open-pollinated kinds so far as vigor and trueness to type are concerned. Like F_1 classes they are available in both Multiflora and Grandiflora types.

The classification of petunias is very mixed and the list of varieties under each heading is so extensive it is difficult to start listing these without leaving out some very good forms. Furthermore, the list changes yearly which adds to the confusion. Keep

Cascade Series

Cherry Tart

nations, and Star Dust (colors bright and varied from soft pink to deepest rose as well as blues and violet) with distinct star markings.

Open-Pollinated. Old line-bred favorites are not as vigorous or as true to type as the newer F_1 hybrids but some types are still popular and good bedding varieties. Listed in many catalogs under P. *hybrida nana compacta* or dwarf bedding plants are such names as: Moonstone, light ivory-yellow; Rosy Morn, rose with a white throat; Blue Bedder, improved mid-blue; Violacea, deep velvety purple; Fire Chief, bright scarlet; and Lipstick, carmine-rose.

Grandifloras. Grandiflora means large or showy-flowered. These types produce vigorous plants 15 in. in height with a spread of 20-24 in. Some have fringed flowers up to 4½ in. across. There are many fine varieties in straight colors, bicolors or mixed.

F_1 Singles—Plain or Smooth Edged, Fringed, and Ruffled. The plain-edged

ground, and Meteor, scarlet red and white.

F_1 Doubles. The carnation-like flowers are freely borne on dwarf, compact plants. Excellent for bedding or pots. These doubles were the first F_1 hybrids. Although not as free-flowering as other types their ruffled and frilled blooms are lovely and they are excellent used in planters, window boxes or hanging baskets. Cherry Tart, a brilliant rose-pink and white variegated; Strawberry Tart, pure white and strawberry red; Peppermint, with rose-pink veins on soft pink flowers; and Snowbird, pure white are representative of the F_1 Double group.

F_2 Singles. Superior to the open-pollinated varieties in vigor and trueness to color, this group offers an improved bedding strain, 15 to 18 inches in height. Silver Blue, a soft light blue is replacing Sky Chief; Snowball, is a fine white; and choices in mixed colors include Colorama (from white to deepest blue and red), some starred combi-

Fire Dance

Grandifloras have the same growth habit and flower size as the fringed Grandifloras but are smooth edged. Favorites in this group are Bingo, a wine-red and white; Dazzler, a carmine; Popcorn and White Cloud are white; and a purple is Purple Prince.

The fringed and ruffled Grandifloras have flowers up to 4 in. across. Of variable habit they are not bedding plants but useful as interplants in shrub borders or used in pots and planters of various types. Appleblossom, a soft appleblossom-pink, slightly variegated from light to intense salmon-pink; Ballerina, a soft glowing salmon; Fire Dance, brilliant scarlet with a bright golden throat; Maytime, a soft salmon-pink; and Prima Donna a bright rose with darker veins represent a few of the fringed and ruffled types. Snow Lady and White Magic are dwarf (12-15 in.), early, free-flowering well-fringed whites.

Cascade Petunias (F₁ Single Grandifloras) will eventually supersede the old Balcony (*P. hybrida pendula*) type. These large single-flowered Grandifloras may be used in all locations where the Balcony type was used: in planters, raised beds, window boxes, hanging baskets and urns and will give a much greater show of color all summer. Bred with planters specifically in mind, with a trailing habit, the strain is available in pink, white, red, or mixed. Sugar Daddy is a cascade type, plum colored and penciled an orchid-purple.

F₂ Singles. A good Grandiflora F₂ single type is Carnival with variegated flowers in a mixture of white and reddish pink, blooms waved and ruffled.

F₁ Doubles. The F₁ Double Grandifloras are very showy with large double flowers on vigorous plants and can be had in blue, lavender, purple, crimson, pink, rose, salmon, and white; or mixtures and bicolors.

Pan-American All-Double plants branch freely, are sturdy and compact, free-flowering with large blooms, deeply fringed, in straight colors or mixed. Canadian All-Double Cotton Candy is a soft creamy salmon suffused with pink and heavily fringed. Canadian Queen is a rose-pink and Blue Moon a dark blue. Available in a mixture too. Sa-

kata's (Japanese) All-Double Gaiety is an example of a pink and white bicolor. Dwarf and compact with medium-large fringed double flowers. Victorious (All-America) is an All-Double dwarf; available in purple, orchid, pink and white.

Giants of California. This Grandiflora group comes in both dwarf and tall kinds. They are among the largest flowering petunias, heavily ruffled with veined throats. The blooms average 5-6 in. across and include white, orchid, salmon, deep rose, wine-red and magenta. Sometimes grown effectively in masses but best suited to containers and raised beds. The Ramona strain is available in light and dark shades or mixed, a good representative of the Dwarf Giants. The first F₁ hybrid Giant of California was Frolic which grows to a height of 15 in. with huge flowers, in a complete range of color.

PHACELIA CAMPANULARIA—California Bluebell. Waterleaf Family.

A lovely little velvety-leaved annual from California much grown for its brilliant royal-blue, bell-shaped flowers about 1 in. in diameter. In the center of the flower are 5 purple stamens terminating in white anthers. Erect, branching stems bear oval, pointed, irregularly-toothed leaves which appear

Phacelia campanularia

wrinkled, are frequently margined with red and when bruised have a rather pleasant odor. Plant grows to 9 in. in height and remain in bloom for a long time. Excellent for edging border or paths or for sowing in drifts in the rock garden. Splendid pot plant for the cool greenhouse. Not satisfactory for cutting.

Hardy. Sow seed in fall or early spring where plants are to bloom. Some say plants do not take transplanting; others have been successful. Germination requires 12 to 30 days depending upon time of sowing. Flowering begins about 12 weeks after sowing and continues for 14 weeks or more. Autumn-sown plants will flower earlier than those sown in the spring. Certain percentage of seedlings will die off during winter so do not thin until April or May. Prefer a sheltered, sunny position and a light, sandy soil. Thin to 6 in. apart. Pinch back when young to develop compact, well-formed plants. Will not do well if the summer is dull and cool.

Varieties: Var. *alba* has pure white flowers, not as attractive as the type.

PHASEOLUS COCCINEUS (*P. multiflorus*)—Scarlet Runner Bean Vine. Pea Family.

A tall fast-growing vine, actually a perennial in tropical America, grown as an annual for ornament in the North. It has attractive pea-like flowers of a showy brilliant scarlet, followed by an abundant crop of beans that are edible when young and green. Thought to be the original of the beans grown by the Aztecs. Although really a pole bean its flowers are so attractive it is frequently used for covering fences and to screen out unsightly objects. Vines climb 8-10 ft. by midsummer.

Of easy culture. Sow seeds at the base of the trellis upon which they are to grow, when soil is warm, and 2 weeks after frosts are past. The seeds are quite large and will germinate quickly in 4 or 5 days in warm soil. Will do well in any well-drained warm garden soil, sandy rather than heavy. Subject to the usual garden pests so spray or dust with an all purpose insecticide. Pods are dark green, long and flattened. They should be eaten when about 4 in. long, before they become tough and fibrous with age.

PHEASANT'S EYE—See *Adonis annua.*

PHLOX DRUMMONDI—Annual Phlox. Phlox Family.

Half-hardy annual; a native of Texas and one of the most widely cultivated of all an-

Phaseolus coccineus

Phlox drummondi Gigantea Art Shades Mixed

nuals. Many interesting named forms on the market. The varieties and color range are legion. The newer kinds have large flowers in big showy terminal clusters. Used in broad masses annual phlox makes a fine showing in the border, in the rock garden or as a ground cover, over a long period of time. Various colors may be combined to form a veritable rainbow. As an undergrowth for the barer-stemmed annuals or bulbs such as gladiolus a phlox planting is invaluable. Plants grow 1-1½-ft. tall and there are dwarf forms which make good edgers. Available in clear soft pink, rose, crimson, scarlet, salmon, violet, and white often with contrasting eyes. Some have frilled flowers. Attractive in arrangements if individual flowers are kept picked off as they wilt.

To hasten blooming sow seed indoors in March or 6 to 8 weeks before outdoor planting is safe or where wanted, as soon as trees leaf out. Thin to 6-8 in. apart. Seedlings resent transplanting so handle carefully keeping ball of soil around roots. Like full sun and ordinary or light well-drained garden soil. Pinch back to keep plants bushy. Bloom 58 to 76 days from seed. Cut fading flowers promptly to lengthen blooming period. Space 10-12 in. apart.

Varieties: Seedsmen advertise many novelties. Var. *grandiflora* is one of the taller annual phlox containing the whole range of phlox colors, plants are 15 in. tall, excellent for cutting. Glamour (All-America) is a tetraploid, a vigorous plant about 14 in. tall. Flowers are salmon-colored with a deeper center ring and a white eye. Gigantea Art Shades Mixed, plants 10 in. tall with large heads of bloom (white eye) in soft pastel colors. *Nana compacta*, plants 8 in. high are free blooming and includes Isabellina, a buff-yellow. Twinkle with starred flowers (All-America) and Globe are around 6 in. tall and 8 in. across with flowers in mixed colors, excellent low edgers.

PHYSALIS ALKEKENGI (*P. francheti*)—
Chinese Lantern. Nightshade Family.
A Eurasian perennial but easily grown from seed in one season and usually treated as a tender annual. Actually a showy weed, with inconspicuous flowers; grown mostly for its

Physalis alkekengi

large ornamental orange-red papery husks which are prominent in the fall. A fast spreader, it is best placed in a remote out of the way corner or in the cutting garden. Cut in the autumn before frost and before rains disfigure ornamental husks. Provide useful material for dried winter arrangements.

Sow seed outdoors early. Not particular about soil but plants enjoy an open, sunny position. Thin to 12 in. apart. Self-sows and can easily become a pest unless all pods are kept picked. Long, creeping, underground stems can also become a nuisance so you may want to dig them up and divide roots or start a new crop from seed each year.

PIMPERNEL—See *Anagallis linifolia*.

PINCUSHION FLOWER. See *Scabiosa atropurpurea*.

PINK—See *Dianthus*.

PLATYSTEMON CALIFORNICUS —
Cream Cup. Poppy Family.
A beautiful California wild flower now in

cultivation and useful as a low-growing annual. Rarely exceeds 12 in. in height and it forms a dense, spreading cluster of grayish-green narrow leaves often clasping the stem and smothered in spring and summer with a profusion of solitary saucer-shaped flowers in creamy-white, deepening to yellow in the center. The poppy-like flowers measure 1 in. or more and are borne on long stems well above the foliage. Bloom from July to September. Attractive little plant for edging the border or for sowing in drifts in the rock garden. Attractive for cutting but quickly fade.

Hardy. Seed carried mostly by Western seedsmen. In fall or in early spring sow seed where they are to grow, in full sun, in a light, well-drained rather sandy soil. Thin to 4 in. apart.

Varieties: Var. *crinitus* is a more hairy plant than the type and the flowers are often tipped with pink or green.

POLYANTHUS—See *Primula polyantha.*

Polygonum orientale

Platystemon californicus

POLYGONUM ORIENTALE — Prince's Feather. Buckwheat or Rhubarb Family.

A large-growing hardy annual from Asia and Australia with graceful, drooping sprays or pendants of densely clustered, bright pink or rose-colored flower spikes, 3-4 in. long. The plant grows to a height of 5 ft. Its large, broad, oval, pointed leaves, 6-10 in. long, are coarse and hairy and the tall branching plants make excellent background material. The attractive flowers are produced freely from July to October and are excellent for cutting. The stalk is tan with red-brown joints every 6 in.

Sow seed in fall or early spring outdoors where they are to flower. They like a good well-drained garden soil, in full sun or partial shade. Thin 12-18 in. apart depending upon the variety.

Varieties: Var. *variegatum* has green leaves marked with white and var. *pumilum* is more compact than the type.

POOR MAN'S ORCHID—See *Schizanthus wisetonensis.*

POPPY—See *Papaver*.

POPPY MALLOW—See *Callirhoe pedata*.

PORTULACA GRANDIFLORA — Rose
Moss. Purslane Family.
A very popular Brazilian annual much prized
for its ease of culture and profusion of bloom.
For a quick-flowering carpet in a hot, dry
sunny place there is nothing better. Does
equally well where summers are short and
cool. Excellent for rock work on banks, along
a driveway strip, as a ground cover, following spring bulbs or in urns or patio planters.
The little solitary flowers about 1 in. wide,
single and double, in many colors, open
when the sun strikes them in the morning.
The glossy-petaled rose-like flowers come in
clear yellow, white, scarlet crimson, orange
and rose. Double kinds are most charming
and in many ways superior to singles. Plants
are of a creeping habit, 6-8 in. high, the
leaves moss-like and almost hidden by the
flowers. Easy to move, so useful for filling
in dry, bare spots.

Portulaca grandiflora

Broadcast the very fine seed mixed with
half dry sand and press into the soil only
lightly or merely rake in. Likes full sun. Any
soil will do, preferably on the poor side. Will
tolerate a variety of conditions. If given water and a little attention at the start plants
will thrive. Left alone without spacing, will
produce sheets of midsummer color. An occasional weeding is the only care needed.
Often self-sow, once planted persist from
year to year. However, only small portion of
double kinds come true to seed. The seeds
which resemble iron filings have a metallic
lustre and are produced in a small, boxlike
capsule. When ripe the lid falls off and re-
veals them.
    Varieties: It is possible to buy separate or
mixed colors in singles and doubles. Jewel
has large single dazzling crimson flowers.

POT MARIGOLD—See *Calendula officinalis*.

PRICKLY POPPY—See *Argemone grandiflora*.

PRIMULA POLYANTHA — Polyanthus.
Primrose Family.
A group of garden hybrid primroses perhaps
derived from crosses between the oxlip (*P.
elatior*), the cowslip (*P. veris*) and the English primrose (*P. vulgaris*). A hardy perennial easily grown from seed. The forms have
been greatly improved, especially in the
color range, which in addition to the original yellow now includes pinks, crimsons,
flame colors, blue and white, many of which
come true from seed. They grow about 12 in.
tall and the flower clusters are usually profuse. Suitable for the rock garden, beds or
borders, and make admirable pot plants for
the cool greenhouse. Lovely in drifts under
spring-flowering ornamental trees or planted
with bulbs.
    The most easily grown of all the primroses
and frequently raised from seed, the reason
for including here. Plants may also be
propagated by division after flowering. Sow
seed thinly indoors in March. Germination
takes around 18 days (55°-60° F.). Place
young seedlings in cold frame and keep

shaded, cool and moist. By mid-May prick out and plant in a cool, shaded location outdoors. Good flowering plants will be ready for planting in their permanent position by October and will come into flower the following spring. They like a rich, well-drained, moist soil and some shade.

Varieties: Giant and Colossal Strains have large flowers in heavy trusses. Seed packets come in mixed colors. The Pacific Strain may be had in separate colors or mixed.

PRINCE'S FEATHER—See *Amaranthus hybridus* and *Polygonum orientale.*

QUAMOCLIT PENNATA (*Ipomea quamoclit*)—Cypress Vine. Morning-Glory Family. Showy and graceful, tender annual, growing 10-20 ft. high, from tropical America, naturalized in the southern states and widely planted in California. It has dark green, feathery or fern-like foliage and is grown mainly for its starlike scarlet flowers borne all summer long. Fast growing, it makes a very dainty and attractive display on a trellis, wall or other support.

For culture see *Q. sloteri.*

Varieties: Var. *alba* has white flowers or buy a packet of mixed seed with both scarlet and white.

Q. sloteri (Ipomoea cardinalis)—Cardinal Climber. An annual hybrid twining vine of great charm derived from crossing two tropical relatives (*Q. pennata* and *Q. coccinea*) of the morning-glory. For a quick temporary screen or effect on a trellis or against a wall this dainty vine is very useful. The glossy rich green fern-like foliage is dotted with small tubular star-shaped fiery scarlet flowers somewhat like small morning-glories with white centers which appear in midsummer and continue until frost. Flowers remain open except during the hottest part of the day. Plants will grow from 10-20 ft. in length. A good climber to grow in pots in winter or anywhere that graceful foliage is desired.

Soak hard seeds in hot water overnight before sowing, after they have been filed or nicked with a knife to let moisture enter. Sow seed outdoors where wanted when dan-

Primula polyantha Pacific Mix

Quamoclit sloteri

Rehmannia angulata

ger of frost is over or for an earlier start, sow seeds indoors 6 to 8 weeks before outdoor planting is possible. Transfer seedlings to permanent site in a warm, sunny location in any average well-drained garden soil. Space 2-4 ft. apart or where needed. Plants cannot take frost. Do not feed, as growth will go to leaves instead of flowers. Usually listed in catalogs by common name, Cardinal Climber.

Varieties: Hearts and Honey is scarlet with a yellow center.

RAGWORT, PURPLE—See *Senecio elegans.*

RAINBOW CORN—See Grasses, Ornamental.

REHMANNIA ANGULATA — Rehmannia. Figwort, Snapdragon or Foxglove Family.
Showy Chinese perennial but not hardy enough to survive northern winters where it is raised as an annual. Has lovely, long, bell-shaped flowers but is not often found in gardens or seed catalogs. The rosy-purple flowers are over 3 in. long, produced on long terminal racemes or in the axils of the leaves. The flower stems tower 3 ft. above the low rosettes of foliage which have numerous sharp teeth or a few toothed lobes. They make good cut flowers and are equally valued in the garden for planting among low annuals, their flower stems producing an unusual display.

Start seed early indoors for a good start since, the larger the plants, the more flower stems may be expected. Sow indoors in February for bloom in July and August or in hotbeds in March or if sown in May young plants may be raised which can be carried through the winter in cold frames to start blooming early the next summer. Watch out for white fly. Plants have a suckering habit and send up young plants which may be potted for winter storage and carried over in cold frames.

Varieties: Var. *tigrina* has spotted flowers and var. *tricolor* has purple flowers which later become violet-rose, the whitish throat spotted with purple.

RESEDA ODORATA—Mignonette. Mignonette Family.

An annual from North Africa much grown in old-fashioned gardens as the most fragrant of all outdoor flowers. The enchanting sweet odor is quickly lost when picked unless some of the newer varieties are grown. Plants grow 1-1½ ft. tall, and are rather loose and sprawling, not showy as a garden plant. Inconspicuous flowers are small in compact spike-like clusters and usually dry up as soon as the weather becomes hot. Foliage is a soft light green. Plant in little groups here and there, perhaps by the doorstep, or a window for fragrance and to cut for arrangements to use with other flowers. Grow in pots for sunny windows. Mignonette will attract the bees.

The seed is very small. Sow sparingly and give a very light covering. Sow in May and for a succession of bloom sow every 2 weeks up to the middle of July. Loses some of its fragrance in very hot weather. Thin to 6-10 in. apart and pinch back to make plants bushy. Mignonette does not transplant easily. Must keep roots covered with a ball of soil. Will bloom 60 to 70 days from seed. Likes full sun or partial shade and is a lime lover. Grows best during cool weather in spring and fall. A dressing of bonemeal early in the season is helpful.

Varieties: Usually the smaller flowered kinds are more fragrant than the giant forms. Sweet Scented is one of the most preferred for its fragrance. Machet is also very fragrant as is *R. odorata grandiflora*.

Reseda odorata

RICINUS COMMUNIS—Castor-Bean Plant. Spurge Family.

A vigorous, quick growing, tree-like plant from the tropics grown mostly in the garden as a striking foliage plant for summer bedding, for background and in dense masses to screen unsightly building or objects. Rather tropical in appearance. Rarely exceeds 5 ft. when grown as an annual although it reaches 40 ft. or more in its native habitat. Slender terminal clusters of small, unattractive flowers are of no consequence. For variation in the large, divided leaves see varieties listed below.

Ricinus communis

Tender. Soak seed in tepid water for 24 hours before sowing to insure rapid and even germination. Pre-soaked seed will germinate in about 15 to 18 days. Sow indoors for early start, 6 weeks in advance of planting out. Plant several seeds in a small pot. When of sufficient size pull out all but the best one. Plant seedlings out when settled warm weather has arrived and space 3-4 ft. apart.

Requires an open sunny position and a rich fertile soil. Need plenty of water and fertilizer for good growth. Staking of the main stem is advisable since it can be easily damaged by high winds. The seeds, which yield castor oil, are poisonous if eaten. Keep away from children.

Varieties: Since they are grown for their foliage, specify color foliage when ordering from seedsman. Differ in having red, bluish-gray, red, maroon, purplish, and reddish-yellow stems and variegated leaves. Hundreds of varieties in cultivation, often incorrectly listed as distinct species. Some of the most valuable for garden purposes include:

var. *africanus* with large, grey-green leaves

var. *borboniensis arboreus* with red stems and blue-gray leaves

var. *cambodgensis* with dark, often purplish stems, and leaves

var. *coccineus*, with dark red leaves

var. *gibsoni*, a small variety with dark red, metallic foliage

var. *hybridus panormitans* or *pamormitanus*, a large variety with bluish leaves

var. *laciniatus*, a variety with leaves deeply cut and slashed

vars. *macrocarpus*, *macrophyllus* and *purpureus* with purple red leaves

var. *sanguineus* with reddish-purple leaves and stems

var. *zanzibarensis*, a striking variety with bright green, white-veined leaves.

ROCK JASMINE—See *Androsace lactiflora*.

ROCK PURSLANE—See *Calandrinia grandiflora*.

ROCKY MOUNTAIN GARLAND — See *Clarkia elegans*.

ROSE MOSS—See *Portulaca grandiflora*.

ROSE OF HEAVEN—See *Lynchnis coelirosa*.

RUDBECKIA BICOLOR — Annual Coneflower. Composite Family.
An erect, robust annual from Texas. Flowers have yellow rays, often purplish-black at the base with a black or brown cone in the center. Differ from other daisies and called coneflower because of their high centers (disk-florets). Both the type and its varieties grow to a height of 1-2 ft. or more.

Striking plants for the border, producing a great profusion of showy flowers when many others have stopped flowering. Plant wherever vigorous growth will not crowd less rampant plants. Splendid for cutting.

Easy to get started. Hardy. Sow seed outdoors where they are to flower. Thin to 6 in. apart. Must have a sunny, open position but any good garden soil will do. Will bloom about 15 weeks after sowing, at their best from August to October. Taller ones will need staking if position is exposed. Will

Rudbeckia bicolor

stand hot, dry conditions very well. Demands little care. Cut flowers freely and don't let them go to seed for an abundance of bloom.

Varieties: Var. *superba* (Erfurt coneflower) has larger flowers and var. *semiplena* has semi-double blooms. Kelvedon Star is long lasting, a deep yellow with a mahogany zone and brown cone or center. Most of the hardy perennials can be grown as annuals if you wish to do so.

RUDBECKIA HIRTA SELECTIONS—
Gloriosa Daisy. Composite Family.
Selections of *R. hirta,* the popular black-eyed Susan, native to the United States, with large single or double flowers are preferred over most species. They bloom the first year from seed and are often perennial, especially in well-drained soil. Vigorous, erect, bushy plants and free-blooming they grow to 3 ft. or more in height and are excellent grouped in masses in the garden for color. The big daisy-like flowers, carried on sturdy stems, are long lasting and excellent for use as cut flowers.

Salpiglossis sinuata

Hardy. If seed is sown early in the spring, plants will bloom from late summer until fall. Open field plants, they prefer full sun, but most any garden soil will do. Space 2 ft. apart. Hot, dry summers do not trouble the gloriosa daisy. Keep the dead flowers picked for continuous bloom.

Varieties: Singles have huge blooms 5 in. and more in diameter, flowers are yellow, mahogany and bicolored with dark centers. Doubles average 4 in. across, flowers are a rich golden yellow (semi-double and double), some are dark centered. Goldflame is a large single, orange with brown centers.

SALPIGLOSSIS SINUATA — Painted
Tongue. Potato or Nightshade Family.
A Chilean annual grown for its velvety, richly varicolored, petunia-like flowers with delicate patterns in gold or contrasting colors traced upon its petals. Flowers are borne upright on slender but strong branches 2 ft. tall and bloom generously in shades of maroon, purple, blue and scarlet during July and August, usually until frost. Plants are

Rudbeckia hirta selections, Single Gloriosa Daisy, Two Black-Eyed Susans not very promising in appearance when young, but develop and send up clusters of elegant flowers on long stems, graceful and long lasting cut for decoration indoors. Grow 2½-3 ft. tall and may be used at the background of the border. A dwarf form about 20 in. tall is sometimes used in borders.

Salpiglossis is not as easy to grow as some annuals. Seed is extremely fine, almost microscopic. Mix with sand and sow indoors 8 to 10 weeks before outdoor planting is safe. Scarcely cover seeds. Will germinate in about 8 to 9 days. Transfer seedlings outdoors. Will bloom 106 to 112 days from seed. Sowing on milled sphagnum moss is good for salpiglossis. Like full sun or partial shade, good well-drained sandy garden soil and a cool growing season with not too much moisture. Do not like hot, humid weather. Space 8-18 in. apart, depending upon variety. Pinch out centers of young plants to encourage branching. May need staking to keep plants erect in an exposed area.

Varieties: Emperor is a 30 in. tall strain with beautiful colors and velvety texture in mixed colors. Bolero, an F_2 Hybrid, is shorter, 2-2½ ft., and bushier, also in mixed colors. The Dwarf Compact strain is a more compact plant and branching. Ideal for beds or borders and for cutting.

SALVIA—Mealy or Mealycup Sage. Mint Family.

The salvias listed here are perennials best grown as annuals, often listed in seed catalogs as Salvia, Scarlet Sage and Perennial Salvia or Blue Sage.

S. *farinacea*—Blue Salvia. A perennial from Texas, not truly hardy in the northern states, so it is treated as an annual. Grows from 2-3 ft. tall, has light, violet-blue flowers on long slender spikes, excellent for cutting. This salvia self-sows freely so when once established will form fine clumps of plants. Blue Bedder is an old-time and still popular variety which grows 2-2½ ft. tall. Is more compact than the type, with splendid spikes of deep Wedgwood-blue flowers which dry well. Royal Blue, White Bedder and Royal White are popular and grow to 3 ft.

The perennial salvias or blue sage (S.

Salvia splendens

farinacea and *S. patens*) may be treated the same as *S. splendens* (see below). Set plants about 12 in. apart. The roots may be dug and stored out of reach of frost over the winter since they are good for more than one season if protected.

S. *patens*—Blue Sage. This half-hardy perennial, native in the mountains of Mexico, grows to 2½ ft. high and has large gentian-blue flowers, unexcelled for depth of its ultramarine blue shade. Does not bloom as profusely as scarlet sage. Cambridge Blue is a good variety with beautiful rich sky-blue flowers. Plants grow 2 ft. tall.

S. *splendens* — Scarlet Sage. A showy, shrub-like perennial from Brazil, not winter-hardy except in frostless regions, grown as an annual since it flowers freely from seed the first year. It has been grown by the millions as a summer bedding plant but was so overplanted and misused many people are prejudiced against it. The brightest of reds, it will overpower other colors, particularly delicate pastel shades, so must be used with care and discretion. A grouping of plants by themselves among rocks on a bank will brighten up the area. Or a clump highlighted against a background of broadleaved evergreens or a light silvery-gray mass of *Artemisia* foliage will add a dramatic touch to the landscape. Used in combination with white petunias or white verbenas the results may be very effective. It does not last well as a cut flower.

Dwarf and tall varieties are cataloged, varying in height from 12 in. to 3 ft. The taller kinds may require staking. The scarlet tubular flowers, including the colored flower bracts, are arranged in showy terminal spikes that rise above the dark green foliage. Pinch the early growth to develop bushy, compact plants.

Scarlet sage takes longer to grow than most annuals so either buy young plants or start seed indoors in late February or early March, keep where temperature is between 70° and 80° F. Soaking the seed will help it germinate faster. Will flower in 75 to 106 days from seed. Set seedings outdoors when settled warm weather arrives, in full sun, in ordinary garden soil. Space 15-30 in. apart depending on whether dwarf or tall varieties. Needs plenty of water. Can be grown all winter in the house from cuttings taken from stock plants salvaged from the garden at the approach of frost.

Varieties: St. John's Fire is an excellent dwarf variety, 12 in. tall; Bonfire is an old favorite still good, reaches 2-3 ft. Fireball and Fireworks are early blooming dwarf plants that make good edgers. The Welwyn strain is offered in separate colors of pink, white, lavender and maroon. Evening Glow (All-America 1964) has brilliant old rose shaded lavender with coral tongue flower spikes, bushy growth, 15-18 in. Pastel varieties are also available in Evening Glow (All-America), old rose; Pink Rouge, salmon rose-pink; Salmon Pygmy, pink with orange corolla and White Fire, creamy white.

SAND VERBENA—See *Abronia umbellata*.

SANVITALIA PROCUMBENS — Creeping Zinnia, Trailing Sanvitalia. Composite Family.

An attractive free-flowering Mexican annual with long trailing stems and low growing, prostrate. Its oval, pointed leaves are about 1 in. long and covered with short hairs. The bright golden-yellow, purple-centered daisy-like flowers are numerous, each measuring about 1 in. across, single and double-flowered, reminding one of tiny zinnias. Rarely exceed 6 in. in height. Useful for edging borders and paths or for low masses in the border. Bright and showy in the rock garden or as a seasonal ground cover. A good plant for the cool greenhouse. Start blooming in June and continue until frost.

Hardy. Sow seeds in fall or early spring outdoors, in full sun, in a light well-drained soil. Thin to stand 6-12 in. apart. Do well in rather dry, hot positions. Many of the autumn-sown plants will die off during the winter so do not thin until spring.

Varieties: Var. *flore-pleno* has very attractive double flowers.

Sanvitalia procumbens

Saponaria calabrica

SAPONARIA CALABRICA (*S. multiflora*) —Soapwort. Pink Family.

A little annual from Italy and Greece with dense, branching stems and smooth oblong or lance-shaped leaves, the plant rarely exceeding 9 in. in height. Sown in drifts its small attractive loose clusters of deep rose-colored flowers about ½ in. in diameter completely cover the foliage creating a lovely carpet of color. Showy plants for edging or sowing in drifts on sunny slopes. Also may be used in rock garden. Flowers last well cut. Leaves make soap suds when rubbed in water.

Seed may be sown outdoors in early spring where they are to flower. Thin to 6 in. apart. They like any well-drained garden soil and an open sunny location but will take partial shade.

Varieties: Var. *alba* has pure white flowers and var. *compacta* is a dwarf, compact form. Scarlet Queen has brilliant scarlet flowers and is much more attractive than the type.

SAPONARIA VACCARIA — Cow Herb, Cockle. Pink Family.

Also known as *Lychnis vaccaria* and *Vaccaria segetalis*, *V. parviflora*, *V. pyramidata* and *V. vulgaris*. A showy annual from Europe with graceful sprays of loose clusters of deep pink flowers, each about ½ in. in diameter. Although small the flowers are produced in great profusion during the summer and are excellent for cutting. Plants grow to 2 ft. or more, leaves are smooth, broadly lance-shaped. Often becomes a weed in the fields although a desirable garden plant. For culture see *S. calabrica*. Thin plants to 9 in. apart.

Varieties: Var. *alba* has white flowers and var. *rosea* pale pink.

SATIN FLOWER—See *Godetia grandiflora*.

SCABIOSA ATROPURPUREA—Pincushion Flower, Sweet Scabious. Teasel Family.

A most attractive annual from southern Europe. It forms a neat rosette of deeply divided basal leaves, above which rise long slender stems to a height of 2 ft. or more terminating in pincushion-like clusters of small flowers in many colors: lavender, lavender-blue, purple, maroon, salmon, pink, red, rose, pale yellow and white. Below each flower cluster is a row of minute leaflets or bracts. The stamens are light in color and in contrast with the petals appear like pins stuck into the flower. Attractive plants grow to 3 ft. tall, bloom in early summer and attract bees and butterflies. The maroon and blackish-purple forms supply some of the deepest colors among annuals. Cut flowers keep several days; long stems, charming and pleasing colors add to their usefulness in arrangements. The annual scabiosa comes in a wide range of colors, the perennial species come mostly in lavenders and blues.

For early start sow seed indoors 8 to 10 weeks before outdoor planting is safe or sow outdoors where plants are to grow. Do best in full sun in any good, well-drained garden soil. Seeds germinate in 20 days. Plants bloom 90 to 100 days from seed. Thin to 6-9 in. apart, keeping plants closely spaced so they will look less spindly and support each other, and flower heads will have less tendency to droop on their thin, wiry stems. Easy to grow but do not relish extreme heat. Pinch off tip branches to encourage bushier growth. Remove dead flowers as they fade. If seed heads are picked off before they ripen, plants will bloom until frost.

Varieties: Sold in seed packets as Large Flowered Double Mixed; Hybrids, Mixed Colors; Giant Hybrid Mixture; Imperial Giants, Mixed Colors; Dwarf Double Mixed, etc. For separate colors specify color desired. Imperial Giants are kinds without the pincushion effect—broad frilled petals arranged in a ball take the place of the more typical pincushion with tubular flowers. The seed heads are peculiarly bristly. A new race of scabiosa. Plants are 3-4 ft. tall with extremely large flowers.

SCARLET RUNNER BEAN—See *Phaseolus coccineus.*

SCARLET SAGE—See *Salvia splendens.*

Saponaria vaccaria

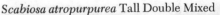

Scabiosa atropurpurea Tall Double Mixed

SCHIZANTHUS WISETONENSIS — Butterfly Flower, Poor Man's Orchid. Potato or Nightshade Family.

Of hybrid origin (*S. pinnatus x S. grahami*) and Chilean parentage this half-hardy annual has many fine colored varieties. The two-lipped flowers are a delight, resembling small orchids or the butterfly, graceful with dainty markings and interesting forms in soft pink, rose, blue, lavender, purple and white with throat markings of deeper tones. Lacy, fine-cut fernlike foliage is nearly hidden under tumbling masses of colorful flowers. Extremely decorative for cutting and keep well. Excellent container plants. Plants grow 1½-4 ft. tall.

Half-hardy. Sow seed indoors 6 to 8 weeks before outdoor planting is safe. Cover only lightly. Seeds are slow to germinate requiring about 20 days. Transfer seedlings outdoors in sun or with filtered shade of high branching trees, in ordinary garden soil, moving each seedling with a ball of earth. Handle carefully since they are easily broken. Space 2-3 ft. apart. Plants do not enjoy hot, dry climate. Pinching back terminal shoots will delay but greatly increase the bloom and correct tendency of plant to become straggly. Plants bloom 70 to 80 days from sowing.

Varieties: Dr. Badger's Hybrids contain all the schizanthus colors. Grandiflora Angel Wings is supposed to be improved over Dr. Badger's, more compact, conical plants of uniform dwarf character. Ball Dwarf Mixture is a dwarf strain.

SEA LAVENDER—See *Limonium sinuatum.*

SEA PURSLANE—See *Atriplex hortensis.*

SENECIO CINERARIA — Dusty Miller. Composite Family.

An old-fashioned favorite grown for its gray woolly-white foliage. Frequently listed in catalogs as *Cineraria maritima (candicans)* or as dusty miller. A perennial from the Mediterranean region, so quickly effective from seed it is usually treated as an annual. Its glistening white foliage makes it useful for the border, for bedding, or as an accent.

Schizanthus wisetonensis Dr. Badger's Hybrid

Senecio cineraria

Silene armeria

Silybum marianum

The flowers which come in late summer are yellow. Sow seed indoors in February or March. Set plants out in May, 1 ft. apart, in full sun.

Diamond is an improved strain, one of the best dwarf dusty millers. Var. *aureo-marginatus* has yellow-edged leaves.

S. *elegans* — Purple Ragwort, Purple Groundsel. A showy long-season annual from South Africa with erect stems, plants about 18 in. tall or more and completely covered with purple, crimson or white flowers, much like a cineraria. A spendid plant for the border or for bedding out. A good edger and a good cut flower in the cooler climates of the United States. A good cool greenhouse plant.

Half-hardy. Seed should be sown outdoors early where plants are to grow, then thinned to 8 in. apart. Blooms well only in cool, moist areas. Any ordinary well-drained garden soil and sun will meet the other requirements.

Varieties: Several very fine named varieties with single or double flowers are listed in catalogs. Var. *alba* has pure white flowers, var. *roseus* rose-colored and var. *purpureus* has deep purple blossoms.

SHELL FLOWER—See *Molucella laevis*.

SILENE ARMERIA—Sweet William Catchfly, None-so-Pretty. Pink Family.
A little known but worthy annual useful in the rock garden and border. A showy plant from southern Europe. The erect stems, 1-2 ft. in height, bear oval pointed or lance-shaped bluish-gray foliage, the lower ones spatula-shaped. Flowers are produced in dense, terminal compound cymes or clusters in colors of bright pink or rose; flowers measure about ¾ in. in diameter.

Hardy. Sow seed in fall or in early spring where they are to flower. Germination takes 12 to 24 days. Flowering starts 10 to 16 weeks after sowing and continues for 6 weeks or more. Prefer a light, well-drained, slightly acid soil and an open sunny location. Thin to 8 in. apart. Will often persist from self-sown seeds. Staking of tall kinds may be necessary if area is exposed.

Varieties: Var. *alba* has pure white flowers and vars. *grandiflora* and *splendida* larger flowers than those of the type.

SILYBUM MARIANUM—Lady's, Milk, or Holy Thistle. Composite Family.
From the Mediterranean region but now naturalized in California. A thistle-like annual which is sometimes biennial. Grows to 4 ft. in height with flat rosettes of 2½ ft. long, glossy leaves, the margins wavy and spiny

with white spots and veins on the upper side. Large purplish-red or rose-purple, faintly sweet-scented flower heads are 2½ in. across, solitary and nodding, surrounded by rings of stout spiny bracts. Grown as an ornamental plant for its silvery leaves. Also grown as a vegetable, its roots, leaves and flower heads being edible.

Hardy. Seeds should be sown in fall or early spring outdoors where plants are to grow. Of easy culture with ordinary garden soil and full sun. Flower in July or August.

SNAPDRAGON—See *Antirrhinum hybrids.*

SNOW-ON-THE-MOUNTAIN—See *Euphorbia marginata.*

SOAPWORT—See *Saponaria calabrica.*

SOUTHERN STAR—See *Oxypetalum caeruleum.*

SPECULARIA SPECULUM—Venus-Looking-Glass. Bellflower Family.
Also known as *Campanula speculum.* A showy plant from Europe and western Asia about 9-12 in. tall with erect stems bearing smooth, oblong, marginally toothed leaves and clusters of saucer-shaped violet-blue or white flowers about ¾ in. in diameter, 2 or 3 to a cluster. An attractive edging plant.

Specularia speculum

Useful for cutting although flowers do not last long in water.

Sow seed outdoors in fall where they are to grow. Prefer a light, well-drained soil in full sun or partial shade. Seed sets freely and if ground is left undisturbed large numbers of young seedlings will spring up.

Varieties: Var. *grandiflora* has larger flowers than those of the type and var. *grandiflora alba* is the same with white flowers. Both may be had with single or double flowers. *Florepleno* added to the varietal name indicates the double types.

SPIDER FLOWER—See *Cleome spinosa.*

STAR OF TEXAS—See *Xanthisma texanum.*

STARWORT—See *Aster amellus.*

STATICE—See *Limonium sinuatum.*

STOCK—See *Mathiola.*

STRAWFLOWER—See *Helichrysum bracteatum.*

SUMMER CYPRESS—See *Kochia scoparia trichophila.*

SUMMER FIR—See *Artemisia sacronum viridis.*

SUNFLOWER—See *Helianthus annuus.*

SUNFLOWER, MEXICAN—See *Tithonia rotundifolia.*

SWAN RIVER DAISY—See *Brachycome iberidifolia.*

SWAN RIVER EVERLASTING—See *Helipterum manglesi.*

SWEET ALYSSUM—See *Lobularia maritima.*

SWEET PEA—See *Lathyrus odoratus.*

SWEET ROCKET—See *Hesperis matronalis.*

SWEET SULTAN—See *Centaurea moschata.*

SWEET WILLIAM—See *Dianthus barbatus.*

SWEET WILLIAM CATCHFLY—See *Silene armeria.*

TAGETES—Marigold. Composite Family. Marigolds, petunias and zinnias are often referred to as the "big three" all-purpose, basic annuals. A native of Mexico, marigolds are widely grown for their brilliant, showy flowers and undemanding, reliable performance in the garden. Erect and branching and highly aromatic (objectionable to some). Seed catalogs list innumerable varieties which show a wide variety of petalage, habits of growth and sizes, from 6 in. to 4 ft. The prevailing colors are yellow, gold and orange. However they also come in dark reds and maroon or in combinations of yellow or orange and red, maroon or mahogany. New varieties are constantly being introduced and some now available are claimed to be odorless.

Plants grow quickly and are seldom bothered by pests or diseases, furnishing quantities of flowers throughout the summer months for both the garden and the house. When used as a cut flower remove the bottom leaves to avoid contaminating the water. Their stiff stems, bright colors and good keeping qualities make them a valuable cut flower.

Plants are effective massed in drifts, the smaller ones in front, the taller kinds at the back; as an edging; or in raised beds; in fact in any place that will take yellow and orange for quick, colorful effects. They will show up in all their brilliance in the fall when most other flowering plants have gone by.

Half-hardy. Buy young plants or sow seed in a warm spot in early spring where plants are to grow or for earlier flowers start seed indoors 7 to 9 weeks before outdoor planting

Tagetes patula Double, Gypsy Mixed

is safe. Seeds will germinate in about one week. Transfer seedlings outdoors when settled weather has arrived, in full sun. They like a light well-drained soil. *T. erecta* requires a somewhat richer soil than the other species and can take more moisture or watering. Marigolds do not object to transplanting and are quite adaptable to less favorable conditions. Thin or space tallest kinds 18-24 in. apart, dwarfer ones 12 in. Require sun for good blooming but can take hot, dry location. Pinching back will encourage branching and heavier bloom. Can pretty well take care of themselves but light colored kinds may attract Japanese beetles. Taller varieties seldom need staking but a stout support early in growth will keep them neatly upright if they are in an exposed area. The more flowers you cut for indoor decoration the more bloom you will get in the garden.

T. erecta—African Marigold. These are the tallest of the marigolds growing to 3-4 ft in height. In seed catalogs they are listed under such headings as Chrysanthemum-Flowered, Carnation-Flowered, Gigantea, Doubles, Dwarf, etc. with varieties of varying colors from yellow to orange, pink, cerise and red. Seeds may be purchased in straight colors or mixed. Some have much doubled or even quilled flower heads, a few varieties are said to have scentless foliage.

Dwarf. African varieties are 8-12 in. high. The Cupid series includes plants 8-10 in. tall with showy chrysanthemum-type flowers, 2½-3 in. across, odorless foliage, flowers in yellow, orange, and gold. Spun Gold (All-America) is early and has golden-yellow flowers profusely borne on dwarf bushy plants, 12 in. tall. Fully double blooms are 2½ in. across, petals nicely incurved. Spun yellow is similar to Spun Gold except for color. Many feel the common name "African Marigold" is confusing since these are North American in origin. Some have suggested "American Marigold" or "Giant Flowered American Marigold."

Tall. African varieties grow up to 3-4 ft. and are frequently later blooming. New F₁ Hybrids are superior to the older varieties. Include Gold Coin Series which produce

fluffy blooms up to 5 in. in diameter on plants 3 ft. tall; blooms carried on top of the foliage and produced in incredible numbers. Climax hybrids bloom in midsummer and have huge flowers 4-5 in. across with ruffled or frilled petals in yellow, orange, gold and primrose. Plants are covered with blooms from top to bottom. Available in both separate and mixed colors. Primrose Climax is a soft creamy primrose-yellow, Yellow Climax a bright yellow and Golden Climax a deep golden yellow. Toreador (All-America) is a popular deep golden-orange of the Climax type. Early to bloom and productive. Flowers 3-3½ in. across, plants 3 ft. high.

Crackerjack Mixed is early and tall with giant blooms in orange, gold, canary and primrose, strongly double. Carnation-Flowered kinds include excellent inbred varieties such as Alaska, pale primrose white, and Hawaii, a rich orange. Plants are 2-2½ ft. tall, loosely petaled flowers 3 in. or more across. Chrysanthemum-Flowered have plants 2-2½ ft. tall with petals tightly incurved, blooms 2½-3½ in. across.

T. patula—French Marigold. The French marigold has the typically golden and yellow flowers but are often marked with crimson and maroon. Smaller than *T. erecta*, the

Tagetes patula Dwarf Single, Naughty Marietta

Thelesperma burridgeanum   *Thunbergia alata*

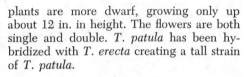

plants are more dwarf, growing only up about 12 in. in height. The flowers are both single and double. *T. patula* has been hybridized with *T. erecta* creating a tall strain of *T. patula.*

Dwarf Doubles include the Petite Series (All-America) which is a class of extra dwarf doubles bred for uniform growth, early bloom and a profusion of flowers. They grow 6-8 in. tall, spread to 12 in., and make neat, trim edging plants. Colors include yellow, orange and gold, available separate or mixed. Also Petite Harmony, gold crest with mahogany ray petals; and Petite Spry, golden yellow with maroon collar. Other good extra dwarf (6 to 8 in.) types include Butterball, butter-yellow; Fireglow, deep mahogany red with varying amounts of gold in centers; Helen Chapman, gold with red touch at base of petals; Lemondrop, compact, canary-yellow; Spry, yellow bordered mahogany; and Sunkist, orange. Harmony is an early golden yellow bordered maroon-red, 12-14 in. tall. Others in this height group include Rusty Red (Fandango), huge deep red blooms; Tangerine, orange companion to Rusty Red; and Color Magic, large flowers variegated yellow-gold and mahogany. Sparky, gold edged with red is very striking and bright.

Dwarf Singles. Dainty Marietta is similar in size of bloom and markings to Naughty Marietta but only half as tall, 6 in. Naughty Marietta has 2-2½ in. yellow blooms with mahogany base. Red Head, 12 in., is rich golden, edged maroon and with rich mahogany.

T. tenuifolia (T. signata) pumila. This is a small compact form rarely exceeding 8-10 in. in height with fern-like foliage and tiny 1 in. yellow flowers marked at the base with orange. A fine edging plant. Lulu is compact and ball-shaped, 7 in. tall with bright yellow flowers. Golden Gem has the same habit as Lulu but is bright orange. Ursula is similar to Lulu in habit with golden orange flowers and bright orange zone.

TAHOKA DAISY — See *Machaeranthera tanacetifolia.*

TASSEL FLOWER—See *Emilia sagittata.*

THELESPERMA BURRIDGEANUM — Cosmidium. Composite Family.
A very fine annual from Texas. The coreopsis-like ray flowers are broad and deep orange in color with a yellow margin; the disk-

flowers are purple. Once considered a hybrid between *T. trifidum* and *Coreopsis tinctoria*. The slender stems about 12-18 in. in height bear finely divided leaves and flower heads which measure 1½ in. across. Attractive plants for the border and for cutting. Similar to coreopsis and will bloom all summer in the sun.

Sow seed outdoors early where plants are to grow. Prefers a light sandy soil and a sunny location. Thin to 6 in. apart.

THISTLE, LADY'S, MILK or HOLY—See *Silybum marianum*.

THUNBERGIA ALATA—Clock Vine, Black-Eyed Susan Vine. Acanthus Family.
A perennial from tropical Africa grown in the North as an annual, blooming in late summer and autumn, although a slight frost cuts their top growth to the ground. This low-growing, dainty, twining climber has perky black-eyed flowers, 1½ in. across, in colors of orange, yellow, cream and white. The vine is easy to grow and attractive. Its tendency to trail makes it highly effective in hanging baskets or draping the front of a window or porch box. The rustic appearance of the vine makes it useful in rock or wall work where it cascades gracefully. Also useful as a ground cover or it can be trained to a low trellis or fence. Tying at intervals will keep the vine in place.

Plant seed outdoors where they are to grow in warm soil, in a sunny location. With warmth and moisture growth is rapid. If grown in containers feed about every 4 weeks to maintain the rich green color of the foliage.

Varieties: Seeds are usually only available in mixed colors. Var. *alba* has white flowers. Var. *aurantiaca* has orange flowers with a characteristic black "eye." Will grow downward or along the ground unless encouraged to climb. *T. gibsoni* is another species sometimes listed in catalogs with rich deep-orange flowers.

TIDY TIPS—See *Layia elegans*.

TITHONIA ROTUNDIFOLIA (*T. speciosa*)—Mexican Sunflower. Composite Family.
Native of Central America and Mexico. The type is not successful in regions with a short growing season but has given rise to several excellent early varieties which will start blooming in mid-July. Unless the early varieties are chosen the plants are frequently frosted before they bloom. It is one of the few annuals that will bloom through August and September despite intense heat and dryness. Plants are robust growing to 4-6 ft. tall. The daisy-like flowers are 3-4 in. wide with orange-scarlet rays and tufted yellow centers. Leaves are velvety, large and often 3-lobed. Imposing when used as temporary hedges or tall background annuals, and excellent as cut flowers. Although foliage is coarse, flowers are so vivid you do not notice the leaves.

Half-hardy. Sow seed indoors in pots and transfer outdoors when soil is warm. Germination takes place in about 10 days (60°-65°). Like a full sun and any good garden soil. Thin to 2-4 ft. apart.

Varieties: Var. *grandiflora* is exceptionally fine with large flowers. Torch (All-America) grows 4-6 ft. tall and is a brilliant orange-scarlet often 4 in. across.

Tithonia rotundifolia Torch

Torenia fournieri　　*Trachymene caerulea*

TOADFLAX—See *Linaria macroccana.*

TOBACCO, FLOWERING, JASMINE or **ORNAMENTAL**—See *Nicotiana alata.*

TORENIA FOURNIERI—Wishbone Flower. Figwort Family.

A bushy annual 8-14 in. high from Cochin, China. A little gem, easy to grow and a very useful plant for summer and fall. Blooms in part shade. The gloxinia-like flowers in sky blue with violet or lavender lower lips and a yellow throat are borne in profusion in July and August up until frost. In the center the stamens are arranged in the shape of a wishbone. Foliage is a bronzy-green. Garden effect is not showy but flowers have beauty and interest and plants are good edgers and effective planted in containers and hanging baskets in half shade. In Florida torenia is used as a substitute for the pansy which is cultivated only with difficulty that far south; young plants come up from self-sown seed in the rainy season.

Tender. Seeds are very fine and when carefully sown indoors, 8 to 10 weeks before outdoor planting is safe, will give excellent plants that will bloom all summer long. Transfer seedlings outdoors in partial shade (except where summers are cool and short) in a reasonably moist but not wet, well-drained garden soil. Will transplant readily. Space 6-8 in. apart. Plants like humidity, tend to fade quickly in a dry atmosphere.

Varieties: Var. *grandiflora* has larger flowers than the type. Var. *alba* has white flowers. Var. *compacta* is dwarf.

TRACHYMENE (*Didiscus*) **CAERULEA**—Blue Lace Flower. Carrot Family.

This Australian annual is frequently seen in florists' windows but easily grown in the home garden. Its minute, lacy flowers are arranged in flat-topped umbels suggesting a blue edition of Queen Anne's lace or wild carrot. Not too outstanding in the garden but decorative when cut. Flowers are about 2½-3 in. in diameter and plants ½-2 ft. high. They last exceptionally well as cut flowers.

For early bloom sow seed indoors 6 to 8 weeks before outdoor planting is safe. Use paper pots for easy transplanting. Or sow

Tropaeolum hybrid, Golden Gleam

seed outdoors in spring when soil is warm, in full sun, in rich soil, where plants are to grow. Thin to 9-10 in. apart. Get more profuse bloom if plants are reasonably crowded. In hot climates they will stop blooming or die. Seedlings resent transplanting and like cool weather. Pinch out the tips of young plants to make them branch more.

Varieties: White and pink varieties are available from specialty seedsmen.

TREE MALLOW—See *Lavatera trimestris splendens.*

TROPAEOLUM HYBRIDS — Nasturtium. Tropaeolum Family.
This old-time flower is a half-hardy annual from Peru that comes in two forms, a dwarf bushy kind and a tall climbing, twining strain that needs a wire or trellis support. Colorful and easy to grow they give quick and effective results. Few other annuals bloom so rapidly from seed. Flowers come single, semi-double and double and although typically orange-yellow or yellow-red they may be had in pale primrose-yellow, creamy white, geranium-scarlet, sulphur-blotched red, deep garnet and vermilion. The leaves are roundish in outline and borne in abundance. Seed is available in straight colors or packets of mixed colors.

Compact, dwarf kinds are excellent for small beds and edging. A packet or two of seed scattered on a sunny, cleared piece of ground will supply a vivid splash of color with little or no work. The trailing types are unexcelled for verandas, trellises, to cover old stumps, fences, rough ground or any unsightly object. Grown on a wire mesh frame in a container on the patio, with sun, it makes a luxurious climber with lustrous foliage and flowers in profusion. It is a real eye-catcher, and may attract some humming birds. Nasturtiums are also excellent for cutting and fragrant in some varieties. The more freely they are cut the more freely they will produce. The young flower buds and unripe seeds are enjoyed by some for their pungent flavor. Seed pods may be picked when green and put in vinegar for pickles.

Of easy culture requiring almost no care except to watch for aphids. Look at the undersides of the round leaves and on tender

VII. Opposite   *It is hard to go wrong when grouping calendulas, for their colors harmonize as easily as do those of marigolds. Plants of the Pacific Beauty strain used here are especially good together. Deep orange Flame, foreground, goes well with paler Apricot Beauty, front left, and with Lemon Beauty, center.*

ew growing tips for any infestation and spray with a good insecticide. If they become infected with black lice use a spray containing nicotine or pyrethrum on the soil, stems and leaves in early morning. Seeds are large; cover to a depth of 3 times their own diameter. Sow when ground is warm (will rot in cold, damp soil), when trees leaf out. Space dwarf types 12 in. apart, tall kinds 2-3 ft. apart. They are difficult to transplant. On large areas where individual seeding is impossible, work the soil first, then broadcast seed and lightly rake it in. For pots use 4 to 6 seeds in a 6 in. pot, then thin seedlings to 3 plants. Nasturtiums prefer full sun and will grow in a poor soil, giving big returns on dry gravelly banks. Rich soils or shade produce more foliage than flowers. They prefer cool sections to hot ones but will not stand frost. Pull them out with autumn's first frost. In mild climates they seed themselves and may live over like perennials.

Varieties: Old-fashioned single mixed may still be had. Newer kinds have double, sweet-scented flowers. Those of the Globe and Gem groups come in assorted colors with big, double and semi-double flowers on a mound-like plant 12 in. high and 18 in. wide. Gleam nasturtiums have giant, fragrant, long-stemmed blooms up to 2½ in. across on 18 in. plants, excellent for beds or cutting. Colors run through mahogany, salmon, gold and orange and may be had in straight colors or mixed. Scarlet Gleam (All-America) and Golden Gleam (All-America) are bright showy colors. Cherry Rose has double flowers held up above the foliage, a unique habit among nasturtiums. Fiery Festival has dazzling scarlet blooms and dark green leaves. Tall trailing forms may be had in mixed colors; blossoms are single or semi-double.

URSINIA ANETHOIDES – Ursinia. Composite Family.

Little grown South African perennial usually grown as an annual since it is only half-hardy. A bushy plant about 18-24 in. tall with wiry stems and finely cut leaves. Beautiful, orange-yellow, daisy-like flowers are 1-2 in. wide, numerous but solitary, borne on long stems well above the foliage. The flowers are marked at the base of the rays with a ring of deep purple. Showy plants for bedding or for sowing in drifts in the border. Flowers good for cutting; however, they open in full sun and close again in the evening. In dull weather they have a tendency to remain closed. Grown as a pot plant in the cool greenhouse.

Sow seed indoors for an early start or outdoors when warm weather has arrived, in full sun, in any light well-drained rather poor soil. Thin to 8-10 in. apart. Flowers 11 weeks after sowing and continues to bloom for 10 weeks or more. May die in areas of great intense summer heat.

Ursinia anethoides

VIII. Opposite *The Mammoth Russian Sunflower is a dramatic plant for an informal garden and also a source of bird food. Jays will often strip the seeds from the head as soon as they are mature, so any heads you wish to save should be protected. Like most sunflowers, the Mammoth Russian will grow on any soil, but makes its greatest size on rich, manured land.*

VENIDIUM FASTUOSUM — Venidum. Composite Family.

A little-grown South African annual with showy brilliant orange flowers about 4 in. in diameter. The ray flowers are purple-brown at the base and the disk a deep, shining black. The flowers open in the morning and close at night even when cut for the house, and remain partially closed on dull days. Small gray-green wooly lyre-shaped leaves and flower buds are covered with dense, cobwebby white hairs which give the plant an attractive, silvery-white appearance. It grows to a height of 2 ft. or more. Excellent plants for the border, they are also splendid for cutting and good greenhouse plants.

Easier to grow in California than in the East. Half-hardy. In the East sow seed indoors 8 weeks before outdoor planting is safe. Be sure soil is warm before seed is sown. Germination takes about 6 days. Transfer seedlings outdoors in a warm, sheltered sunny position in a light well-drained soil. Space 12 in. apart. Flowering begins about 12 weeks after sowing and continues for 7 weeks or more. Do not overwater. In East plants are subject to stem rot. In California and similar climates sow directly outdoors. Plants like heat, sun and drought. Staking may be necessary if in an exposed position.

Varieties: Flowers are usually yellow but several varieties are now cataloged ranging in color through buff, yellow, orange and white. In each case there is a purple-black ring of color in the center. All usually listed in catalogs as var. *hybridum*.

VENUS-LOOKING-GLASS—See *Specularia speculum*.

VERBASCUM — Mullein. Figwort, Snapdragon or Foxglove Family.

The verbascums are mostly hardy biennials and include some handsome garden plants suitable for the large border, the wild garden or edging shrubbery. As a biennial sow seed in August or September for flowering the next summer. Grow best in a light well-drained soil and partial shade. Do not like wet, cold soil.

Verbascum

Venidium fastuosum

The Harkness hybrids grow to 6 ft. in height with immense spikes, well furnished with large pure yellow flowers.

Verbascum phoeniceum—Purple Mullein. A well known 2-4 ft. biennial from south-eastern Europe and Asia. Flowers freely the first year from seed and may be grown as an annual. It forms basal rosettes of dark green leaves, the margins with coarsely rounded teeth, hairy or downy below, and smooth on the upper surface. From the center of the rosette rise long leafy stems ending in stiff purple flower spikes. Each flower is about 1 in. across and bears a cluster of purple-wooly stamens in the center. The tall dense flower spikes are an interesting contrast to the wooly leaf rosettes, which are very decorative. Will take high winds so can be grown near the windy shore. Excellent cut.

Likes a sandy well-drained loam and partial shade. Flowers earlier than the other species, in May or June. Plant 12-24 in. apart. In favorable positions plants may self-sow but will not come true from such seed.

Varieties: Var. *album* has white flowers.

Other hybrids may be had in mixed colors of pink, rose, salmon, lilac, violet and white.

VERBENA (*hortensis*) HYBRIDA—Garden Verbena. Verbena Family.

A race of beautiful hybrids, parents South American perennials, but grown here mostly as a half-hardy annual since it blooms from seed the first year if started early indoors. Sprawling or trailing, the many-branched plant may spread 18-24 in. and some tall ones reach 12 in. in height. Has bright green or gray-green leaves with toothed margins and the fragrant small flowers are in flat compact terminal clusters in shades ranging from lightest pink to red, light lavender-blue to deep violet, white and cream. Many flowers have contrasting centers. The rich colors of the verbena are very showy and have been a garden favorite for generations, furnishing a profuse, continuous, colorful display all summer long even in hot, dry places. They are quite adaptable. Good for holding a bank, covering bare spots after bulbs have finished blooming, for massing in the front of a border, for use in rock gardens or for planting in

Verbena hybrida Dwarf, Erect

a container for a sunny spot on the terrace. Attractive as cut flowers.

Seeds appear not unlike small twigs and are slow to germinate. Sow indoors 8 to 10 weeks before outdoor planting is safe. Transfer seedlings outdoor only after settled warm weather has arrived. Will bloom 88 to 106 days from seed. Florists sow in February for bloom in May, when they sell the small plants in flats. Space 10-16 in. apart. Plant in full sun in any good garden soil. Pinch taller types back early in their growth to promote bushiness. Keep flowers cut so plants will not go to seed. Will tolerate high heat. If the foliage turns whitish, use a dust containing sulphur. If wanted for next year it is possible to dig up the tuberous root before frost, pot it up and carry through the winter indoors.

Varieties: Giant, Tall Erect, Bush Type and Dwarf kinds are all available, both in straight colors or mixed. Spectrum Red (All-America) is in the Giant class. Dwarf Upright Rainbow Mixed is a lively blend of colors, most with a large eye of contrasting color. Sparkle is a dwarf, 9 in. tall, bright red with a white eye; Crystal is white and both are excellent for edging or the rock garden. Salmon Queen, Snow White and scarlet Firelight are bush type growing 8-10 in. tall and 12 in. across. Some others 8-10 in. include Calypso, a novelty blend of striped and blotched colors; Delight, a coral-pink; and Splendor, deep reddish-purple with white eye. Royale, large flowered violet-blue with eye, and Torrid, a deep red with white eye, are 12-18 inches.

VINCA ROSEA (*Catharanthus roseus*)— Madagascar Periwinkle. Dogbane Family.
A tender, short-lived perennial from tropical Madagascar, *Vinca rosea* is much grown for bedding purposes and for pot plants and treated as a tender annual. A sturdy-stemmed bushy plant, 1-2 ft. tall, it has attractive, dark green glossy leaves. Its pink, rose and white flowers, 1-1½ in. across, are borne 2 to 3 in a cluster, some with a darker or contrasting eye. Not good for cutting.

A slow grower so for certainty of bloom, north of Philadelphia, sow seed indoors 8 to 10 weeks before outdoor planting is safe.

Vinca rosea

Germination takes 10 days (65°-70°). When weather is settled transfer seedlings outdoors in full sun or partial shade in any ordinary well-drained garden soil. Space 6-12 in. apart. Keep soil moist but not overwatered. Feed occasionally. *Vinca rosea* does better in warm than cold regions. Thrives in hot, dry weather and is not troubled by insects or disease.

Varieties: Seed packets may be purchased in straight colors or mixed. Var. *alba* has white flowers; var. *oculata*, white with a red center. New upright dwarf forms 10-12 in. tall, are good, splendid for bedding, and include Coquette (Little Pinkie), with a tolerance to heat and drought with glossy, deep green leaves and attractive rosy-pink blooms; also Bright Eye which is a pure white with a rose eye. Rose Carpet is creeping or trailing in habit, with rose-colored flowers. Makes a good ground cover.

Vinca major variegata is a variegated trailing evergreen widely used for window boxes and sold by florists. Easily propagated by cuttings or division. Not hardy in the North, often a ground cover in the South.

Viola corunta Mixed

VIOLA CORNUTA — Viola, Bedding or Tufted Pansy. Violet Family.

A short-lived perennial from Spain and the Pyrenees these little relatives of the pansy are informal and cheery, easy to grow and with many uses—as an edging plant, as clumps in the rock garden or as a ground cover under shrubs. One kind reseeds itself so readily it is called Johnny-jump-up. Their flowers are usually smaller than pansies and they form more tufted, mounding plants. Culture is similar.

Hardy. Set out plants in early spring about 4 in. apart or grow from seed sown in early spring or late summer. Violas need rich, moist soil and although they do not like hot, dry summers they bloom better in hot weather than pansies. They do well in partial shade. Flowers should be picked as soon as they fade. Cut back plants lightly in summer and water in dry weather for good bloom.

Varieties: Both seeds and plants are available. Some favorites include: Arkwright Ruby, ruby-crimson; Blue Perfection; Chantreyland, apricot; Eileen, royal blue; Jersey Gem, violet-blue; John Wallmark, soft lavender and Vixen, creamy yellow.

VIOLA TRICOLOR HORTENSIS—Pansy. Violet Family.

All pansies are perhaps derived from the European *V. tricolor*, a perennial species, but as now developed they are best treated as annuals or biennials. They come in colors of rich velvety blue, gold, red and white, the petals usually blotched or striped. The appealing flowers are flatish and look like uplifted faces. The plants have a tendency to sprawl, grow to 8 in. in height, with leaves mostly basal and heart-shaped.

A universal spring-time favorite the pansy is useful for edging, as a filler in the border or ground cover, and attractive used in combination with spring flowering bulbs. Attractive cut and used in arrangements.

Without a cold frame or 45°-60° greenhouse the pansy is not easy for the home gardener to propagate. Purchased plants ready to put out are the easiest solution. They transplant without difficulty. To have a long blooming period they should be set out as soon as possible after danger of heavy frost is past; they tolerate light frosts. The site should be cool and moist with a rich, well-drained soil. Pansies will not bloom in full shade but will do rather well in half-shaded places. Space 6 in. apart. To encourage bloom remove all flowers as fast as they fade and cut or pinch back if plants become leggy. Never let pansies dry out and fertilize every 3 or 4 weeks. Cool, early spring weather is the best growing time; the summer heat usually kills them. When this happens pull them out and plant something else in their place.

The better varieties are shy seed bearers so good pansy seed is expensive, but buy the best for the most attractive colors and most satisfying results. Pansy seed is good for only 9 months. Old seed will not germinate properly. When the temperature is above 70° pansy seed will not germinate. Seed sown in August will bloom in early spring.

Sow seed in August, ⅛ in. deep, in ½ rich loam and ½ sand, well mixed. Carry the seedlings over the winter in a cold frame, cool greenhouse (45°-60°) or well mulched outdoors. As soon as possible in the spring transplant to permanent site, spacing 6 in. apart.

Viola tricolor hortensis Mixed

Varieties: Many excellent strains are available. A few of them are Swiss Giants, favorites with large flowers, available in several straight colors, bicolors or in a mixed assortment; Maple Leaf Giants; and Engelmann's Giants. Masterpiece has very frilled and ruffled blooms. Newer developments are Color Carnival with many red and wine tones, Masquerade in a light colored orange and the Early-flowering French Giants are popular. Arcadia Mixed is a popular giant-flowered type available in a mixture of pastel colors.

VIPER'S BUGLOSS— See *Echium plantagineum.*

WALLFLOWER—See *Cheiranthus cheiri.*

WHITECUP—See *Nierembergia rivularis.*

WILD CUCUMBER—See *Echinocystis lobata.*

WIND POPPY—See *Meconopsis heterophylla.*

WINGED EVERLASTING—See *Ammobium alatum.*

WISHBONE FLOWER—See *Torenia fournieri.*

WOODRUFF—See *Asperula orientalis.*

XANTHISMA TEXANUM—Star of Texas. Composite Family.
An erect, branching annual about 2-3 ft. tall from Texas. It has narrow, oblong or lance-shaped leaves and showy citron-yellow daisy-like flowers about 2½ in. in diameter, borne on stems at the end of the branches. The lower leaves are toothed along the margins. An attractive plant for sowing in large drifts in the border. Its flowers are excellent for cutting. Flowers freely from July to September.
   Hardy. Sow seed where they are to grow in a light, fairly dry soil, in an open sunny position. Staking will be necessary if in an exposed position. Thin to 12 in. apart.

Xanthisma texanum

Xeranthemum annuum

XERANTHEMUM ANNUUM—Immortelle. Composite Family.

Interesting everlasting; an erect, bushy plant about 2-3 ft. tall from the Mediterranean region. Narrow wooly oblong or lance-shaped, sharply pointed leaves are ashy or silvery-green in appearance. Long-stemmed, solitary purple flowers measure about 1½ in. across and are excellent for cutting. Plants are useful in the border. For use as an everlasting cut the silky flower heads just as they start to be fully open, tie together by stem ends and hang upside down in a dry, airy place until quite dry.

Hardy. Sow seed in open in early spring where plants are to grow in a poor, rather dry sandy soil, in full sun. Germination takes about 18 days. Thin to 8 in. apart. Flowering begins about 11 weeks after sowing and continues for six weeks or more. At their best from July to September.

Varieties: Several fine ones are listed in seed catalogs. Var. *ligulosum* has semi-double flowers, var. *periligulosum* fully double flowers and var. *compactum* or var. *multiflorum* are smaller and more compact than the type. Each variety includes several color forms such as *album* (white), *roseum* (rose) or *purpureum* (purple). This and *Catananche,* a perennial, are the best blue or purple everlastings.

ZINNIA HYBRIDS — Zinnia. Composite Family.

Derived from much hybridizing of two Mexican plants: Z. *elegans* is the parent of tall varieties and Z. *angustifolia* parent of the dwarfer types. One of the indispensable staples of the garden. Easy to grow, developing quickly from seed in 6 to 8 weeks and offering a dependable riot of color all through the hot summer weather. Colors include all but blue: shades of orange, yellow, pink, red, purple, lilac, white and bicolors.

A standby for the beginner, both in the garden and as a cut flower, with flowers from the tiny to the immense and plants ranging from dwarf sizes to those 3 ft. high or more. With marigolds and petunias they comprise the 3 annuals with the largest seed sales. Tall kinds with heavy lush foliage make excellent and substantial backgrounds for the varying heights of lower-growing kinds. If pinched back to develop branching, zinnias have the sturdy value of shrubs in a new garden. Used as fillers in a newly planted shrub border they make the planting look well developed and full the first year. Lower growing kinds are excellent for edging. Zinnias massed in smart color choices and heights can be strikingly effective. In bold masses for distant effects, few other annuals can rival them.

Zinnia angustifolia

Zinnia Firecracker

Half-hardy. Sow the large seeds indoors 8 to 10 weeks before outdoor planting is safe for an early start. Seeds germinate in 5 days at 60°-65° F. Transfer seedlings outdoors when settled warm weather has arrived. The young plants are susceptible to frost so do not plant out too early. Large-flowered kinds are difficult to transplant and should be sown where they are to grow or in peat pots. Young plants should be pinched back to make them bushy and well branched, unless huge show blooms are desired. For large prize blooms disbud all but the top, terminal bud. Zinnias flower most freely on a well-drained, moderately rich soil in a sunny location. An open location with good air circulation offers the best chance to escape mildew. Sun, good air circulation and good weather will help prevent mildew, but to be on the safe side spray with a good fungicide, such as Karathane. If chewing insects bother, control with an all-purpose insecticide. Flowering begins about 8 to 10 weeks after sowing and will continue for 10 weeks or more. They are at their best from June until August. For August and September bloom sow seed in May where plants are to bloom. Space or thin to 8-10 in. apart for

dwarf varieties, 12-15 in. for the taller kinds.

Varieties: Breeders have developed all sizes, shapes and colors and seedsmen put out so many new strains and varieties it is hard to keep up with them. The new types and new colors are a continuing source of interest. Some strains are said to be mildew-resistant.

For small gardens there are midget or dwarf zinnias, all of them fine for edgings and low borders, and small arrangements. *Z. angustifolia* (syn. *Z. haageana* and syn. *Z. mexicana*) is the parent of the dwarf types.

Thumbelina (All-America) is a plant 6 in. high, completely covered with semi-double or double flowers 1¼-1½ in. across, in many colors.

Tom Thumb Mixture comes in a variety of colors with small double flowers on compact plants 8-10 in. tall. Lilliput-type bloom.

Cupid Mixture. Small button-like flowers 1 in. in diameter on dwarf, compact plants 12 in. tall, in a variety of colors. Smaller than the Lilliput type.

Button Zinnias. Dwarf, compact, free-flowering plants 10-12 in. tall, in pink or red flowers, 1½ in. in diameter; disease resistant.

Lilliput or Pompon. Dwarf, bushy, compact plants 12-18 in. tall with small pompon-like flowers 1-2 in. in diameter on strong stems, offered in a variety of colors.

Mexican Hybrids often cataloged under *Haageana* (*Z. angustifolia*) are favorite bedding zinnias 14-18 in. tall, flowers single to double around 2 in. in diameter. Good varieties are Old Mexico (All-America), a bushy plant with striking bicolor flowers of deep crimson overlaid golden yellow and Persian Carpet with variegated flowers on a mound-like plant.

Z. linearis is the only single zinnia. It has golden-yellow, orange-tipped flowers about 2 in. in diameter. Plants grow 12 in. tall.

Most intermediate or medium sized plants are variations of *Z. elegans pumila*.

Cut and Come Again. Bushy plants between the Pompons and Giants in size, in a variety of separate colors or mixed. Plants 18-24 in. tall, with medium-sized flowers 2½-3½ in. across, blooms early; a long time favorite. Peppermint Stick is variegated and has flower rays striped in various bright color combinations, a good novelty.

Scabiosa-Flowered Mixed. Plants grow 2-2½ ft. high; medium-sized flowers resembling scabiosa in rich autumn shades.

Dwarf Double Pumila Mixed. Between Giants and Lilliputs in size.

Giant Flowered. *Z. elegans* is the parent of the tall, huge varieties which include the Giants, Dahlia-Flowered, Cactus-Flowered, etc. Dahlia-Flowered and California Giant zinnias are two of the oldest, tallest and largest flowered kinds. Through the last several years, the original difference between Dahlia-Flowered and California Giants has virtually disappeared. Many seedsmen have started selling them all as Giant Flowered. They grow 3 ft. tall or more with blossoms 5-6 in. across. Some kinds are bicolor. Among the Giant Doubles with dahlia-like flowers listed in some catalogs are Canary Bird, yel-

Zinnia Firecracker and Thumbelina

low; Golden Dawn, golden-yellow; Scarlet Flame, scarlet; and Royal Purple.

Cactus-Flowered is a new type zinnia, 2½-3½ ft. tall, with unusual shaggy flowers 4-5 in. in diameter, rays curled upward and quilled or tubular as in the Cactus Dahlias with many good varieties and colors. Several F_1 hybrids are available in the Giant Cactus types. Among these are: Bonanza (All-America 1964), golden orange; Firecracker (All-America 1963), scarlet; Zenith Yellow (All-America 1965), clear mid-yellow; and Trail Blazer, red with yellow centers, resistant to mildew. Other Giant Cactus are: Red Man (All-America 1962), red; Rosie O'Grady, deep rose; Blaze, mandarin red with scarlet orange; and Ice Cream, cream.

Giant Doubles have huge double-flowered heads 4-5 in. in diameter; plants grow 3-3½ ft. tall and come in all colors but blue. Good varieties include Enchantress, pink; Isabellina, cream-yellow; and Purity, white.

Tetra Giant Doubles have very large flowers 5-6½ in. in diameter; plants grow 2-2½ ft. tall; good bedding plants. State Fair is available in a wide color range.

Sanvitalia procumbens, Creeping Zinnia, is not a zinnia but usually cataloged under that heading.

Part II

Growing Annuals from Seed
or Started Plants

1

Useful Facts and
Definitions

PLANT NAMES

In Part I the most important annuals in cultivation today were listed alphabetically by botanical name. These two-part names, mostly Latin, are universally accepted so that even if a garden catalog is printed in French, Italian, or Spanish, for example, the Latin name is an accurate scientific means of identification. Unfortunately there is no single accepted authority on spelling these Latin names, and gardening books printed in English reflect a lack of standardization. However, this inconsistency of spelling does not impair the tremendous usefulness of our binomial system of plant nomenclature.

In addition to a scientific name, most plants have one or more common names, which vary from region to region, and for this reason are inexact and confusing. Nevertheless common names are often colorful and tell something of the way the plant behaves. Since people like to use names which are familiar to them, it is customary for garden writers to list the common name as well as the botanical one.

Plants are classified by family, genus, and species. Those having the same basic characteristics as to the structure of the flowers and particularly their reproductive organs are assigned to the same family, the largest number of annuals belonging to the Daisy or

Composite Family (Latin, *Compositae*). Generally one prominent genus gives the family its name. For example the Poppy Family (*Papaveraceae*) is made up of about 25 genera which include the genus *Papaver* or poppy.

Under the broad family name comes a narrower classification, the genus name (plural, genera) for plants in an even closer relationship. Modifying the genus name is a specific name which tells something more about the habit of the plant—for example, *grandiflora* meaning large flower—or about the place where it was discovered, or the man who introduced it. Sometimes a plant will have a third name to indicate that it is a variation of the species. In Part I the scientific name is listed first, followed by the common name or names and the name of the family. After the first appearance of the genus name, when it is clear which of the many genera the plant belongs to, an initial letter is used with the species name, both in italics, upper and lower case, as *A. acutifolia*.

GEOGRAPHIC ORIGINS

The native habitat or geographic origin of a plant is also of genuine interest to the botanist, indicating to him definite cultural requirements. Seed from a desert region, adapted to survive fierce heat, will not be able to survive our cold; therefore it should never be sown in the autumn, to be killed by our winter frosts.

In the North where winters are severe we grow summer annuals that germinate in the spring, flower during the summer, and die at the onset of winter. The reverse is true in warmer climates where annuals complete their life cycle during the mild, humid winter. Southern gardens grow most of their annuals during the winter. Seeds which in the North are started early indoors to provide a long blooming season, in the South may be started in late summer or early fall.

Many plants which are really shrubs or perennials in their natural environment in warmer climates are grown in the North as annuals since they are not sufficiently hardy to stand cold temperatures.

PERENNIALS GROWN AS ANNUALS

With changed environment, over a period of time, plants change their habits. This ability to adapt to altered conditions is often helped along by plant breeders through proper selection. The environmental conditions of some perennials have been so changed that they are now nearer in habit to true annuals or biennials, and strains exist that will bloom the first year from seed. These changes have been brought about by such practices as sowing perennial seed indoors and then planting out the seedlings as soon as the soil can be worked, to get bloom the first year; by treating seed and artificially subjecting it to low temperatures to hasten germination; by constant selection of plants to breed for an abundance of bloom, with ultimate depletion of food reserves.

SYMBOLS H, HH AND T

The symbols H, HH and T, either in capitals or small letters, are frequently found in descriptions of specific annuals in flower seed catalogs. These letters, indicating hardy, half-hardy, and tender provide a key to the best time for sowing seeds.

Hardy. The term hardy, as applied to an annual, indicates a plant that withstands some frost and usually one which comes up from self-sown seed in the spring. The seed is winter hardy and not injured by the cold, although the plant itself may or may not be winter hardy.

Half-Hardy. As applied to annuals the term indicates that the seed and plant will stand some cold but not hard frosts. The seed should be sown outdoors only when danger of hard frost is past. A light frost will do no harm so long as the seedlings have not yet emerged from the soil.

Tender. An annual listed as tender will not stand any frost what-ever, either as seed or seedling. Seed should be sown outdoors only after all danger of frost is past, preferably after the soil has warmed and the nights have turned mild.

AVERAGE HARD-FROST DATES

These dates were furnished by the United States Department of Agriculture based on their weather records. Allow two weeks either way to meet seasonal differences. *Wait* if the season is late and the soil is not yet warmed up.

State	Last in Spring	First in Fall
Alabama, N. W.	Mar. 25	Oct. 30
Alabama, S. E.	Mar. 8	Nov. 15
Arizona, No.	Apr. 23	Oct. 19
Arizona, So.	Mar. 1	Dec. 1
Arkansas, No.	Apr. 7	Oct. 23
Arkansas, So.	Mar. 25	Nov. 3
California		
Imperial Valley	Jan. 25	Dec. 15
Interior Valley	Mar. 1	Nov. 15
Southern Coast	Jan. 15	Dec. 15
Central Coast	Feb. 25	Dec. 1
Mountain Sections	Apr. 25	Sept. 1
Colorado, West	May 25	Sept. 18
Colorado, N. E.	May 11	Sept. 27
Colorado, S. E.	May 1	Oct. 15
Connecticut	Apr. 25	Oct. 20
Delaware	Apr. 15	Oct. 25
District of Columbia	Apr. 11	Oct. 23
Florida, No.	Feb. 25	Dec. 5
Florida, Central	Feb. 11	Dec. 28
Florida, So. of Lake Okeechobee, almost frost-free		
Georgia, No.	Apr. 1	Nov. 1
Georgia, So.	Mar. 15	Nov. 15
Idaho	May 21	Sept. 22
Illinois, No.	May 1	Oct. 8
Illinois, So.	Apr. 15	Oct. 20
Indiana, No.	May 1	Oct. 8
Indiana, So.	Apr. 15	Oct. 20
Iowa, No.	May 1	Oct. 2
Iowa, So.	Apr. 15	Oct. 9
Kansas	Apr. 20	Oct. 15
Kentucky	Apr. 15	Oct. 20
Louisiana, No.	Mar. 13	Nov. 10
Louisiana, So.	Feb. 20	Nov. 20
Maine	May 25	Sept. 25
Maryland	Apr. 19	Oct. 20
Massachusetts	Apr. 25	Oct. 25
Michigan, Upper Pen.	May 25	Sept. 15

State	Last in Spring	First in Fall
Michigan, No.	May 17	Sept. 25
Michigan, So.	May 10	Oct. 8
Minnesota, No.	May 25	Sept. 15
Minnesota, So.	May 11	Oct. 1
Mississippi, No.	Mar. 25	Oct. 30
Mississippi, So.	Mar. 15	Nov. 15
Missouri	Apr. 20	Oct. 20
Montana	May 21	Sept. 22
Nebraska, W.	May 11	Oct. 4
Nebraska, E.	Apr. 15	Oct. 15
Nevada, W.	May 19	Sept. 22
Nevada, E.	June 1	Sept. 14
New Hampshire	May 23	Sept. 25
New Jersey	Apr. 20	Oct. 25
New Mexico, No.	Apr. 23	Oct. 17
New Mexico, So.	Apr. 1	Nov. 1
New York, W.	May 10	Oct. 8
New York, E.	May 1	Oct. 15
New York, No.	May 15	Oct. 1
N. Carolina, W.	Apr. 15	Oct. 25
N. Carolina, E.	Apr. 8	Nov. 1
N. Dakota, W.	May 21	Sept. 13
N. Dakota, E.	May 16	Sept. 20
Ohio, No.	May 6	Oct. 15
Ohio, So.	Apr. 20	Oct. 20
Oklahoma	Apr. 2	Nov. 2
Oregon, W.	Apr. 17	Oct. 25
Oregon, E.	June 4	Sept. 22
Pennsylvania, W.	Apr. 20	Oct. 10
Pennsylvania, Cen.	May 1	Oct. 15
Pennsylvania, E.	Apr. 17	Oct. 15
Rhode Island	Apr. 25	Oct. 25
S. Carolina, N. W.	Apr. 1	Nov. 8
S. Carolina, S. E.	Mar. 15	Nov. 15
S. Dakota	May 15	Sept. 25
Tennessee	Apr. 10	Oct. 25
Texas, N. W.	Apr. 15	Nov. 1
Texas, N. E.	Mar. 21	Nov. 10
Texas, So.	Feb. 10	Dec. 15

State	Last in Spring	First in Fall
Utah	Apr. 26	Oct. 19
Vermont	May 23	Sept. 25
Virginia, No.	Apr. 15	Oct. 25
Virginia, So.	Apr. 10	Oct. 30
Washington, W.	Apr. 10	Nov. 15
Washington, E.	May 15	Oct. 1
W. Virginia, W.	May 1	Oct. 15
W. Virginia, E.	May 15	Oct. 1
Wisconsin, No.	May 17	Sept. 25
Wisconsin, So.	May 1	Oct. 10
Wyoming, W.	June 20	Aug. 20
Wyoming, E.	May 21	Sept. 20

HYBRIDS, TETRAPLOIDS AND POLYPLOIDS

You will find annual varieties listed in catalogs under terms that may be new to you such as F_1 and F_2 hybrids, tetraploids or polyploids.

F_1 and F_2 Hybrids. These hybrids have been developed in many annual plants. The F_1 hybrids are the result of carefully controlled crossing, frequently by hand-pollination of two different parent strains. A new crop of seeds must be bred each year, using the same crosses to obtain identical varieties. The result is larger, stronger plants and flowers; increased vitality; more blooms and earlier flowering dates.

The F_2 hybrid is the result of the cross-pollination of two F_1 hybrids. They are superior in size of bloom and plant vigor to most inbred or open-pollinated kinds, but lack the controlled perfection of their F_1 parentage. The seeds are less expensive.

The Tetraploids and Polyploids. The hereditary nature of the living plant organism is controlled by microscopic structures inside each cell called chromosomes. Scientists have discovered that they can artificially double the number of chromosomes in plants by the use of chemicals. The best known of these is colchicine, a poison extracted from the autumn crocus (*Colchicum*). The seedlings of treated parents are sometimes superior in vigor, size of flower, fruit, and seed, with taller and heavier stems. These improved strains may be called tetraploids. The Tetra Snowdrift alyssum is 1 foot tall and better for cutting than the other annual alyssum, only 3 to 6 inches in height.

Polyploids are the result of an additional increase in the number of chromosomes in the plant. New Century zinnias are polyploids.

ALL-AMERICA SELECTIONS

This program, started in 1932, is sponsored by several seedsmen's organizations to test and evaluate new flower and vegetable introductions of commercial plant breeders. The seeds are sown, grown and tested in cooperative trial grounds, in various climates throughout the United States and southern Canada before they are placed on the market.

An All-America Seed Selections Committee, experts in the field, judge and compare introductions most critically. You can be sure that any variety with the "All-America Selection" emblem was a winner and therefore considered of outstanding merit by the judges.

Visitors are always welcome at any of the A.A.S. Demonstration Gardens and trial grounds. Demonstration gardens are located in:

California—Los Angeles State and County Arboretum, Arcadia

Colorado—Horticultural Arts Society, Colorado Springs

Georgia—Callaway Gardens, Pine Mountain

Illinois—University of Illinois, Dept. of Floriculture, Urbana

Kentucky—University of Kentucky, Lexington

Massachusetts—University of Massachusetts, Waltham Field Station, Waltham

Michigan—Michigan State University, Hidden Lake Gardens, Tipton

Missouri—Flower and Garden Test Garden, Kansas City

New Jersey—Rutgers University (Extension Service), College of Agriculture, New Brunswick

New York—Sterling Forest Gardens, Tuxedo

Ohio—Kingwood Center, Mansfield

Pennsylvania—Hershey Estates, Hersey; Longwood Gardens, Kennett Square

Virginia—Norfolk Botanical Gardens, Norfolk; Virginia Polytechnic Institute, Blacksburg

Wisconsin—Whitnall Park, Hales Corners, Milwaukee

Canada—Canada Dept. Agr. Central Exp. Sta., Ottawa, Ontario; Edwards Gardens, Toronto, Ontario

1965 represents the first season of All-Britain flower trials, after several years of study, planning, correspondence and cooperation from the experienced All-America Selections group.

THE SEED-GROWING BUSINESS

Few realize the tremendous responsibility and risk involved in growing seed for the market today. The plants, subject to all the hazards of weather, pest and decay must be grown so they come to perfection of flowering and continue on to produce the necessary crop of seed. The seedsman must know the exact best time to set and harvest a crop. Then the entire crop must be harvested, cleaned and delivered to the distributing center in time for the spring demand—assuming, of course, that a demand will exist for the seeds on which so much time and money has been expended.

In addition, mother seed or stock must be selected each year to preserve the standard of the variety as to color of flower, habit of growth, earliness and other characteristics. The old-fashioned hand flail is still used, mainly for threshing small quantities of valuable stock and mother seed, but research in new commercial practices and ingenious mechanical devices cut down the expensive hand labor and are helping solve many of the current problems.

To insure thorough ripening and harvesting, the bulk of the seed is now grown in the warmer and more dependable climates of California. With weather problems thereby reduced, and with increasing mechanization, the contemporary gardener gets clean, viable seeds which will produce good plants for his garden.

NEW INTRODUCTIONS

Every season, through discoveries from the wild and horticultural breeding and selection, new plants are offered to the gardening public. Before they make their appearance in the seed catalogs or on the seed racks, these introductions have had years of study, intensive research, and patient detective work. Not all of the new plants are worthy, since selling garden material is highly competitive and newness itself becomes a commodity. However, hybridizers strive for such desirable qualities as earlier or later blooms, more freely blooming flowers, more compact growth habits or more resistance to heat and disease. Color is always considered. Thus hybridizers are now and have for years been working for a clear, white marigold, a blue zinnia, and many other tones and hues new to that particular species.

When it is clear that the new plant has one or more characteristics to distinguish it from others in the same species, it may be put on the market as variety Golden Beauty or Snowball or Crimson Glory or Marie Hamilton or Mrs. John Smith. It is under these or similar varietal names that a huge number of new plants is introduced each year. Of course these new plants add an element of excitement to gardening, and avid gardeners eagerly await descriptions and pictures of current offerings.

NAMED VARIETIES

Listing named varieties in a book is always tricky not only because so many new ones are introduced each year, particularly in popular annuals such as petunias, zinnias and marigolds, but also because as the new ones come in, old varieties may be dropped. Therefore it is not always possible to buy seeds of old-time favorites, much as every seedsman tries, of course, to keep abreast of demand. To find the latest and best varieties available, consult reliable seed catalogs issued each season and keep up-to-date by reading gardening pages in magazines and newspapers.

TOXIC ANNUALS

Some plants are injurious to man and animals, producing irritation, distress, or even death if taken internally. We are all familiar with poison ivy and the deadly mushroom. Fortunately, not many garden annuals are dangerously poisonous, although relatively harmless plants can cause trouble, if taken in too large quantities, as happens at times with livestock. Some parts of a plant may be more injurious than others, as the seeds of the castor-bean plant are more deadly than the remainder of the plant. Not all persons are equally affected by the same poison. Some skins are highly susceptible to the skin-irritant in poison ivy, others practically immune.

Fortunately, the bad taste of injurious plants will prevent the child, in most cases, from more than a nibble. They may, however, swallow berries without chewing or tasting them. If there is the least suspicion a child has swallowed poisonous berries or eaten the leaves call a physician at once. With symptoms of pain, headache, vomiting, drowsiness, or convulsions give the child prompt and expert care. The identification of the source of the trouble is important, so, in case of poisoning, get a specimen of the plant eaten at the same time you rush to call the doctor.

Plants with a milky juice such as the milkweeds and spurges are potentially dangerous, often causing severe irritation of the skin or alimentary canal, if taken internally. Alkaloids are abundant and dangerous in the potato or nightshade family and some members of the buttercup and figwort families. Any medicinal plant may be poisonous if a considerable amount of it is eaten. The following plants could cause trouble if eaten:

Datura—(all parts, seeds deadly)
Delphinium—Larkspur (foliage)
Digitalis—Foxglove (foliage dangerous)
Euphorbia species (juice dangerous)
Lantana (berries)
Nicotiana species (leaves)
Ricinus communis—Castor Bean Plant (all parts, seeds deadly)

OTHER SOURCES FOR GARDEN INFORMATION

Garden centers sponsored by garden clubs, the clubs themselves, horticultural and one-plant societies, flower shows, and botanical gardens and arboretums make important contributions to the community by disseminating reliable horticultural information. County extension workers, supported by public funds, can be extraordinarily useful in helping analyze soil, suggesting controls for diseases and pests prevalent in the community, giving lectures to interested groups and in many similar ways. And don't neglect your bookstore or public library as sources for useful, pleasurable and reliable information about specific plants as well as every aspect of gardening.

2

Annuals from Seed

With few exceptions, annuals reproduce entirely from seeds, and flowers are the means by which they make seeds. The seeds vary widely in size, from the very fine ones of petunia and snapdragon to the larger ones of cosmos, marigold, nasturtium, sunflower and zinnia. Nature has endowed them with a wonderful diversity in form which helps in their natural distribution. Some have "wings" and "parachutes" which aid in their air travel by wind and breeze. The "hooks" and "burrs" on others attach themselves to animals. Some seeds have impervious coats enabling them to survive digestion in animals' stomachs, others are "floaters," being buoyant and waterproof, suited for transportation by water.

Seeds also come in an infinite variety of textures. Some are soft, others are extremely hard; some require only a few days to germinate, others a month or more. All need the right combination of air, heat, and moisture, usually germinating in darkness or subdued light, although a few will not germinate unless first exposed to light.

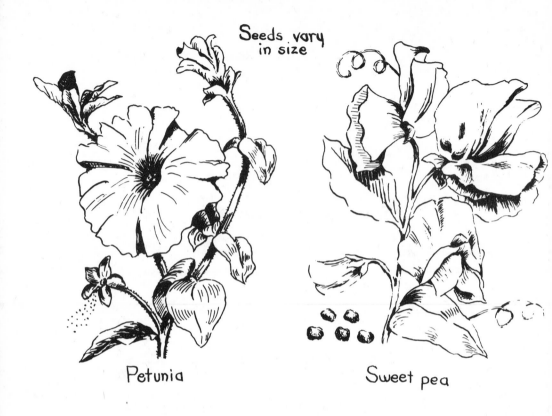

Seeds vary
in size

Petunia

Sweet pea

WHY START FROM SEED?

For many people the experience of growing plants from seed has great appeal and gives deep satisfaction. The experienced gardener does not find this process difficult and has the big advantage of being able to grow plants not usually available in nursery flats. The flower arranger can also grow some of the uncommon, less known annuals for exhibition or for home decoration. It is less expensive to grow annuals from seed than to purchase the young plants and a few seed packets will produce enough plants for your own garden and to give to friends and neighbors.

Growing flowers from seed is the perfect way to interest children in gardening. A child who pokes a few nasturtium seeds into the ground gets a big thrill out of watching what happens, providing it happens fast enough. The novice, the new gardener, is fascinated and pleased to cover bare ground with seed and watch the results. Many retired professional men who find gardening a new and fascinating field like to start from seed.

HOW LONG CAN SEEDS BE STORED?

Few seeds will sprout as soon as mature; most remain dormant for a "rest period" which varies with differing plants. The period is necessary for certain chemical changes, related to the ripening of the nutrients stored in the seed and for the maturing embryo. The seeds of many plants germinate poorly if more than a few weeks old, although some will sprout well even after being stored for 10 years.

Seeds keep best in a dry, cool place in an airtight container. Though dormant, they are living organisms and must be properly handled for satisfactory results. Their vitality, or lack of it, is dependent upon their maturity (well ripened), harvesting under favorable conditions (dry), and proper storage. Always plant the very best seed you can get.

Good fresh seed bought from reliable dealers will give you the right start. Never buy seed more than 3 months in advance of planting since old seed may lose much of its vitality under ordinary home conditions and may produce poor seedlings. Always keep seed dry and cool until you use it.

The cost of the seed is a very small percentage of the cost of growing any crop and it is silly to spend time, labor, and money for fertilizers, pesticides, etc., which are the real costs of gardening, on any but the best. Therefore use the best kinds such as F_1 hybrids and buy it fresh for the greatest satisfaction.

SEED FROM YOUR OWN GARDEN

For many gardeners, the deepest satisfaction comes from self-seeding annuals which reappear year after year as do larkspur and cornflowers. These old-timers are pulled up after the plant has gone to seed, the seed which is scattered in the process starting its own life cycle. However, many garden flowers have been extensively hybridized and their seeds may not produce plants typical of their parents, so it is usually best to buy fresh seed packets as needed rather than to trust seed from your own garden.

PELLETED SEEDS

Pelleted seeds are a new development. Seeds are individually coated with an inert material that will absorb moisture from the soil when the seeds are planted, at which time the material disintegrates. A fungicide or a repellent against animal pests is sometimes mixed with the material. Nutrients may also be incorporated to accelerate growth in the early stages. Sometimes dyes are used to indicate the flower color of the plant. The added bulk makes the seeds easy to see and they can be handled individually, which cuts waste by allowing spaced sowing. Seed-starting procedure differs slightly from the regular method. Follow seed packet directions.

WHAT MAKES SEED GERMINATE?

Most annual flower seeds take between one to three weeks to germinate. If they are viable they will germinate, but the length of time required will vary depending upon both internal and external factors. Moisture, temperature, and oxygen must be available in the right amounts for changes to take place within the seed. As it takes in water the seed coat softens and the seed swells, enzyme activity increases, dissolving stored food, making it available to the growing embryo.

Moisture. Water or moisture is essential at the time of sowing to saturate the seed and enable the embryo to draw on the hitherto unavailable food reserves. Once germination has taken place moisture is still necessary for the continuing growth of the young embryo and the production of a vigorous young seedling. Seed beds should be moist at the time of sowing and in addition, retentive of moisture to supply the further needs of the young plant. An even distribution of moisture must be maintained.

Temperature. Temperature affects the rate at which the chemical changes take place and so affects the rate at which the embryo grows. However, the temperature requirements vary between species. Some germinate best at low temperatures, others at high ones. The optimum temperature depends to a large degree upon that experienced by the plant in its natural environment. Those from temperate and Arctic climates germinate best at comparatively low temperatures; plants from tropical or sub-tropical regions at high ones. Some plants germinate readily at constant temperatures, others require a fluctuating range, varying between night and day.

Oxygen. An oxygen or air supply is essential for good seed germination. Without it the stored food reserves cannot undergo the chemical changes necessary to make them available to the young embryo. Therefore seed beds should be porous, the upper surface unable to cake, to allow air and moisture to come in contact with the seed.

Soil. Whether soil is acid, alkaline, or neutral has little effect on the germination of the seed, although its effect is important on the subsequent growth of the young plant. The best soil for starting seeds is loose, well drained, fine textured and low in nutrients.

Other Factors. Other factors affecting seed germination include the viability, age, and stage of maturity of the seed. Also any methods the gardener may use to chemically stimulate seed germination.

OPEN GROUND OR FLATS?

Seeds may be sown in the open ground or started in flats and other containers. Each method has its advantages. Plants grown from seed where they are to remain are less work and often flower sooner than flat-grown plants, since some growing time is saved by eliminating the shock of transplanting. The plants may be more vigorous and have a longer blooming period than the same seed started in flats.

Sowing seed in flats or containers gives you better control. You can control the soil mix and move the flats around so the seeded flats get the right amount of sun and shade. Watering is easier and you notice disease or pest damage more quickly and can take corrective steps before there is much loss. Fine seeds such as petunia and snapdragon are usually started in flats.

PREPARING THE GARDEN FOR A NEW PLANTING

In Autumn. Careful soil preparation is important for good seed germination and good plant growth. However, once the soil has been well prepared little effort is required to keep it in good condition for successive plantings. For new beds, start preparation in the autumn if at all possible. For a large area stir up the soil with a power cultivator. For small, average-garden areas, spade by hand. Turn the soil over completely to a depth of 8 to 10 inches. Break up any large clumps with the back of the spade or a shovel. Remove any large stones or trash and turn under grass, leaves or any vegetative matter that will readily decay. Pull out any weeds that show up before they set seed.

Some soils will need lime before flowers are planted. If you would like a test made, with a trowel dig up samples of the soil to a depth of 4 to 5 inches, mix these together, dry the mixture at room temperature, and submit about one-half pint of the mixture in a clean container to your county agent's office. Mark on the container your name, address, and what you wish to grow. He will let you know what the soil needs for the desired plant.

In Spring. Before planting, with another spading, thoroughly work into the soil organic matter (such as peat moss, compost, leaf mold or well-rotted manure), sand, fertilizer and lime, if needed. When the soil is thoroughly mixed, level and smooth the surface by raking.

For ordinary garden soil, use a two-inch layer of organic matter, a one-inch layer of sand (from building supply yard or river sand), a complete fertilizer at the rate recommended on the container, and 5 lbs. of ground limestone per 100 sq. ft. if needed.

One usually spreads 1½ to 2 lbs. of commercial fertilizer (a pint jar holds about 2 lbs. of 5-10-5 fertilizer) for every 100 sq. ft. of garden. The 5-10-5 formula indicates the percentage of nitrogen, by weight, phosphoric acid (the source of phosphorus) and water-soluble potash.

Prepare the garden for planting

Garden is ready for spading if soil crumbles when squeezed

Use spade fork to work in humus, sand, fertilizer and lime (if necessary)

Complete fertilizer

sand 1"
Humus
SOIL

With iron rake level surface and create a fine loose seed bed

To Improve Light, Gravely, Sandy Soil. Add plenty of organic matter, one-fourth by volume (1 peck organic matter to 1 bushel sandy soil). This will keep the soil from drying out too rapidly and help it retain plant nutrients. If the soil is heavy clay, it can be lightened by using twice the amount of organic matter and sand. Poor subsoil can be made into a good garden loam by annual additions of organic matter and sand.

Before seeding or planting, the soil should have time to settle or be made firm by treading or rolling; prepare it a week or two before planting if possible. There should be no hollows anywhere underneath so that the roots can go straight down and come into intimate contact with the particles of the soil. Since the roots need air as well as moisture, soil should not be worked when too wet and sticky; this will cause packing and seal out the air, preventing proper ventilation.

Soil must be friable—easily crumbled when you pick up a handful—so that air can penetrate. When the above directions for soil preparation are followed and completed, the beds are then ready for seeding or planting with young seedlings or purchased started plants.

FOR PLANTING IN ESTABLISHED BEDS

If you are planting in bulb beds after bulbs have flowered, or in shrub beds which should have been properly prepared, just scratch ½ inch of peat moss into the surface of the soil before sowing the seed. To do this break up any lumps in the peat, spread over the surface and work or scratch into the soil with a rake or a hoe, whichever tool you prefer. If you are planting annuals in an old shrub bed, loosen soil and add some fertilizer before scratching in the peat moss.

WHEN TO SOW SEED OUTDOORS

You can sow annual seeds directly in the open ground where the plants are to grow or you can start them early indoors—under fluorescent lights or in a window—and set them out after the weather is settled.

Fall For Hardy Annuals. Many so-called hardy annuals produce larger plants, earlier and finer flowers if sown in the fall where they are to flower. Seeds planted in the fall should be buried just a little deeper than those sown in early spring, and should be put into the ground only when the weather has turned cold, just before winter arrives. The purpose of fall planting is not to germinate the seeds then, since many of the seedlings would be too immature to survive the winter successfully. The seeds remain dormant but are ready for the earliest possible germination in the spring, well before the earliest chance for outdoor sowing.

Fall or Early Spring For Hardy Annuals. Hardy annuals may be safely sown outdoors, in the open, in fall or early spring, as soil conditions permit, even though frosts are not yet over. This group of annuals frequently self-sow, especially if winters are not too severe. The seeds are generally winter-hardy in areas no colder than Boston. A light fall mulch of one inch or so, never enough to check the seedlings, may prove beneficial in severe climates.

In this group are some of the annuals that require a long growing season to flower, some that need cold temperatures for their seeds to germinate and a few that resent transplanting and are better started where they are to flower.

Winter For Hardy Annuals. In areas where snows come and go there will be days in January or February when the top soil is thawed enough for planting seed. However, the ground is generally too wet to work at this time; the beds should have been made ready for midwinter planting in the fall. Seeds planted in midwinter will develop early in the spring and come into flower as quickly as those sown early indoors or in a cold frame, producing the earliest possible crop of flowers. See "Average Hard-Frost Dates," page 143.

Early Spring For Hardy Annuals. For early outdoor planting sow hardy annuals six weeks before the last spring frost.

Self-Sown Volunteers. If you wish to grow annuals from self-sown volunteer seedlings that come up around the mother plant, it may be necessary to remove mulch from the bed for a while in the spring, if the mulch is thick and of a coarse material. If fine or mostly decomposed, self-sown seeds will come right through whatever remains. If you want the self-sown seedlings, delay the application of a spring mulch until the seedlings have grown high enough to survive it. Self-sown seedlings will not come true, generally. Petunias revert to type, double bachelor's buttons revert to single, etc.

After Frosts For Tender Annuals and Biennials. Annuals that are tender and bloom reasonably quickly from seed are planted directly outdoors after all danger of frost is past. They are juicy-leaved kinds and can stand no cold, either in the seed or plant stages. Plant out only when settled weather comes and the trees are in leaf. For an earlier start, these annuals may be sown indoors.

Biennials, similar in many ways, are treated in much the same way. Like perennials they take two growing seasons to reach the blooming period; however, like annuals most of them flower once and then die. Some biennials as hollyhock and foxglove reseed themselves so readily you have a new supply of plants each year. As a general rule biennials bloom earlier than most annuals, spring and early summer are usually their peak flowering seasons. Sow biennials in May and June, as early as is practical so there is time for the plants to become well established by fall.

A cold frame or a suitable place in the garden should be reserved as a seed bed for such plants, a sheltered position which can be shaded as required. The soil should be clean, free of weeds and well cultivated before sowing. Sow in shallow drills and as soon as the seedlings can be handled prick out and place in nursery rows 12 to 15 inches apart, with plants 6 to 9 inches apart in the row. Transplant to permanent location in the fall. Some mulch or protection may be advisable.

DEPTH TO SOW

Most people sow annuals too thickly. It is important to carefully follow the directions on the back of the seed packet for depth and rate or amount of seed to use, etc.

Do not bury seeds too deeply. The tiny sprouts are not able to lift very much weight through the surface. As a guide, cover seeds to a depth equal to two to three times their diameter.

Larger seeds are sown more deeply to receive sufficient moisture but not too deeply to exclude air. Sow the fairly large seeds of such plants as the cornflower, cosmos, four o'clock, marigold, morning-glory, nasturtium, sweet pea, and zinnia directly in the bottom of a ¼-inch furrow. Fine seed may be sown on the surface and just gently pressed in. It does not need to be covered.

BROADCASTING SEED

For covering a waste area or sunny slope, broadcasting is an ideal method: put seed in saucer or hand and scatter evenly, with fingers, over soil where seeds are to grow.

SOWING IN ROWS

Generally, sowing in rows is preferable since seedlings can be identified, thinned, and weeded more readily.

Make a narrow, shallow groove (called furrow, row, trench or drill) in soil with the back of a rake or handle of hoe. To make a straight line, tie twine to two sticks set at each end of the furrow; use twine as guide line for planting. Sow seeds sparsely in the drill so seedlings will have room to develop and to allow space for early thinning. Overcrowded seedlings do not make the best plants and cause more work because they need extra thinning and transplanting. Of course it is important to sow enough seed to insure a good covering of plants. Place enough seed to cover the furrow in a saucer or in the palm of your hand and distribute it evenly with forefinger and thumb. Do not make the furrow until you are ready to plant.

HOW TO SOW SEED IN OPEN GROUND

To prevent caking of top of soil, mix sand with the surface layer of soil to make narrow furrows about ½-inch deep and fill the furrows with milled sphagnum or some other sterile seeding mix. (Outdoors, vermiculite is apt to get soggy.) Sow the seed and cover it as recommended on the seed packet, with surface layer of soil, sterile seeding mix, or whatever pulverized material you are using. Label each variety. Gently tamp soil down with a board or rake to eliminate air pockets.

Adjust water nozzle to a fine mist spray, and water the area thoroughly. A strong jet of water will disturb the seed and make puddles of water. Go back and forth over the seed bed until the soil is well soaked. Water again when the soil looks or feels dry. More watering will be necessary when the weather is hot or windy. If there is danger of drying out, seeds blowing away, or birds eating them covering may be advisable but often this is not necessary. Care must be used in covering and the cover removed

Sowing in the open ground

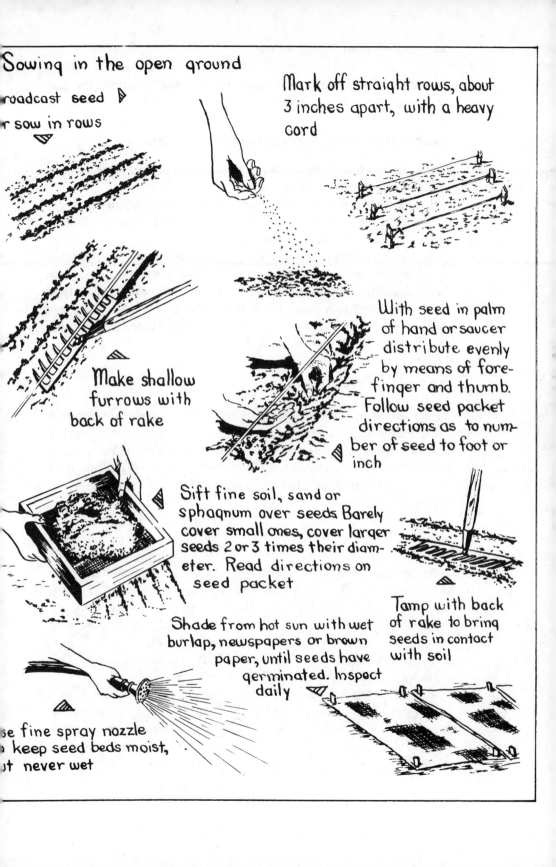

roadcast seed ▷
r sow in rows ▽

Mark off straight rows, about 3 inches apart, with a heavy cord

Make shallow furrows with back of rake

With seed in palm of hand or saucer distribute evenly by means of fore-finger and thumb. Follow seed packet directions as to number of seed to foot or inch

Sift fine soil, sand or sphagnum over seeds Barely cover small ones, cover larger seeds 2 or 3 times their diameter. Read directions on seed packet

Tamp with back of rake to bring seeds in contact with soil

Shade from hot sun with wet burlap, newspapers or brown paper, until seeds have germinated. Inspect daily

se fine spray nozzle keep seed beds moist, t never wet

as soon as seeds begin to germinate so as not to injure the tiny seedlings. Set out bait if snails or slugs are a problem.

BASIC STEPS IN PLANTING SEED IN OPEN GROUND

Since annuals have only one short season to complete growth, they should be given the best conditions possible.

1. Select an open site with plenty of air and light and a bright sunny location or light shade. (Few annuals will succeed in dense shade or under the drip of trees.)

2. Prepare soil bed in autumn by turning over soil 8 to 10 inches deep. Spade again in spring. Add organic matter (and ground limestone if needed). Let soil settle. Make shallow furrow to hold seed. Sow seeds to a depth of no more than 2 or 3 times their size and cover them if so recommended. Label. Water with spray. Weed. Spray with water as needed.

PLANTING IN FLATS

Best method to use for expensive or very fine seed; for seed that takes a long time to germinate; for seed requiring a long growing season; for hot weather annuals that you want to start early when the ground outside is still too cold or wet; when only a couple of dozen plants are needed; and for perennials and biennials being grown as annuals.

To take full advantage of this method you should have some sheltered place in which to protect seeded flats, and later the small transplants, from inclement weather. Many gardeners start seeds in flats under fluorescent lights in the basement, in kitchen or spare bedroom windows, or in glass-enclosed, heated porches. The nearer the light the better the seedlings, otherwise they become too leggy reaching for light. After seedlings appear, keep turning the flats to keep the baby plants upright. A cold frame, hotbed, sun-heated pit or greenhouse, although not essential, can be helpful. It depends on how interested you are.

When To Start Seeds. Start the seeds a month or more before the nights have become frost free, the date for setting these seedlings out in the garden. Fine seeds like the petunia, *Salvia farinacea,* and snapdragon will require more time and should be sown earlier than the large and coarse ones. Cool-season annuals like

Sowing in flats and other containers

1. Cover drainage holes or cracks with sphagnum

Add favorite germinating mix: level and firm gently

2.

3. Make shallow drills ⅛ to ¼ inch deep, rows 2 inches apart, using piece of lath, ruler or pencil

Sow seeds as directed on seed packet

4.

5. Cover lightly with layer of germinating mix

Tamp lightly

6.

7. Label properly

For small area use a rubber-bulb syringe

8. Water carefully

9. Soak container from below in large basin of water. When top of soil feels moist, remove from water.

To maintain humidity for germination cover with polyethylene food sack

To start Heavenly Blue morning glories, place seeds on a moist paper towel, seal in polyethylene bag, a substitute for nicking the seed, and when sprouted plant individually, shoot sprout downward

stock and the sweet pea require an early start before hot weather sets in. Perennials or biennials being grown as annuals should be started very early inside to insure flowering. There is more risk involved in damping-off with seeds that must be sown extra early, as in January, so special care must be taken with such early sowings.

Planting Mix. Most gardeners have their own pet soil mix. (Professionals like milled sphagnum.) The important thing is to use one that is loose, drains well and will not cake, yet holds moisture. A clean, coarse river or builder's grade sand was the favorite for years but sand requires frequent watering and is heavy to lift.

Some gardeners prepare a mixture of equal parts coarse sand, leaf mold or peat moss, and garden loam screened through ¼-inch mesh. To help prevent damping off (collapse of seedlings caused by a soil fungus that attacks them, produced by wetness and insufficient drainage) treat the mixture with a commercial fungicide. This is recommended if soil-born diseases are present.

Or, rather than treating the entire seeding mixture, the seeds may be treated by pouring a small amount of fungicide powder into the seed packet and shaking it to coat the seeds. Follow directions on the package. Most of the larger seed companies sell treated seeds. However, the treatment protects only the small area around the seed and as the roots grow out, they come in contact with the soil; if it does harbor any diseases it will contaminate the new plant.

Seeds may also be started in a sterile medium such as finely ground sphagnum moss, vermiculite, or perlite—much used in recent years. The Agricultural Experiment Station at North Platte, Nebraska, has combined one part dry sphagnum (rubbed through a ¼-inch mesh screen) and two parts each of vermiculite and perlite with good results. The sterile, soil-less medium eliminates danger of damping-off and produces sturdy seedlings with big healthy root systems that suffer little in transplanting. The combination seems to eliminate the disadvantages of any one used alone—for example, the root injury sometimes incurred in removing seedlings from sphagnum moss, the packing and waterlogging with vermiculite, or the poor growth with perlite alone. Since young seedlings have few roots and leaves and are able to take little food from the earth at this stage, apply soluble fertilizer sparingly.

If you are planning to sow seeds in flats in early spring, before

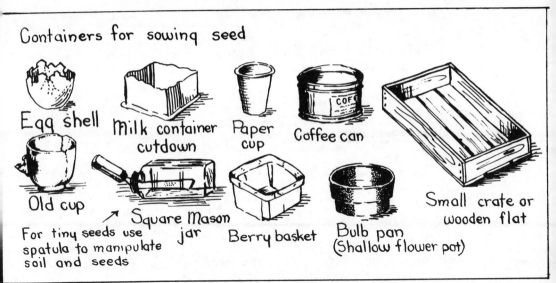

Containers for sowing seed

Egg shell — Milk container cutdown — Paper cup — Coffee can — Old cup — Square Mason jar — Berry basket — Bulb pan (Shallow flower pot) — Small crate or wooden flat

For tiny seeds use spatula to manipulate soil and seeds

the ground is warm enough to work, store a quantity of soil for this purpose. Moisten it about once a month to keep it in good condition but do not keep it wet or it will sour.

To store soil as the commercial florist does, fill flats with soil and stack them by alternating them in a tier, crosswise, so they may be easily watered from both ends, without any adjusting or moving of the flats.

Containers. Flats, seed pans, shallow cut-down milk cartons, coffee cans, earthen pots, wooden boxes and any other shallow containers may be used, but be sure to punch drainage holes in containers that do not already have them. Seedlings require little soil but ample drainage. Flats are commonly used by the professional. Clean container thoroughly before using it and provide for crocking over the drainage holes, with pieces of a broken flower pot, pebbles or sphagnum moss. Trays for surplus water from drainage holes also will be needed.

The actual planting. Fill the container to ¾ inch from the top with milled sphagnum or favorite seeding mix, soak from bottom; let settle. Mark off rows with a ruler or a piece of lath, pressing it ⅛ to ¼ inch deep into the mix. A pencil also serves as a convenient tool for marking rows. Space rows about 2 inches apart. Sow seeds in the little furrows and cover with seeding mix. Firm so there is good contact between seed and mix. Label clearly. Fine seeds need not be covered.

Water carefully with a fine mist to prevent disturbing the seed. You may soak the seed container from below in a sink or large basin (especially good for very fine seed). Keep the seeding mixture moist (but not wet) at all times. If it were thoroughly moistened at the time of seeding, it may not be necessary, in the case of fast germinating seeds, to water again until the seedlings appear.

Cover container with a sheet of polyethylene plastic and shade or use wet newspaper or wet brown paper to insure a moist atmosphere and protect from the direct rays of the sun. Place in a warm (60° to 75° F.) spot, never in direct sunlight. A basement, heated back porch or cold frame will do. Lift the covering morning and night every day after the second day to see if the seeds have started to germinate. Remove covering as soon as seedlings appear, to give them air. Now they need light.

Water with a fine spray or by setting the flat in a pan of water. Feed every week to 10 days with a complete fertilizer, first feeding at one-half strength, subsequent ones at full strength. Remember, the amount and frequency of feeding controls the growth. Large-seeded plants may be grown in peat pots, 2 to 4 seeds in each pot.

COLD FRAME AND HOTBED

These outdoor frames, although not essential, can be helpful in many ways for sowing seeds, rooting cuttings, hardening-off seedlings before planting outdoors, for safe storage, and to get a head start in the spring. A cold frame furnishes a protected area for seed beds and, with covering removed, provides good light for growth of seedlings.

In early spring before outdoor sowing is possible and again in August and November seeds may be sown in pots or flats and put in the cold frame. It is a handy place for rooting cuttings in early summer, and in winter will carry over stock plants not reliably hardy outdoors, to provide spring cuttings. A hotbed is a heated cold frame but most amateurs prefer to manage with the latter, starting a month later and requiring only sun heat.

The site for the cold frame must be well drained, in a sheltered corner; if possible the frame should slope toward the south in order to get as much sun as possible in the early part of the year.

Use Cold Frame To Get Early Start With Seedlings

Annuals can be sown directly in cold frame 2 to 4 weeks earlier than outdoors

Sowing in flats or pots makes it easier to use cold frame later for transplanted or potted seedlings

A height of 18 inches at the rear and 12 inches in the front will afford a good slope to shed rain and catch the sun's rays. To insure good drainage, plan to have the soil 2 to 3 inches higher than the soil level on the outside of the frame. Use 6 inches of a good soil mixture inside the cold frame or for small quantities sow seeds in pots or flats filled with soil and set them in the frame on a base of sand or cinders. This base provides good drainage until the seedlings are ready for transplanting.

GIVE SEEDLINGS LIGHT, WATER AND FERTILIZER

Light. As soon as seedlings appear, when growth starts, remove covering and shift them to good light. Outdoors, shift flats to a brighter, more open location, perhaps under a high-branching tree, but still not in full sun. If you have a fluorescent light set-up, this is ideal for seedlings grown indoors, as it is possible to control conditions closely and get excellent results.

Watering and Fertilizing. After growth has begun and the covering has been removed, the tiny plants must be watered and fertilized. Extra care must now be taken to see that the seedlings never become really dry. Water in the morning, so any surplus moisture will be drained off by evening. To feed and water at the same time, mix one tablespoon of a soluble fertilizer with one gallon of water. Indoors use a rubber-bulb syringe to apply the solution in a fine mist, with no danger of washing out any of the little seedlings, or place the container in a shallow pan of water keeping the level of the water below the rim of the container. Allow it to soak until the surface of the soil is moist. Avoid any excessive moisture.

TRANSPLANTING THE SEEDLINGS

Preliminary Thinning or Pricking-Out. This should be done as soon as young seedlings have developed two sets of true leaves and are just large enough to handle. Seedlings must be thinned to allow them sufficient light, air, water, nutrients and space to develop fully, and to avoid any struggle for existence or danger of becoming tall, leggy, disappointing specimens. Never let them get too large for easy transplanting. Fill flats with a slightly richer mixture than the one in which the seed was germinated. Two parts of garden loam, 1 part river sand and 1 part peat moss is good. Then with a pencil, small plant label, or knife blade carefully lift tiny seedling; hold by a leaf between thumb and forefinger and insert in hole of appropriate depth, spacing plants 1½ to 3 inches apart each way, according to their size. This first transplanting is known as pricking out.

Gently firm soil around the roots, leaving the surface soil loose. When flat is filled, water, and place in light shade for 2 or 3 days before moving into half-sun. Keep seedlings watered. Gradually expose them to more sun so that by the time they are ready to be set out in the garden, when the plants touch each other, they can take full sunlight without wilting.

Planting Depth. Seedlings of such flowers as the petunia form rosettes with the growing point at the base of the cluster of leaves, at soil level. This type must be replanted to the same depth at which they were growing in the germinating container. If they are buried deeper, the growing point will be buried and the seedling may die.

The other type, like the chrysanthemum and snapdragon with

Preliminary Thinning

Prick out tiny seedlings when there are 2 sets of leaves by separating them from the soil with the aid of a pencil or pot label. Hold by a leaf between the thumb and forefinger

Make holes for young transplants, spacing seedlings about 2 inches apart in each direction

With growing point at tip of stem seedling can be reset deeper

With growing point at base of cluster, seedling must be reset at same depth

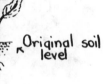

Original soil level

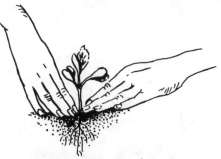

Soil should be gently firmed about the roots without squeezing them leaving the surface soil loose

Cut down milk cartons (not over 4 inches in height) for individual seedlings, placed in a cutdown cardboard box are easily handled. Slit cartons on two sides to remove seedlings

Transplant Seedlings to the Garden

When seedlings have grown larger and are touching each other they are ready to set out in garden where they are to grow

In spacing consider the habit and size of the plant and read directions on seed packet.

In hot dry areas set plants closer together to help shade soil and keep it cool

When transplanti... from flats cut like a cake. The square of soil will protect the roots

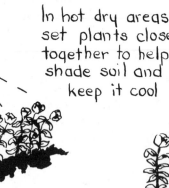

In humid areas space seedlings farther apart to allow ground t... warm up and allow good air circulation to prevent mildе...

Firm soil around seedlings when reset

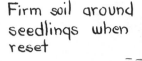

Water

During hardening-off period cover plants for about one week with small berry or fruit boxes or flower pots to prevent wilting from the hot sun

A practical portable shad... can easily b... made from laths nailed one inch apart, on : by 3's, set on 10 inc stilts

an upright stem, has the growing point at the tip. When pricked out such seedlings can be planted a little deeper than they were originally, since the growing point is at the top of the stem.

Second Thinning and Transplanting. When seedlings begin to crowd each other, they are ready to be transplanted into the garden or into pots. With proper timing this will come when the trees are leafing out and danger of frost is past.

Carefully water the soil several hours before transplanting, so it will adhere to the seedling roots. Choose a dull, cloudy day for setting out the plants, preferably in the early morning or, next best, late afternoon. The plants then have the night hours in which to recover from the initial shock of transplanting. This is especially true of annuals with large leaf surfaces like marigolds, petunias, and zinnias.

If the seedlings have been grown in flats, the soil in the flat can be cut like a cake and each plant carefully lifted, with a block of soil around its roots, and set into its permanent location. Dig good-sized straight-sided planting holes. Work up the soil at the bottom of the hole to make a soft cushion for the roots to penetrate.

Hardening-Off. With young seedlings any changes should be gradual, so a short hardening-off period with a certain amount of protection from the sun and weather is advisable when plants are first set out. If the weather is hot you can shade from direct sun for a few days with cardboard, shingles, or burlap, newspaper, or wrapping paper supported on stakes. A good-sized portable lath frame is excellent. Easy and inexpensive to make, it will shade a number of plants at once, stores easily and can be pressed into service at a moment's notice. It can also be used to provide part shade for flats or young seedlings.

Spacing. Plants vary in their habits and size and should be spaced accordingly. Calendulas thinned to 12 inches apart will form bushy, branching plants covered with flowers. A more slender-growing annual like Virginia stock prefers the support of neighboring plants and needs only to be thinned a few inches. When thinning or setting out started plants, give them the recommended distances between plants as indicated on the seed packet. Proper spacing is necessary for best growth and development as well as appearance.

Climate may be a reason for some variation. In cool-summer areas use the spacing instructions on the seed packets but in hot, dry, inland climates it helps to space the plants closer together. They then shade the ground and in this way keep the soil cooler and moister around roots of the annuals. In coastal or humid areas allow space for plenty of air and for the ground to warm up. This will help prevent mildew.

SUCCESS WITH SPECIAL KINDS OF ANNUALS

Annuals Which Resent Transplanting. (See Part I.) These should either be sown directly in the beds or borders where they are to grow and then thinned to the proper spacing, or if they must be started early inside, they should be started in individual pots, preferably the peat or manure pots, that can be planted in the ground right along with the seedlings.

Fine Seed. Thoroughly water the soil before sowing, thus eliminating the danger of washing away the tiny seed. Then place the fine seed on the surface of the soil and press it gently with a flat piece of wood or the palm of your hand. Some gardeners find it helpful to first mix seed with sand to avoid over-sowing. Sown out in the open, small seeds are best covered with burlap or some type of sacking which can be sprinkled from time to time. Remove sacking immediately when the seed begins to germinate. For the young seedlings temporary shading from the hot sun is necessary for the heat may cook and kill the sensitive young plants.

For Slow Starters and Short-Time Bloomers. With some flowers you must wait 2½ to 4 months to get bloom, from time of sowing. Others may die down quickly (see Part I). Time your sowings so each lot of seedlings will be ready to set out at the right time. It is not a good idea to hold seedlings back in flats. They may become root-bound and suffer a check in growth, from which plants never entirely recover. Also they frequently become too large for satisfactory transplantings.

The way to find the optimum planting-out time for one's own garden is by keeping good records, rather than by trial and error. Arrange times for sowing so the times for thinning and transplanting are spaced to best advantage for you and your garden.

3

Annuals from Started Plants and Cuttings

Although planting seed is the favorite way to grow annuals, many gardners prefer to buy young plants from local nurserymen. Still another way to insure a supply of flowers for your annual garden is to propagate your own stock from cuttings. Both procedures are described in the following paragraphs.

FROM STARTED PLANTS

The simplest, easiest and most satisfactory procedure for many is to start with purchased young plants. By buying started plants from the florist or garden center you may have annuals blooming in your garden several weeks earlier than if you sow the seeds. This is particularly true of plants that are rather difficult to grow from seed, petunia for instance, or those that need several months to bloom or are slow to germinate like candytuft, coneflower, gaillardia, gloriosa daisy, lupine, scarlet sage, and verbena and others as mentioned in Part I. Transplants, properly handled, begin to bloom shortly after planting out and are a real boon to the busy gardener.

SHOPPING FOR YOUNG PLANTS

1. Shop early, as soon as settled weather arrives, so you will have a good choice in variety and quality.

2. Know what you want and need in kinds, varieties, and color. Make a list with the number of plants you need of each kind, for your space. If there are more than you want in one flat, maybe you can buy in partnership with a neighbor.

3. Avoid the temptation of choosing plants already in bloom. Blooms will soon fade. Younger plants will have a chance to adapt to your garden before the buds open and so will stay in bloom longer.

4. Choose compact, well-branched small plants. A small, compact plant will usually have a larger, better root system than those that are tall and leggy.

5. Foliage is an excellent indication of general health. Strong, vigorous plants have good crisp green leaves. Avoid weak-looking plants with drooping, yellowing or browning leaves, or any that may have been nipped by the frost.

6. Many small garden centers and nurseries will be glad to supply the annuals you want, if you let them know far enough ahead to produce the plants themselves or buy them from their wholesale distributors.

CARE IN SETTING OUT

With plants in flats it is important to remove them very carefully when ready to plant out, and to disturb the roots as little as possible. On small plants the slender roots dry quickly when exposed to the air, hot sun, or wind. They will be badly damaged and may be set back as much as 2 to 3 weeks unless the ball of soil is kept intact around the roots.

1. Set out started plants the day you buy them. If this is not possible store them in a cool, shaded spot and keep watered, but plant in your garden as soon as you can.

2. To remove young plants from the flat, slice downward in the soil between the plants and lift out each plant with a block of soil surrounding its roots. Immediately set the block of soil in the planting hole prepared for it (see page 170).

3. If in fiber pots, remove the fiber pot, keeping the square of soil intact around the plant roots, then set soil and plant in the planting hole.

4. If in peat pots, simply place pot and all in the ground. The peat pot will break down and improve the soil around the plant.

5. When the plants are set out, water them. Use one tablespoon of an all-purpose fertilizer in one gallon of water for watering the young plants.

ANNUALS FROM CUTTINGS

It is possible to propagate many plants inexpensively by taking cuttings or slips from one parent plant, and with this method you will have sizeable plants more quickly than if you planted them from seed.

It is important to encourage the cuttings to root by placing them in a moist rooting medium. Although our earlier book, *Propagating House Plants* (Hearthside Press Inc.) gives full details, we repeat here the section on making an effective window-sill greenhouse.

From June to August outdoor plants may be propagated by cuttings in this way. Cuttings made in May when plants go outdoors will furnish sizeable specimens for winter use. Take cuttings from plants like fuchsia early in August before the wood begins to harden. In the fall it is possible to make cuttings of ageratum, dimorphotheca, impatiens, petunias and snapdragons for winter bloom. Many gardeners keep their geraniums going by taking cuttings in the fall. Cuttings made from indoor plants in January, February, and March are a good source of early flowering bedding plants for the border.

Making a Window-Sill Greenhouse. If you have a northern window that gets plenty of light, but no direct sun, you have an ideal spot for rooting cuttings. A plastic freezer bag, without any holes, makes a perfect enclosure, since polyethylene plastic film has the capacity to retain moisture, while permitting air to pass through it. This miniature plastic greenhouse requires little equipment and is so easy to do.

To prepare the rooting mixture use two parts of peat moss, by volume, to one part of clean, salt-free sand. Screen the peat moss through a ¼ inch wire mesh and thoroughly mix the two materials. Add enough water, so that when well mixed, a handful squeezed in the hand will hold together, but not drip water.

For 5 to 6 cuttings choose a 2 qt. plastic bag and fill the bottom with rooting mixture to a height of 4 inches. Firm mix with fingers.

Cuttings should be made when stems are neither too soft and succulent nor too mature. The stem should snap when bent, but hang by a bit of tissue. Select young, vigorous stem tips, cutting 2- to 4-inch lengths, depending upon the type of plant. Make a diagonal basal cut, with a sharp knife, just below a node (the joint of a stem or junction of leaf and stem). Remove any flowers or buds and any lower leaves. A cutting should have at least two buds (undeveloped shoots, stems or foliage).

From one inch above the base, make a very thin slice off the side of the cutting, then dip the base in a root-inducing hormone powder, carefully following directions on the package. The slice taken off the side gives the hormone a better chance to work.

Insert cuttings, so leaves barely touch, 2 to 3 inches deep in the rooting mix in the plastic bag. Lightly sprinkle the cuttings, just enough to dampen the foliage. Use a rubber band to tightly seal the top of the bag. Place miniature plastic greenhouse on northern window sill until cuttings are rooted.

Impatiens will root in only a few days. The length of time varies depending upon the type of plant and its particular root growth. Some may require 10 weeks or more. Check on root growth by removing a cutting. If the roots are ½ to 1 inch long they can be transplanted to pots. The cuttings should, however, first be hardened off—conditioned to a less humid atmosphere by gradually opening the bag over a period of several days. At this time some watering may be necessary, just enough to keep the rooting mixture as moist as it was when the bag was closed tight.

4

Annuals Under
Fluorescent Lights

Gardening under artificial lights has become a very exciting and rewarding hobby for many. With a fluorescent-light garden it is possible to ignore the seasons and grow annuals indoors during the winter months, just as gardeners with greenhouses have been able to do.

ABOUT FLUORESCENT LIGHTING

Light is essential to plant growth. All the colors that make up sunlight, as revealed in the rainbow, are necessary in the proper proportions, blue and red rays having the greatest effect on plant growth. Briefly, blue light helps to regulate the chemical conversions in the plant system and makes the plants grow bushier. Red rays aid in seed germination and initiation of roots in cuttings, stimulating growth and bloom. A proper balance of red and blue lighting is important to good growth and flowering.

Fluorescent tubes are the main source of light for indoor gardening. Incandescent bulbs are also used by some as a supplement, but are objectionable because of the amount of heat they give off, which also dries the air, reducing the humidity. Standard fluorescent tubes are available in lengths from 18 to 96 inches in natural white, warm white, soft white, cool white and daylight.

The warm white contains more red and the cool shades such as daylight more blue rays so a combination of one warm white and one daylight is advised for plant growth. A reflector, no more than one foot above the tubes, is needed to spread the light downward over the plants. Paint the inside of the reflector with a flat-white paint to diffuse more light.

There are now on the market special fluorescent lamps, combining the red and the blue rays in proper balance, developed for the purpose of growing plants. They are superior to the standard ones for growing seedlings, rooting cuttings and for getting growth started. It must be remembered that these growth lamps speed growth, therefore step up the feeding and watering frequency to keep pace with the increased growth rate.

Because the heat of the fluorescent lamp is spread over the length of the tube, it is scarcely noticeable. The light produced from 3 to 4 inches at each end of the tube, gives off less light rays than the center, which gives off the most light rays, and most nearly approximates sunshine; therefore plants requiring the most sunshine (generally the flowering ones) should be placed beneath the center area. Those requiring less sunshine can be placed in the lower light intensity at the ends of the tubes. Incandescent bulbs give off more heat, so if used, plants must be placed farther away from this light source, from 2½ to 4 feet below or they will cook. Never use only incandescent bulbs as such light will produce tall, spindly specimens that bloom prematurely and deteriorate rapidly.

A BASIC SET-UP

Vernon Johnston and Winifred Carriere in *An Easy Guide to Artificial Light-Gardening* recommend 10 to 20 watts of plant growth fluorescent light or 20 to 40 watts of combined standard fluorescents for each square foot of light-garden area and state that a square foot will accommodate around 48 seedlings from sprouting until ready to transplant; or four mature plants six inches in diameter. Fluorescent fixtures are available in 1-,2-,3-, or 4-channel widths; the length of the tube governs the wattage, so the higher the wattage, the longer the tube. A 20-watt tube is 24 inches long.

Two 20-watt plant growth fluorescent lamps or two 40-watt standard fluorescent lamps, one warm white and one cool white, in a double channel (48 inches long), with a reflector, planned so

Seeds Grown Under Lights

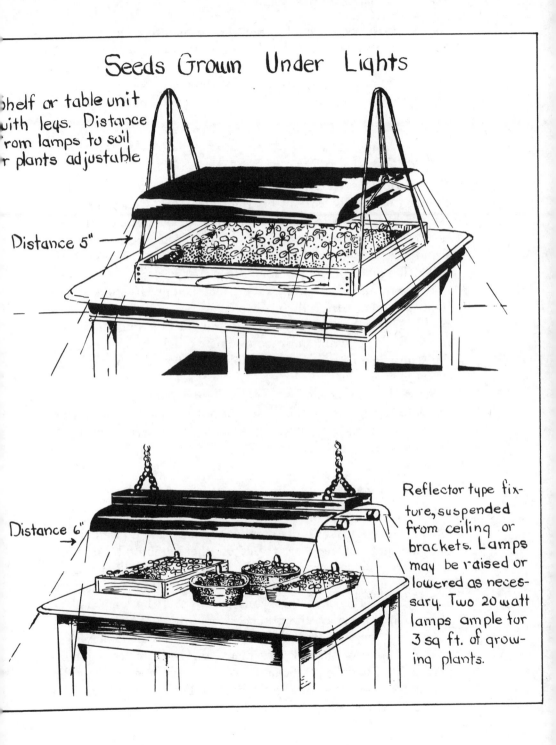

Shelf or table unit with legs. Distance from lamps to soil or plants adjustable

Distance 5"

Distance 6"

Reflector type fixture, suspended from ceiling or brackets. Lamps may be raised or lowered as necessary. Two 20 watt lamps ample for 3 sq ft. of growing plants.

the lamps can be lowered or raised conveniently, and a table, is the basic set-up necessary for the beginner. An automatic timer to turn off and turn on the lights, automatic watering devices and other accessories are all available for those who become enthusiasts and have need for them, when away from home or on vacation.

DAY LENGTHS

Photoperiodism refers to the response of plants to the length of the day, especially as it affects their blooming. Generally in the temperate zones there will be from 12 to 16 hours of daylight during the growing season, and most plants from such regions demand 12 to 16 hours of light for normal flowering. These plants, called long-day plants, comprise most garden annuals.

In the tropics or sub-tropics there may be only 10 hours of daylight. The plants from these regions are referred to as short-day plants. They often will not flower if brought to a long-day region or will delay flowering until the waning daylight promotes it. The chrysanthemum is a typical example of a short-day plant, hence its fall flowering.

Since photoperiodism has been better understood many growers simulate the appropriate light conditions by shading or by electric illumination, controlling the day length by turning off lights after the desired number of hours.

LIGHT REQUIREMENTS

When annuals are grown under fluorescent light, the needed light intensity varies, just as it does outdoors. Those that do well in partial shade outdoors need less than those that require full sun. Most annuals require sun or a high light intensity. As seedlings, therefore, they are placed 4 to 6 inches below the lights and in the center of the lighting area. As plants grow, raise the lamp and as plants mature increase the distance from 6 to 10 inches.

The wax begonia, coleus, fuchsia, impatiens and pansy are good examples of shade-loving plants that require less light intensity. They may be placed at both ends of the tubes or along the two edges where there are less light rays. For mature plants raise the lights as necessary, to 8 to 12 inches.

SEEDLINGS UNDER LIGHTS

Plants like the celosia, cosmos, dahlia, marigold, morning-glory, salvia, sunflower, and zinnia like 16 hours of light, but no more. There has not been sufficient experimentation to date to determine whether seeds germinate faster in darkness or light. Considerable testing is being done by agricultural experiment stations, seed and lighting companies at this time, but germinating seeds under fluorescent lighting is still in the experimental stage. It is known, however, that germinating seeds should have some dark period in each 24 hours, for better assimilation and growth processes. If you want to try light, use 16 to 18 hours of light, the remainder in total darkness. A 24-inch tube will take care of a seed-flat area 32 inches long by 24 inches wide.

All the practices that apply to growing seedlings under natural lighting still hold true and must be observed when using artificial lights. For those who like to grow annuals from seed, starting seedlings indoors under lights will give the outdoor garden a generous head start. Young, immature plants need more light than mature ones. Seedlings should be closer to the source of light than developed plants. Sun-loving seedlings are grown 4 to 6 inches below the center portion of the lights. Place the shade-loving annuals, requiring less intense heat, under the ends of the tubes and along both edges or sides, where the light rays are less. Of course, there are many gradations outdoors in the amount of sun or partial shade annuals receive; this is equally true indoors with artificial lighting. This is why we say 4 to 6 inches from the light. If plants are stretching upward, getting leggy, put them closer to the light. If they lean away from the source of light move them farther out from center, and if they lean toward it, move them in a little. As the seedlings grow, raise the lamp as necessary, keeping the distance to the top of the leaves 4 to 6 inches.

Most annual seedlings grow fastest with a day temperature of 70° to 75° F. and a night temperature of 60° to 65° F., the temperature ordinarily maintained in the home. A higher temperature will produce spindly plants. Good air circulation is essential too.

In general allow 6 to 10 weeks growing time from seeding to planting size, although the time varies considerably with each individual annual. Fast-growing annuals such as dahlias, marigolds, and zinnias only require 5 weeks. When side branches are showing and leavès of neighboring plants touch each other, the plants should be given more space. Transplant them to flats in potting soil. When ready for the garden, remove the flats to a cold frame or sheltered outdoor spot for a few days of hardening off before planting in their permanent outdoor location.

Asters, bachelor's buttons, carnations, cleome, coreopsis, gypsophila, lobelias, lupines, pansies, petunias, stocks, scabiosas, nicotianas, and torenias all do especially well started under lights. Marigolds and salvias will also do well but should be started about a month later than the others as they tend to develop rank growth.

CUTTINGS UNDER LIGHTS

Cuttings from last summer's annuals root quickly under light. As a rule it is better to take cuttings of a coleus or geranium, rather than bring the whole plant into the light-garden. By this means these plants can be carried over from year to year. Cuttings of fuchsias and impatiens are easily rooted. Remember that cuttings will produce plants like the parent plant; they come true.

Using a sharp knife, make cuttings from tip growth, 3 to 4 inches in length, depending upon the variety and size of stem. Remove the lower leaves. Dip the cut stem into a hormone powder for quick rooting and insert cutting ½ to 1 inch in the cutting bed, a flat filled with 3 to 4 inches of sterile rooting medium such as clean, sharp sand or equal parts of sand and peat moss or vermiculite or perlite. Keep rooting medium moist but never wet. In a few days roots should start to develop. When they have shown a good start, transplant to a potting soil in an appropriate pot. A polyethylene tent around a new cutting will keep in the moisture. Cuttings do well in low-light intensities and can be placed toward the end zones or tucked in between other large plants.

MOVING PLANTS OUTDOORS

Even the most enthusiastic winter gardener, unless an apartment dweller, likes to move outdoors for the pleasant summer months. When taking plants outdoors for the summer, from a flourescent light-garden, harden them off by placing the plants in an unheated, protected area such as a porch or cold frame for a week or two. Bringing them in in the fall does not require this same process, although it is a good idea to bring them in before you turn the heat on for the season. If the plants were plunged into the soil in pots they will be easy to lift. Many of the annuals such as impatiens, petunias, coleus and geraniums can be potted up and kept growing indoors under lights. Place mature plants 8 to 12 inches below the light, depending upon their light requirements. If the plants are too large take cuttings and root them. Some plants like the geranium should be given a rest period. Place it in a cool, dark place and give it just sufficient water to keep it alive. In the spring, repot geraniums using fresh soil, water it and put it under fluorescent lights for a few weeks. Plants will come back miraculously well.

5

Good Garden Practices

FOR CAPACITY BLOOM AND TO PROLONG THE SEASON

For a continuous and prolonged display of bloom in the garden many annuals can be seeded at various intervals throughout the growing season. Start some plants early by sowing the seeds indoors in March and then transplant the seedlings to small pots or outdoors when settled weather permits. Seeds for later flowers may be sown in the open ground in May. If you need late color, seeds may be sown later. Sweet alyssum, baby's breath, bachelor's button, candytuft, cape marigold, coreopsis, love-in-a-mist, love-lies-bleeding, mignonette, annual phlox, and swan river daisy are annuals with a short season of bloom especially suited to successive sowings throughout the growing season. Biennials in the same category include the English daisy, foxglove, sweet william, and wallflower.

Good garden practices will also add immeasurably to the prolonged display of color. The usual life pattern of an annual is to grow, flower, set seed, and die all in one season. They are free-bloomers but there is a point in their life cycle when tissues begin to harden, growth stops, and seed development begins. Hot weather hardens the tissues prematurely. This is why annuals in coastal regions bloom longer than in hot inland gardens. Tissues harden if the supply of nutrients gives out before the plant is mature. Cold nights and drying winds have the same effects. Lack of water and damage to the plant by disease or garden pests are further contributing factors.

Anything the gardener can do to prevent annuals from completing their cycle of producing seeds will prolong their bloom. Even after natural hardening has started you can still encourage more flowers to develop by removing the faded blossoms. This prevents the development of seeds. To forestall premature hardening of the tissues and prolong the blooming season of annuals:

1. Select annuals suited to your climate. Nasturiums grow very well in cool climates and do not do so well in hot-summer areas. Zinnias do well in hot-summer areas and do not do so well in cool climates.

2. Feed annuals almost as soon as they are in the ground. Regularly once a month is not too often. Water deeply and repeat whenever the top one or two inches of soil dries out.

3. Use a summer mulch to conserve moisture and reduce the competition from weeds, also to keep the soil surface cool. A healthy, vigorous plant will help shade its own roots.

4. Control pests and diseases. Sweet peas will bloom 4 to 6 weeks longer if not allowed to mildew. The same thing applies to calendulas and zinnias.

5. Keep faded blooms picked off. Make this a regular chore, daily if possible. Annuals that produce heavy masses of flowers early in the season will wear themselves out and die back unless all seed pods are removed before they mature. This can become quite a task with flowers such as poppies, which develop seeds rapidly, or with those whose flowers are small and the seed pods scanty in number, like phacelia or forget-me-nots. Such annuals may be used like perennials to give color for a short period of time; they should then be replaced with later-blooming species.

FEEDING DURING THE GROWING SEASON

The amount of fertilizer used should be determined by the soil, its previous treatment, and the requirements of the crop. If you are in doubt, consult your county extension agent or state experiment stations. The idea with annuals is to keep them growing fast. Many good all-purpose fertilizers under various trade names are on the market today. These chemical fertilizer have a numerical formula of three figures as 5-10-5 which indicates the percentages in alpha-betical order of nitrogen, phosphorus and potassium. Some are compounded for fast action, others release their elements gradu-ally over a long period. Superphosphate is a useful fertilizer for annual flowers. Too much nitrogen causes plants to make tall, spindly soft growth, an abundance of foliage, and poor flowers.

Always work or rake the fertilizer into the soil and then add water to dissolve it. Fertilizers must be soluble in water to be available to the plants. In general use 2 to 3 lbs. of fertilizer for every 100 sq. ft., ⅓ at the time of planting, ⅓ when first growth starts and ⅓ just as the plants commence to bloom. Never over-use fertilizers because there can be injury from over-application. Always carefully follow directions on the bag or package.

Old-timers prefer to broadcast the fertilizer by hand. Apply along the sides of rows, with a trowel, being careful to avoid burn-ing young foliage. Do not have fertilizer on foliage since it may kill or injure the leaves. Sprinkle overhead after feeding to wash fertilizer from foliage so leaves will not burn. Rake in fertilizer, and water immediately after application.

In porous soil or very rainy seasons, additional fertilizing may be needed. Sprinkle light applications around each clump and gently hoe fertilizer in, then water.

WATERING

Water is essential for the intake of nutrients from the soil. If prop-erly prepared, the soil should hold moisture and watering should only be necessary during dry spells. You must water in dry weather, if you want a good crop of flowers. Plants give off large quantities of water from their leaves, but if the soil is kept loose at the top and not allowed to cake on the surface, rain will enter and there should be little loss of moisture.

Light sprinklings do more harm than good; water thoroughly or not at all. More plants are injured by light sprinkles, a little dribble each day, than by drought. Water well, when needed, really doing a good job of it and then wait until the soil is dry before watering again. A soil soaker applies moisture with little evaporation or runoff. The water seeps slowly into the ground where it is needed. Deep watering encourages deep rooting. Shal-low-rooted plants will need more frequent watering than deep-rooted ones. Overhead watering is satisfactory until buds start to open. After blossoms unfold, always water from underneath.

CULTIVATING AND MULCHING

About a week or so after planting, cultivate, lightly digging into the top inch of soil with a scratcher or hoe to uproot any young weeds. Occasional cultivation throughout the season will remove any weeds and maintain surface mulch of loose soil. Hoe gently, since deep cultivation may damage shallow-rooted annuals.

A summer mulch may be used to keep the weeds down. Spread an inch or two of mulch loosely over the border between plants. These mulches tend to discourage weeds and conserve moisture in the soil. Apply only after the soil has first been well soaked. If a few weeds do come up, pull them out by hand. The type of mulch you use will be determined by your location and what is available at a reasonable cost. Look around and see what your neighbors are using and do some experimenting on your own. Some suitable mulches include leaves, pine needles, buckwheat hulls, straw, salt hay, grass cuttings, peat moss, coconut fiber, cocoa shells, ground corncobs, burlap and prepared paper.

TO PREVENT DISEASES AND PESTS

Annuals are comparatively free from attacks by garden pests since their short life tends to discourage a build-up in insect population. Two factors that will encourage trouble should be noted. Annuals grown with other plants already infested will soon be infested. A single species or variety grown in large numbers, in the same location, year after year, may also run into difficulty. Remember it is easier to prevent trouble than to cure it so observe all the necessary preventive steps.

1. Healthy plants build up a resistance to attack. Weak plants are susceptible.
2. Maintain good housekeeping and clean, sanitary practices. Keep down the weeds, remove yellowed leaves or stems, destroy by burning any diseased or infested parts.
3. Rotate susceptible plants with non-susceptible ones.
4. Provide well-prepared soil and adequate drainage.
5. Maintain a good, well-balanced nutritional status of the soil.

6. Allow for plenty of light and air among the foliage.
7. Use a summer mulch to conserve soil moisture, and water in dry weather.
8. Spray or dust as necessary to prevent the spread of disease to other plants.

TO CONTROL DISEASES AND PESTS

Since the publication of Rachel Carson's book *Silent Spring*, the careless use of pesticides in this country has become a major concern. New and valuable regulations restricting their use have been made, particularly in connection with vegetables and edible plants. With chlordane, for example, there is a long residual action in the soil, even present the year after application. This is unimportant in the flower garden, but anyone planning to grow vegetables should ask the county agent or extension service what materials are safe to use.

The insecticides we have listed are meant only for the flower garden and should always be used with the utmost care, and with meticulous attention to the directions on the label. If your flower garden is close to a vegetable patch (your own or a neighbor's) and if you have children or pets, you might well decide that pest damage is preferable to the use of strong poisons.

There are "all-purpose" or combination sprays and dusts on the market that will take care of just about any pest or disease. These multi-purpose compounds accomplish in one operation what would otherwise require separate applications. They may be used in either liquid or powder form, whichever you choose. For the amateur, dusting is usually preferable, since dusts are handier in small quantities for quick jobs. Always read all information on the

All-purpose dusts help keep plants free of insects and disease

container carefully and use only as directed by the manufacturer. All dusts and sprays are poisonous to a greater or lesser degree. Be alert to the dangers that lie in the careless or ignorant handling of these compounds.

If ants become annoying, treat the soil around the plants with a dust or solution of chlordane or lindane. Ants may spread fungus spores so should be eliminated.

Aphids. These plant lice live on plants and suck their juices, causing curled and distorted leaves. Aphids are one of the main carriers of virus diseases, so get rid of them. Watch for them on the young growth, buds, and undersides of leaves of calendulas, chrysanthemums, larkspur, lupine, nasturtiums, poppies, rudbeckia, and sweet peas. Use an insecticide such as malathion, Black Leaf 40 (highly poisonous), rotenone or pyrethrum (both have low toxicity to humans). The latter two, and malathion, should not be kept over from season to season as they lose their value after long storage.

Beetle, Asiatic Garden. The most effective insecticide for the control of Asiatic Garden Beetle, Blister Beetle and Japanese Beetle is carbaryl, the chemical name for Sevin. The Asiatic Garden Beetle is a night-feeding brown specimen about ⅜ in. long that is related to the Japanese Beetle and eats the leaves of the China aster, cosmos, dahlia, and verbena. Dust or spray with carbaryl (Sevin), DDT, methoxychlor, rotenone and lindane (poisonous, so handle with care).

Beetle, Blister. A long, thin black beetle that eats the foliage and flowers of the calendula and China aster. Control same as Asiatic Garden Beetle.

Beetle, Japanese. Hand pick, knock the insects into a can containing water and kerosene, and spray with carbaryl (Sevin), or combined DDT and malathion, or methoxychlor. Also treat the soil. Chlordane may be applied to the soil as a dust or granules as well as a spray to control beetle grubs. This will also discourage moles that live on grubs.

Cutworms. These insects chew off the plant near the surface of the ground. Dust plant with DDT or methoxychlor, and soil with chlordane or lindane.

Leaf Hoppers. Winged leaping insects which suck the juice of plants. They attack the underside of leaves of dahlias. Carrier of viruses so kill them by using DDT or methoxychlor, malathion (relatively safe to handle) or lindane.

Leaf Miners. Chewing insects that make tunnels in the leaves of flowers such as columbine, sweet peas and verbena. Use malathion, DDT, methoxychlor or lindane (poisonous so handle with care).

Mealy Bug. A sucking insect covered with a white, woolly protective substance and found at the joints and undersides of leaves on such plants as coleus, geranium, heliotrope, and lantana. They suck the juices from the stems and leaves stunting and killing the plants. If only a few mealy bugs are present pick them off with a toothpick or kill them with a swab of cotton or a matchstick dipped in rubbing alcohol. Spray or dust plants with malathion, repeat application 2 or 3 times at 2 week intervals, until infestation is under control.

Stalk Borers. This is a one-inch-long, striped gray caterpillar that tunnels or burrows in the stems of flower stalks. Hand pick and kill or dust or spray with DDT, carbaryl (Sevin) or one of the other insecticides. Borer sometimes infect the China aster, cosmos, dahlias, hollyhocks, and zinnias. Get rid of all weeds, old stems and rubbish to control and prevent their occurrence.

Thrips. Minute insects which cause flowers to be malformed and blotched with brown or white. Spray developing growth of plants subject to thrips such as annual chrysanthemums and foxglove at weekly intervals, as soon as they attain 6 inches in height, with DDT, methoxychlor or malathion.

Whitefly. This is a small, white, winged sucking insect which attacks the underside of leaves and lays eggs there. Leaves of infested plants become pale, mottled or stippled, plants lack vigor, turn yellow and die. Leaves become sticky with honeydew and often are coated with black sooty mold. Watch for whitefly on ageratum, coleus, geranium, gourds, heliotrope, impatiens, and lantana. To control dust or spray with DDT, malathion or lindane.

Mites. Cyclamen mite and Red Spider mite are both destructive pests of garden flowers. Cyclamen mite is a minute animal usually invisible to the naked eye. It lives between the bud and flower scales and causes stunted and distorted leaves and flowers which soon become darkened and otherwise discolored. These mites are particularly destructive to delphinium and primrose but may also infest snapdragon, petunia, and geranium. Heavily infested plants should be destroyed. Regular thorough spraying with endosulfan

(Thiodan) or Kelthane when the infestation begins will often hold the pest in check.

Red Spider mites are small but can usually be seen with the naked eye when they move. They thrive in hot, dry weather and multiply rapidly with favorable conditions. They usually live on the underside of the leaves and may enclose several leaves and buds in a flimsy web. Infested leaves develop a mottled yellow appearance with stunted growth. Hollyhock and foxglove are favorite hosts but almost all garden flowers may be infested.

Aramite and Kelthane are specific miticides and frequent applications of malathion and other organic phosphate insecticides will hold them in check.

Nematodes. These tiny eelworms tunnel through the feeding roots, causing irregular swellings or nodules. Infested plants are stunted, weak in growth and pale green. If infested, discard the entire plant and do not plant in the same area. Consult your County Extension Agent about nematicides used to fumigate soil.

Slugs. These are shell-less snails abundant around seedbeds, seedlings, rock gardens, and shaded spots. They eat large holes in the foliage at night and leave slimy trails. Dust metaldehyde on the soil.

Botrytis. The control of fungus diseases depends generally upon the use of fungicides. In this fungus disease gray mold forms on the affected plants; sometimes found on geraniums, marigolds and pansies. Cut away the affected parts and burn, and reduce the water. One of the copper fungicides should be used to spray the soil and young shoots when they start to grow.

Damping-Off. Good drainage and good air circulation will prevent damping-off disease in seeds and seedlings. Captan is useful to check this fungus growth.

Mildew. A thin, dirty-white felted mass or growth which forms on the leaves, stems, and buds of affected plants as dahlias, petunias, sweet peas, verbena, and zinnias. Control with Karathane, (also called Mildex) or sulphur. Sulphur, both a fungicide and insecticide, has been largely replaced by ferbam (Fermate), phaltan and Karathane. Karathane will not burn foliage at high temperatures and is much safer in hot weather than sulphur. Karathane is compatible with Aramite, captan and malathion for a combination dust or spray. Any of the fixed copper compounds (COCS) are good fungicides for mildew. Once mildew gets a foothold it is not easy to control. Experienced gardeners who keep records know which plants are subject to mildew and just about the time it usually hits and schedule preventive measures accordingly.

Mosaic Disease. A virus disease characterized by mottling of the foliage which sometimes effects dahlias, petunias and stock. Segregate susceptible kinds. Use an insecticide to destroy insects which are capable of transmitting the virus from infected to healthy plants.

Rust. This causes spots or discoloration on leaves and stems. Sometimes found on China aster, hollyhock, and snapdragon. Control with captan, maneb (Manzate) or zineb (Parzate).

Wilt. Sometimes attacks China aster and dahlias. A fungus and bacterial disease characterized by wilting and withering of leaves. Make tip cuttings of strongest shoots in the fall or spring and burn the old clumps.

Yellows. A virus carried by leaf hoppers causing aster plants to become stunted and yellow, flowers greenish. Get rid of leaf hoppers with DDT or malathion.

The U.S. Department of Agriculture, Washington, D. C. has a concise folder (No. PA-589 revised May 1964) entitled "The Safe Use of Pesticides in the Home and in the Garden." A postcard with your name and address and a request for the folder will bring this pertinent information free to your home.

ORGANIC GARDENING

Organic gardening has attracted much attention in recent years. It is not a new concept, but a very old garden practice, which stresses the use and preservation of humus using, among other natural materials, animal manure, compost and heavy mulching of hay and grass clippings (6-8 inches thick) instead of chemical fertilizers. The use of these organic materials is good horticultural practice and will increase soil moisture-holding capacity and plant food content. It must be remembered, however, that plants so grown are not immune to pest attack.

PINCHING AND DISBUDDING

Pinching. To promote good branching, with thumbnail and finger pinch out the top or terminal buds or shoots of young plants such

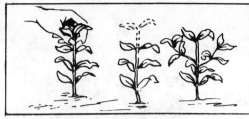

Pinch to make annuals branch. Use thumb and forefinger to remove top inch or so of growth. Do not pinch cockscomb, poppies, stock or balsam.

as ageratum, browallia, calendula, chrysanthemum, dianthus, perilla, petunia, phacelia, phlox, salpiglossis, schizanthus, snapdragon, verbena, and the zinnia. Pinching develops bushier plants, reduces the ultimate height and causes more abundant, smaller bloom. Since pinching will somewhat delay flowering, if you wish, pinch out about half of the plants, allowing the others to bloom naturally.

Do not pinch balsam (impatiens), cockscomb, everlastings or stock whose beauty depends upon a rocket spike of bloom. Many annuals, if given the proper space to develop naturally, will branch freely and do not need pinching.

Disbudding. If you are interested in growing larger flowers, the side buds should be removed, a procedure called disbudding. This concentrates the strength in the terminal bud and is practiced with such flowers as the carnation (not the cluster-flower type), chrysanthemum, and dahlia when large blooms are wanted for exhibition purposes. Pinch off the side or lateral buds as soon as they form, leaving only the terminal or top bud.

STAKING

Only the taller, more slender annuals which tend to bend in strong winds should require staking, unless the garden area is in a windy, exposed location. Supports should be inconspicuous and loose enough to let the plants develop naturally. Keep everything looking natural and unsupported.

If staking will be necessary, give careful and early attention to the young plants that need it. After the final thinning, place twiggy sticks, inserted firmly in the ground, among seedlings in a bed. Plan height so the plants, when fully grown, will grow above the supports. Many professional gardeners use small branches (sticks of branches) to keep small plants upright if they need an inconspicuous support. If handled properly they are not seen. Bamboo canes painted green, with green raffia for tying, are satisfactory if skillfully handled, so plants are allowed to develop fully and completely and hide the supports.

All supports should be inconspicuous and loose enough to let plants develop naturally

Try a plant box (with frame and twine) for growing sweet peas

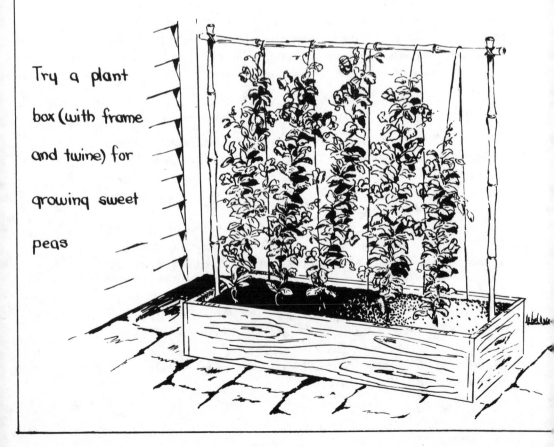

KEEP FLOWERS CUT

For Enjoyment Indoors. Annuals are the best source of summer flowers for the arranger, supplying endless variety in color, form, texture, size, and height. When planning annuals for the garden, think also of the colors that look best in your entrance hall, living room, or dining room and plan for cutting. Many annuals have good long stems for cutting and many are excellent keepers. They will supply quantities of cut flowers without worry about how the garden looks, because the more you cut the better and more profusely the plants flower. And they bloom over a very long period of time if they are kept cut. So why not cut the flowers while they are still fresh, and enjoy them indoors as well as in the garden? When cutting, cut back straggling growth to keep plants trim and in healthy condition. Cut so as to encourage a better-shaped plant and better branching.

For Continuous and Prolonged Bloom. If faded flowers are not removed and the plants are allowed to ripen seeds, annuals will stop blooming; so do not let seeds develop. To continue and prolong the season of bloom, to economize the strength of the plant, and prevent seeding, which is hard work for plants, remove old, faded flowers. This will not only help to keep the garden looking tidy and neat but is essential for continued and prolonged bloom.

However if you are interested in seed pods as decorative material for arrangements, you may want to let some plants go to seed for this purpose. Or leave a few gone-to-seed annuals, especially composites, for winter bird food.

PUT GARDEN TO BED

This is a very easy task with annuals. To tidy up the annual border for winter pull up all annuals when frost comes. If there are no diseases, insect pests, or seeds of weeds, place the pulled-up plants on the compost pile to disintegrate. This organic matter increases the value of the garden soil. Volunteer seedlings and those from seeds planted in the fall will come through the winter without much loss if covered lightly with spruce or fir boughs or pine needles. Give them some protection that is airy. Gather up the stakes and check labels on any fall plantings.

6

Monthly Schedule of
Things to Do

JANUARY

1. Order and study seed catalogs, which start arriving in numbers with the new year. Get out past gardening records, made at garden tours and flower shows, with lists of preferences and prejudices noted. Decide what you want to grow again, what you will discard, and choose at least one new annual to try for the coming season.
2. Read a few garden books.
3. Make paper plans. Roughly sketch any form changes. List annual varieties to be used, height, color and time of bloom of each, selecting a sufficient number of kinds for continuous color. Note when seed should be sown for early and continuous bloom.
4. Place order for seeds early, especially novelties, otherwise the supply may be exhausted.
5. In the South plant ageratum, columbine, larkspur, phlox, poppies, and snapdragons now. Bachelor's buttons, pinks, sweet peas, and sweet william may also be planted.
6. On the West Coast in warmer regions sow sweet peas outdoors in well-drained soil in a sunny location, as well as seed of baby's breath, larkspur, poppies, and other kinds that are difficult to transplant.

7. A fluorescent light-garden in your basement will give you a year-round garden. *An Easy Guide to Artificial Light-Gardening* by Vernon Johnston and Winifred Carriere (Hearthside Press Inc.) gives the basic information about starting one.

Compost piles can still be made. Cover them with an inch or two of soil, leaving a depression in the center to catch rain and hasten decomposition.

FEBRUARY

1. Start seed of the slow-maturing annuals like Chabaud carnations, salvia, and stock now. Seed of the flowering vines, *Cobaea scandens* and *Thunbergia alata,* may be sown late this month for plants to set out in the garden as soon as warm weather arrives. Order seed of dwarf dahlias now for sowing indoors or in a frame in early March.
2. Cold frames should be made ready now. Place in a sheltered area where there is plenty of sunshine; a southern exposure is best. Repair any broken sashes or frames.
3. Check on your garden equipment. Get all tools in shape, ready for use when the busy spring season arrives. Repair window boxes. Look over the items pictured in seed catalogs—plant bands, peat pots, etc. for easy handling of seedlings. Will any of these items make your work easier and more effective? What type of watering equipment best suits your needs? Compare notes now and choose wisely while you have time and are less busy with actual garden work.
4. In the South sow seed of godetias and schizanthus indoors now for an early start, so they will finish blooming before the real hot weather comes. Salvias and torenia are also benefited by an early start.

Flower seeds may be planted all winter. In the cotton belt it will be from March on but seeds may be started indoors in February.
5. On the West Coast cuttings of *Begonia semperflorens* varieties, coleus, and impatiens plants can be rooted for planting later on in window boxes and flower beds.

MARCH

March means activity to the gardener no matter where he lives.

In the South planting is well under way but in the North gardeners are just getting started, busy planting seeds indoors. If you garden under lights in the basement, by March or April start a routine practice of thoroughly ventilating the area at regular intervals to increase fresh air circulation, but avoid drafts or any sudden change in temperature.

1. Annuals which are slow in coming along and may be sown indoors the first half of the month for an early start include ageratum, asters, annual chrysanthemums, cosmos, annual gaillardia, impatiens, lobelias, moonflowers, some morning-glories, nicotiana, petunias, annual phlox, salpiglossis, salvia, scabiosa, snapdragons, stock, verbenas, and wallflowers. Late in the month faster growing kinds may be started indoors or in the cold frame.

   Make a sowing of dwarf dahlia seeds indoors before the middle of the month for bedding use later.
2. Sow the hardy kinds in the open ground.

   Sweet peas should be planted just as soon as the ground is ready. Seed them 2 inches deep in trenches but cover them only slightly, fill in more as they develop. If buried 2 inches at the start they may rot.
3. Set out pansy plants as soon as the ground is ready. They will flower continuously if the blossoms are kept picked. Use the English daisy as an edging for the pansy bed or in a bed by itself.
4. The cold frame may be used now for starting such flowers as annual asters, calendulas, petunias, salpiglossis, snapdragons and stock. Seeds should be started in frames about 4 weeks ahead of outside planting dates. Ventilate the frames on warm days but keep the sash covered with heavy mats on cold nights.
5. If seeds in flats are planted sparsely much tedious thinning will be avoided. Thin seedlings so they will have room to develop. When transplanting is necessary, transfer seedlings to flats and put in cold frame, if you have one.
6. Repair arbors, lattice work and fences and do any necessary painting, before the vines start to grow. Be sure the staples have not pulled way.
7. Begin a compost heap. Use all dead leaves, grass clippings, wood ashes and the like. Turn occasionally and wet down.

8. In some sections of the country garden work may be started this month. Do not spade or plow soil until it is dry enough to fall apart slowly when a little is squeezed in the hand. If it remains in a lump it is not dry enough.

9. Keep garden record book. Record where and when seeds or plants were purchased and results obtained. Record dates of sowing seed and planting and time of bloom—any information that will be helpful to you for another year.

10. Label all plants properly so you know what you have.

11. Check spray materials and fertilizers and get rid of any chemicals in containers from which the labels have been lost. Memory is not reliable enough.

12. In the South plant castor beans for shade between flower borders and plant marigolds now.

13. On the West Coast set out pansies, if you did not plant them out last fall. Sow seed of hardy annuals like the calendula, candytuft, clarkia, godetia, larkspur, and snapdragon.

APRIL

1. Scatter annual poppy seeds in the borders or anywhere else you wish to have them growing.

2. Plant fast-growing vines like the scarlet runner bean or hyacinth bean, to cover unsightly places, if soil is warm and dry enough.

    Tithonia, the Mexican sunflower, is good next to walls, buildings or behind flower borders and does not mind the heat.

3. If Heavenly Blue morning-glories are wanted early, you may place seeds on a moist paper towel and seal in polyethelene bag; when sprouted, plant individually in pots, shoot sprout downward.

4. Watch for aphids on sweet peas after they have grown about a foot or two. Malathion is effective as a remedy.

5. Spray or dust hollyhocks with captan, maneb or zineb as soon as plants begin to grow to control rust.

6. Cold frames should be left open throughout the day when the weather is warm to harden-off seedlings which will be planted in the open ground later.

7. Have garden soil tested if you are making a new garden. Apply lime and any necessary fertilizer in the correct amounts, early

before the ground is spaded. If tests show need, superphosphate is a good fertilizer for flowers, or use a complete fertilizer if soil is generally poor, unless only poor-soil annuals are to be grown.

8. Keep some reserve seedlings in flats to replace those the cutworms take.
9. In the South apply a complete fertilizer late in the month (one with a high phosphate content).
10. On the West Coast sow seed of low-growing annuals over bulb beds if you intend to leave bulbs where they are.

MAY

Now the gardener's work begins in earnest.

1. Nearly all flower seeds can be sown in the garden during the next few weeks. Fine seeds like petunias may be kept from getting too dry by covering them with newspaper or burlap held in place with stones or soil. Remove the cover as soon as the seed germinates.
2. Sow seeds of annuals between the rows to take the place of tulips and daffodils. Annual phlox, California poppies, nasturtiums and others are good for this purpose.
3. Any plants received by mail or express should be plunged in water or buried in moist earth for a time, if they are badly dried upon arrival.
4. Set out bedding plants and annuals that have been grown under lights or in frames, first enriching the soil sufficiently so the plants will make good growth throughout the summer. Hold some seedlings in reserve to fill in the gaps.
5. When setting out seedlings started in the house or in a cold frame choose a quiet, cloudy day if possible; sun and wind will dry them rapidly. Plant long-stemmed seedlings like cosmos with the roots an inch or so deep but avoid burying the crowns of plants that have their leaves borne in rosettes. Pinch back tall, lanky growths to 2 or 3 sets of leaves.
6. Give sweet peas the support they need before the vines grow tall and fall over (see illustration of support, page 194). Brush may be used and netting is also excellent for the purpose.
7. Watch lupine for lice. Use malathion as a control.
8. Prepare window boxes using sufficient plants to fill the box well.

9. Keep the faded flowers picked from the pansies and violas to encourage new bloom.

10. As *Anchusa capensis* (summer forget-me-not) shows signs of slowing down, the tops should be cut off to encourage new growth and a second crop.

11. If frost threatens protect young plants.

12. Apply a summer mulch if you wish.

13. In the South for hot dry spots try arctotis and dimorphotheca. For late bloom when everything else is gone try sanvitalia.

14. On the West Coast if you want to leave bulbs where they are after they have bloomed, sow seed of ageratum, impatiens, lobelia, snapdragon, viola, and other small annuals.

    Start from seed such annual vines as the balloon vine, co-baea, moonflower, and ornamental gourds. All are quick growing and will provide both screen and shade where needed. They may be grown in containers as well as in the open ground.

    Continue to buy plants of annual seedlings and set them out in the garden or in containers for continuous summer and autumn color. They need sun for best results.

    Pinch back plants like annual chrysanthemum and phlox to make them bushy but not non-branching kinds like lupines.

JUNE

1. Still not too late to make plantings of certain annuals such as bachelor's button, gaillardia, gypsophila, scabiosa, Shirley poppy, and zinnia. It is not too late to plant Heavenly Blue morning-glory seeds but started plants may be obtained from nurserymen.

2. Sow portulaca seed now, a good old-fashioned, low-growing flower for quick results in a hot, exposed situation.

3. Sow seed of biennials for bloom next year.

4. Set out seedlings of annuals for summer bloom. Cut back pansy plants to encourage summer bloom. Shade newly set out seedlings for several days until they become established, especially if the weather is hot.

5. Hollyhock blooms will be improved by thinning the flower buds. Flowers do not last as long on crowded stalks and the tip flowers are seldom good. Continue to spray hollyhocks

with ferbam for rust and mildew.

6. If there are vacancies in the garden they can be filled by buying started plants. Any of the annuals can be safely set out now. Many of them will make good flowering plants before the end of the season if seed is sown at once.

7. Mulch soil around sweet peas to help keep the roots moist and prevent mildew. Deep watering 2 or 3 times a week is needed, as well as mulch and a biweekly use of liquid fertilizer.

8. Cut faded blooms from all plants and pinch the tops of any that need it for bushy growth.

JULY

1. It is not too late to sow seeds of Shirley poppies, mignonette, annual lupines and baby's breath for late flowering.

2. Iceland poppies are readily started from seed at this season. It is better to pick the pods and sow the seeds than to depend upon self-sowing.

3. Sow more seeds of biennials now.

4. English daisy (*Bellis perennis*) may be started from seed now for early bloom next spring. Outdoor beds may be used where the exposure is not too great but it is better to use a cold frame in the North.

5. Columbine, in many varieties, can be started from seed now.

6. Order pansy seed now for the new beds. Many good strains are now available.

7. Bachelor's buttons, which have finished their first blooming period, may often be made to flower again by shearing at least 6 inches from the tops of the plants. Then fertilize and water.

8. In dry weather give dwarf dahlias enough water to soak the ground several inches deep. Apply a water-soluble fertilizer now too, preferably one high in phosphate, as dwarf dahlias are very likely to go heavily to leaves.

9. During dry spells also water the rock garden.

10. Spray with malathion if necessary to keep nasturtiums and sweet peas free from lice. Use application of Karathane to prevent mildew on phlox.

11. Keep the dead and dying foliage of hollyhocks cleared away from around the plants. Keep the under sides of the leaves

well covered with ferbam to prevent the spreading of rust disease. Sow fresh hollyhock seed to get young clean plants free of disease for next year.

12. Keep window boxes cultivated and watered regularly. Use a water-soluble fertilizer; superphosphate is good for flowers.
13. In the South give cleome plenty of space. Blooms well at this time of year. Feed with superphosphate and water zinnias if you want good bloom. For evening scent *Nicotiana alata* is excellent.
14. On the West Coast sow quick-growing annuals for late summer bloom including California poppies, sweet alyssum, dimorphotheca, annual phlox and portulaca. Remove old blooms from annuals and apply a light application of water-soluble fertilizer. Too heavy feedings may stimulate foliage growth.
15. With artificial lights, sow seeds of snapdragons for Christmas bloom.

AUGUST

Throughout the country August brings hot and sticky weather. With it, too, comes the full enjoyment of flowers tended carefully during the spring and early summer.

1. This is about the last call to sow seeds of biennials for early spring bloom; start next year's pansies, canterbury bells, foxgloves, hollyhocks, delphiniums, sweet williams, English daisies, and forget-me-nots by sowing seed now.
2. To insure prolific bloom keep removing faded flowers. Cut fresh flowers for bouquets too. This helps keep the garden neat and increases flower productivity. Gather blooms in the evening and plunge them into water overnight before arranging. Cut buds of Heavenly Blue morning-glory the night before and use them for breakfast table arrangements.
3. Keep seed from forming on sweet william, poppies, coreopsis, and foxglove unless you want them to self-sow and propagate themselves.
4. As soon as hollyhocks have finished blooming, cut them to the ground and burn all tops and leaves. Spray young seedlings with a fungicide to keep them from becoming infected.
5. You can gather many flowers and seed heads now, suitable

for drying and use in winter bouquets. To retain best color, collect flowers when in their prime, before any fading takes place. Cockcomb, gomphrena, gypsophila, larkspur, marigold, blue salvia, strawflower, zinnia, and seed pods are all excellent sources of material. Read *Creative Decorations with Dried Flowers* by Dorothea Schnibben Thompson (Hearthside Press Inc.) and learn the silica-gel method of drying flowers so they remain brilliant and unshriveled.

6. Cut and dry herbs now, just before the flowers open, for spiciest aroma and flavor. Hang leaf herbs to dry, after thoroughly cleaning, in a well-ventilated darkened room.

7. In August flower seeds may be sown in pots or flats and put in the cold frame. It is also a handy place for rooting cuttings.

8. Keep tools sharpened and in good condition.

9. In the South feed dahlias. Calendulas planted now in sheltered locations will bloom in late winter and early spring. Start plants of coreopsis, gypsophila, gaillardias, and valerian now. They will make husky plants by next year.

10. On the West Coast seeds of annuals such as nemesia, calendula, sweet alyssum, pansy, snapdragon, and viola can be sown now for autumn bloom.

SEPTEMBER

1. Sow seed of bachelor's buttons, poppies, and other hardy annuals now for early spring bloom.

2. Pick strawflowers or everlastings such as *Ammobium, Catananche, Gomphrena, Helichrysum, Helipterum* and *Xeranthemum* when the buds begin to open, tie loosely in bunches, and hang heads down to dry.

3. Gourds for winter decoration should be picked before they are touched by frost. The stem should be cut off about 2 inches from the fruit.

4. Small plants of calendulas, lantanas, dwarf asters and petunias potted up now will grow and flower in the living room for some time. It is best they should become well established while the weather is still warm.

5. Violas planted in cold frames now will give good plants for next spring.

6. Make cuttings of coleus, *Begonia semperflorens* and impatiens

plants, if wanted for the house during the winter. Root them in moist sand.

7. In the South use heat-resistant *Salvia farinacea* for violet blue flowers. They will bloom from July into September.
8. On the West Coast lift and discard annuals when past their peak. Place those not diseased on the compost pile. Start to collect kitchen herbs, selecting a few young plants to pot for winter use. Try borage, sweet basil or sweet marjoram for flavoring and nasturtium leaves and seeds for salads.

OCTOBER

1. Fill boxes with leaf mold, good garden soil and sand to store for use next spring when planting indoors in flats and boxes.
2. Gather leaves and garden refuse, except that which is diseased, and add to compost pile, adding lime and commercial fertilizers. Of course this will not decay until warmer weather next spring.
3. When gourds have dried, wash with a disinfectant and wax if you like that type of finish.
4. Remove seed heads of sunflowers before they are fully ripe and spread in a dry, airy place to cure for about 2 weeks before removing the seeds.
5. This is a good time to prepare sweet pea beds for early spring planting. Follow procedure described under *Lathyrus odoratus,* sweet pea.
6. Use the cold frame to carry over young plants such as the Canterbury bell, English daisy, foxglove, forget-me-not, and the pansy (not reliably hardy outdoors) for early spring planting. It is also useful for storing stock plants not reliably hardy outdoors, to provide spring cuttings. With artificial lighting equipment, take stem cuttings or pot up any young plants, divide and pot up larger clumps and bring them indoors for the light-garden. Impatiens responds especially well and is a continuous bloomer.
7. In the South annuals such as malcomia, gypsophila, alyssum, phlox, poppies, and bachelor's buttons may be sown now. Giant Imperial larkspurs should be sown now for April and May bloom. Prepare the ground for sweet peas. Seed may be sown early in November.

8. On the West Coast prepare beds for planting. Planting time varies with the area.

NOVEMBER

1. In New Jersey and states farther south sweet peas may be sown in pots and kept in cold frame over winter or even sown in the open ground in deeply prepared trenches. When the ground is frozen mulch the rows with 3 inches of straw.
2. If pansies started in August can be enclosed with boards and a sash placed over them, they will bloom earlier than pansies left unprotected. There should be a heavy covering of leaves under the glass.
3. Any necessary covering materials should be prepared now, to be used as soon as the ground freezes hard, not before.
4. Grease or oil the metal parts of all garden tools to keep them from rusting. Good anti-rust fluids are now available.
5. Put the cold frame to use by storing in it plants that need protection such as foxgloves, canterbury bells, pansies, English daisies, and forget-me-nots. Late bloom can be had on into the winter by setting violets and pansies in a cold frame.
6. Bring in tools and equipment. Store fertilizer where it will keep dry.
7. Seal containers of spray materials carefully. Wash and dry sprayers. Gather garden stakes, clean to remove dirt, and store carefully in neatly tied piles.

DECEMBER

As we go into December in temperate climates, outside chores come to a close, visible growth is stilled, and the garden is bare except for a bit of brightness in berries or branches and the silhouette of evergreens.

1. Cover hollyhocks and foxgloves lightly with spruce or fir boughs or pine needles. Something airy is safest with evergreen biennials.
2. Ventilate cold frame in which pansies, English daisies, etc. are being wintered until the ground is thoroughly frozen. Then mulch lightly and replace the sash, covering it with straw mats for the rest of the winter.

3. It is safest and better to buy fresh seed each year. In the long run it is cheap and sure, although practically every gardener has one or two kinds of seed he saves. Hybrids very seldom come true.
4. Clean the grounds generally, gathering leaves for the compost pile, shoving them around shrubs for a cover and gradual "enricher" of the soil.
5. Send for seed catalogs.
6. Make winter bouquets.
7. Hint that seeds of newer annuals, mulches, silica-gel for drying annuals, fluorescent-light equipment and a few good garden books would be welcome at Christmas.

Part III

Annuals for Every Garden

7

Designing the Garden
to Include Annuals

"A garden" as defined in Webster's New World Dictionary is "a piece of ground . . . a well-cultivated region . . . a place planted with trees and flowers." And so, of course, it is.

The topography of that piece of ground, the architecture of your house, the needs of your family and your climate all play a part in the design of your garden. Most people want a place that fits the family standards of beauty, and provides seclusion from the world. Their first consideration should be for the overall structure, which involves the placement of trees, shrubs and lawn. Only then is it appropriate to add surface enrichment with flowers.

Annuals, biennials and perennials, properly used and well grown, glorify the landscape, but for the summer scene the main reliance must be on annuals. When planted abundantly, their magnificent colors and profuse bloom are the main feature of many a July and August setting, and they can continue to bring delight until winter comes.

AN ANNUAL BORDER

A border is a narrow ornamental strip of land which edges the house, marks the boundary of a walk or driveway, outlines a patio, surrounds a wall, etc. The border may be mixed (with perennials, annuals, or shrubs) or it may contain only one type of plant. The all-annual border is a most spectacular way to use annuals.

Key	Quantity	Plant		Color	Height
1	4	Marigold	Golden Climax	Golden	30-36"
2	5	"	Primrose "	Soft Primrose	30-36"
3	5	"	Yellow "	Bright Yellow	30-36"
4	4	"	Toreador	Orange	30-36"
5	4	"	Hawaii	Orange	24"
6	4	"	Alaska	Almost White	24"
7	2	"	Orange Fluffy	Orange	30"
8	6	"	Mr. Sam	Yellow	24"
9	5	"	Tangerine	Tangerine	15"
10	4	"	Red Head	Mahogany-bronze-gold	12"
11	8	"	Naughty Marietta	Yellow-Maroon	12"
12	6	"	Spun Gold	Yellow	12"

For Best Border Effects. If thoughtfully done, the border should fit into its overall setting, by skillful relationship to the more permanent features of the garden. It will harmonize with the surroundings in spirit and tie in with the landscape. Annuals that coincide with blooms of nearby trees, shrubs and vines—for example a border edged with pansies, blue phlox and forget-me-nots combined with lilacs and wisteria—offer a harmonious blending. When in bloom, the border should give a finished appearance of subtle blendings and contrast. Some type of enclosure or background, as a fence, wall or hedge, will show the border off to best advantage.

1. The size of the border will of necessity be determined partially by the space available. Narrow borders make maintenance easier but a wide border—8 to 10 feet—is more effective and makes continuous bloom easier to achieve. A border should be at least 3 to 4 feet wide to be effective. Choose annuals in scale with the size of the border.

2. The number and kinds of annuals used will depend upon the size of the bed. Diversity is desirable but avoid a spotty appearance. Don't use too many different kinds. Plant large blocks of harmonious colors, using several plants of each variety together. The larger the border, the larger

Petunias, massed to unify a border of shrubs, perennials and annuals, are all of one color. This creates a better effect than would have been possible had alternating colors been used, as in common practice.

should be the size of the individual groupings. Make sizes and shapes a bit irregular except in formal beds.

3. A curved or irregular edge that fits in with the contour of the land is usually more interesting than a straight one.

4. There should be a gradation of heights. Generally, the tallest plants should be planted toward the back, the smallest, low-growing dwarf or trailing ones in front for edging and the space between filled with those of intermediate heights, but let a few drift out of their group. Some irregularity will avoid a stiff or too-formal effect. Do not let plants be hidden by others in front of them.

5. Make the most of form or variety in shape, especially in the intermediate section. Intersperse spike material with round. Use some of the daisy-like flowers of arctotis, calendula, coreopsis, cosmos, etc.; the rounded cushions of scabiosa; the spires of larkspur, foxglove, snapdragon and lupine; branches of salpiglossis and blocks of petunias and zinnias. A variety in bloom sizes and forms is desirable, yet the transition should be consistent and pleasing, not out of scale.

6. Plan a good sequence of bloom so there will be something in flower throughout the border all through the summer. Avoid using short-season bloomers next to each other. Cool weather annuals usually contribute the earlier bloom but may die out with hot dry weather. California and Shirley poppies, candytuft, clarkia, larkspur, pansies and salpiglossis are good examples. Each section of the border should contain some early-season, some mid-season and some late-season kinds near each other.

7. Choose plants suitable for the site. It is ridiculous to try to grow an annual that needs sun to bloom in a shady location.

8. Space plants with attention to their natural growth and that of their neighbors. Remember some breathing space is necessary for good healthy plants.

CONSIDER COLOR

With the varieties developed in recent years you can get almost the same spectrum of hues from annuals as you can from a color wheel or from prints and fabrics. If varieties are thoughtfully chosen you can have color from early in the season until frost, with an abundance of flowers for garden display and for cutting. Because annuals offer such a varied range of color, your scheme must be well planned or it may look very nondescript.

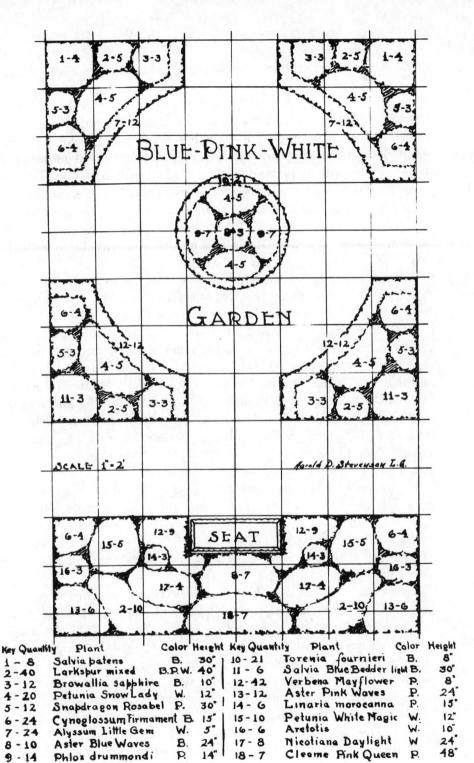

BLUE-PINK-WHITE GARDEN

SCALE 1"=2'

Harold D. Stevenson L.A.

SEAT

Key Quantity	Plant	Color	Height	Key Quantity	Plant	Color	Height
1 - 8	Salvia patens	B.	30"	10 - 21	Torenia fournieri	B.	8"
2 - 40	Larkspur mixed	B.P.W.	40"	11 - 6	Salvia Blue Bedder	light B.	30"
3 - 12	Browallia sapphire	B.	10"	12 - 42	Verbena Mayflower	P.	8"
4 - 20	Petunia Snow Lady	W.	12"	13 - 12	Aster Pink Waves	P.	24"
5 - 12	Snapdragon Rosabel	P.	30"	14 - 6	Linaria morocanna	P.	15"
6 - 24	Cynoglossum Firmament	B.	15"	15 - 10	Petunia White Magic	W.	12"
7 - 24	Alyssum Little Gem	W.	5"	16 - 6	Aretotis	W.	10"
8 - 10	Aster Blue Waves	B.	24"	17 - 8	Nicotiana Daylight	W	24"
9 - 14	Phlox drummondi	P.	14"	18 - 7	Cleome Pink Queen	P.	48"

Many gardeners still simply alternate color blocks, much as was done in Victorian gardens, rather than planning and planting large areas of harmonious colors which drift gently into each other for most effective, pleasing results. This brings to attention the value of growing annuals in straight known colors, rather than buying color mixtures. Random color groupings are not effective for sophisticated gardens and artistic placement of plants to make good transition between colors.

Personal taste will determine whether you choose a blend of subtle, related colors or bold, striking combinations. In general, choose a scheme that pleases you and blends well with the house and existing outdoor masonry and permanent plantings—flowers that tie in with the neighboring flowering shrubs and trees.

Every garden needs contrasts, but they need not be vivid ones. Subdued, neutral hues may be effective foils for each other. To avoid spottiness use a bright contrast for quieter harmonies.

One-Color Garden. In a restricted area or in part shade, a one-color garden can be effective, adding to the sense of space and well-ordered simplicity. Variety may be had in shapes, sizes, heights and textures and in a wide range of tones—pale, vivid and dark. White flowers are luminous and lovely at night and cool and restful during hot summer days. Fragrance, always an asset, seems twice as strong in night air. So a white and green garden, with some fragrant flowers, nicotiana for example, would be pleasing if you spend time in the garden during the evening.

We have seen lovely blue gardens using ageratum, larkspur, lobelia, petunias, blue sage, and morning-glories, but all-blue gardens tend to look cold unless blue-purple is added to give warmth. An all-yellow border for an entire season is possible and satisfying with such flowers as calendulas, yellow violas, marigolds and zinnias, and an edging of dwarf marigolds.

Analogous or Related Colors. Harmonious combinations or blends may be had with closely related colors such as orange snapdragons and yellow marigolds or dull yellow-orange and red-orange zinnias. Choose tints or shades related to the main hue. For a good color range of blues, warm pinks, reds and violets select varieties by color in asters, petunias, etc. In autumn the oranges, reds, rusts, and purples which occur in nature are typical of related or analogous color sequences.

Use of Contrasting Colors. Colors that contrast rather than blend, such as blue and yellow, require more skill to handle but when well done are rich and exciting in their effects. Blue bachelor's buttons or spikes of blue larkspur and the gay orange tones of coreopsis or calendulas are pleasing when combined. In such combinations the duller or less intense colors should be given the larger area, the brighter, more intense colors the smaller area. Pastel tints and deep shades give little trouble but avoid putting strong colors such as magenta, orange, purple and scarlet near each other. Planted in large drifts and seen from a great distance, which grays their brilliance, such color combinations can be natural and lovely, but they are discordant in small areas. If you do find yourself with an unpleasant combination remember any plant can be moved, even in full bloom, providing adequate soil is taken with it.

Blender Colors. In nature we find a jumble of colors, all blending together harmoniously, without objectionable contrasts. The lesson to be learned is the generous use of greens and grays. Sufficient foliage may be a foil or buffer between color pictures. Dark green leaves are an excellent harmonizer of bright flower colors, as red and orange. Gray foliage is excellent with lavenders, blues and pinks. Groupings of white or palest yellow blooms are useful blenders in the garden, and, of course, distance itself is also a harmonizer.

Warm and Cool Colors. There is harmony among warm related colors such as yellow-orange, orange and red-orange; also among the cool related colors as green, blue-green and blue, while the two groups contrast with each other. Warm colors are conspicuous, aggressive, and stimulating; cool colors calm and restful. Something on the borderline between warmth and coolness may have the cheer of warm colors and the calmness of the cool. For restful, quiet, subtle effects and to give a sense of distance combine some of the lovely blues and violets. Soft pinks and salmons are warm colors and can be given zest with an accent of red and purple.

Warm colors as pinks and reds make objects appear nearer, cool colors as blue make them appear farther away. To create the illusion of more space than you really have plant the cool colors (the bluish flowers) in the background and use the warm colors (pink and red) in the foreground.

OBSERVE A FEW COLOR RULES

1. Plant generously of each group for best effects.
2. Plan large areas of harmonious colors, with drifts of bloom melting together to provide transition.

3. For sophisticated groupings purchase seed or started plants in straight colors rather than color mixtures.

4. Strong, vivid colors viewed from across the lawn are grayed by atmosphere, so that even clashing colors can be planted as neighbors. Such colors are also subdued in strong sunlight, which is why hot pinks and oranges are the colors used so often in Spanish design. Vivid colors are magnificent against dark foliage.

5. Soft subtle tones, the pastels, are seen from close-up, around the terrace and near the house. A wooded area is also a good site for pastels and whites which sparkle in contrast. Try pinks and purples against gray rock.

MAKING A PLAN FOR THE BORDER

Don't plan too large an area. You can always add to the border another year. Any part-time (weekend) gardener should be able to handle a border 4 ft. x 25 ft. If one can get at both sides of the border the work is much easier. The size, of course, will depend upon the land available, the experience, know-how and enthusiasm of the gardener, but anyone should be able to manage 100 square feet.

1. Get a pad of cross-ruled paper in the ten-cent store and make a planting sheet with detailed plans of where the annuals are to go. Plan a scale of 1 inch to a foot, or whatever scale is most convenient to give you a good picture of how the border will shape up.

2. Work out one small section or unit of the border until it suits you, then repeat the unit in a sequence at intervals, varying the plan enough to avoid any set look. This repetition of color and plants will give the border unity.

3. For the backbone of the border select six or more basic annuals with long-lasting flowers or foliage, which will remain handsome most of the growing season. Keep in mind heights, colors, shapes and a succession of bloom, so you will have something interesting in flower throughout the growing season. Plan to use each annual in a group of sufficient size to be effective. This will avoid the spottiness and ineffectual results of many small groupings.

4. Plan two or three groupings of the tall basic annuals for the rear and two or three of intermediate height for the middle. Each grouping, block or drift should somewhat follow the shape of the border. Groups of tall plants should come forward in places to avoid any stilted appearance. Plan drifts or blocks of low growing or trailing kinds for edging

Plan an annual border in relation to its site. Here an orderly edging of sweet alyssum repeats the straight lines of the path, with variety provided by stock, snapdragons and petunias.

in the foreground. Then use filler flowers to bridge any gaps between the large groupings.

5. Well-placed accents, which call attention to the best characteristics of the border—its color, form or texture—may be developed by using taller blooms, contrasting forms and lines or a dramatic grouping of color which immediately attract attention, but are still a pleasing part of the complete unit.

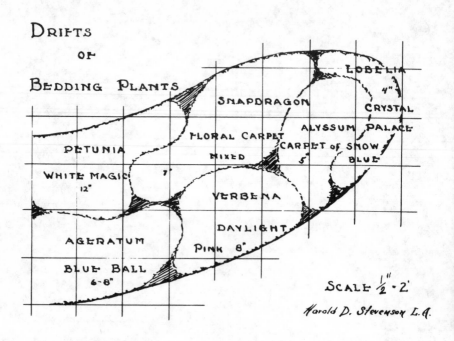

BACKGROUND PLANTS

The size or width of the border will determine, to a large extent, the height of the plants you can use. In a border only 3 to 4 feet wide the tallest plants should not be much over 2½ to 3 feet high. This is a generalization and other factors must be considered. For example feathery plants such as gypsophila can be taller, since their effect is light and airy. Wider borders will take taller plants. The height and sturdiness of many annuals make them useful for background use in the border, or as temporary hedges or screens. Some of the tall ones that measure 3 feet and more are listed below.

Althaea rosea—Hollyhock, to 5 ft.
Amaranthus tricolor—Joseph's Coat, to 4 ft.
Celosia argentea plumosa, Tall—Feathered Cockscomb, to 3 ft.
Centaurea americana—Basket Flower, to 3 ft.
Centaurea imperialis—Sweet Sultan, to 3 ft.
Cleome spinosa—Spider Flower, 3 to 5 ft.
Coreopsis tinctoria, Tall—Calliopsis, to 3 ft.
Cosmos bipinnatus hybrids, Tall—Cosmos, 3 to 5 ft.
Datura metel—Angel's Trumpet, to 3 ft.
Delphinium ajacis—Annual Larkspur, 2 to 4 ft.
Euphorbia heterophylla—Mexican Fire Plant, to 3 ft.
Grasses, Ornamental—mostly 1 to 4 ft.
Helianthus annuus—Sunflower, to 8 ft.
Helichrysum bracteatum—Strawflower, to 3 ft.
Kochia scoparia—Summer Cypress, to 3 ft.
Lathyrus odoratus—Sweet Pea, to 6 ft.
Lavatera trimestris splendens—Tree Mallow, 3 to 4 ft.
Mirabilis jalapa—Four O'Clock, to 3 ft.
Ricinus communis—Castor Bean Plant, 4 to 6 ft.
Salvia splendens, Tall—Scarlet Sage, to 3 ft.
Scabiosa atropurpurea—Pincushion Flower, to 3 ft.
Tagetes erecta, Tall—African Marigold, 3 to 4 ft.
Tithonia rotundifolia—Mexican Sunflower, 4 to 6 ft.
Zinnia hybrids, Tall—3 to 4 ft.

PLANTS OF INTERMEDIATE HEIGHT

Annuals of intermediate height are usually placed in the middle of the border, with some toward the back and others a bit forward to give a natural, pleasing effect. Some annuals, such as the snapdragon, marigold and zinnia, may be had in heights ranging from 6 inches to 3 to 4 feet, so be specific about the height you want; specify dwarfs, varieties of medium height, or giant or tall kinds. Plants that grow 15 to 24 inches in height are considered intermediates and include a large group from which to choose.

Ageratum houstonianum
Anchusa capensis—Summer
  Forget-Me-Not
Antirrhinum hybrids—Snapdragon,
  Semi-Tall
Arctotis stoechadifolia—African Daisy
Browallia speciosa
Calendula officinalis—Pot Marigold
Callistephus chinensis—China Aster
Celosia argentea cristata—Cockscomb
Centaurea cyanus—Bachelor's Button
Centaurea moschata—Sweet Sultan

Clarkia elegans—Rocky Mountain
  Garland
Coreopsis tinctoria—Calliopsis
Cynoglossum amabile—Chinese
  Forget-Me-Not
Delphinium ajacis—Annual Larkspur
Dianthus barbatus—Sweet William
Dianthus chinensis—China or
  Annual Pink
Dimorphotheca aurantiaca—
  African Daisy
Eschscholzia californica—

California Poppy
Euphorbia marginata—
Snow-on-the-Mountain
Gaillardia pulchella—Annual
Blanket Flower
Godetia grandiflora—Satin Flower
(to 3 ft.)
Gomphrena globosa—
Globe Amaranth
Gypsophila elegans—Baby's Breath
Hunnemannia fumariaefolia—
Mexican Tulip Poppy
Impatiens balsamina—
Garden Balsam
Machaeranthera tanacetifolia—
Tahoka Daisy
Mathiola incana annua—
Ten-Weeks Stock
Molucella laevis—Bells of Ireland

Myosotis sylvatica—Annual
Forget-Me-Not
Nicotiana alata—Flowering Tobacco
Nigella damascena—Love-in-a-Mist
Papaver rhoeas—Shirley Poppy
(to 3 ft.)
Petunia
Phlox drummondi—Annual
Phlox, Tall
Rudbeckia bicolor—Annual
Coneflower
Salpiglossis sinuata—Painted Tongue
Salvia farinacea—Mountain Sage
Tagetes erecta—African Marigold
(select medium heights)
Tropaeolum hybrids—Nasturtium
Vinca rosea—Madagascar Periwinkle
Zinnia hybrids (select
medium heights)

Alyssum and petunias serve as edging plants and facers for cleome, snapdragons and tall ageratum.

LOW OR EDGING PLANTS

The ideal edging plant is dwarf and compact and blooms continuously. It gives a neat and tidy finish to the flower border and has a lovely softening effect that is pleasing when edging the border, brick walks, drives or the patio.

Any number of annuals make good edgers, forming lovely mounds of foliage, dotted throughout the summer with attractive flowers. No matter how leggy the stems at the back may be some annual can be found to cover them. If you want a very low edging be sure to get the very dwarf varieties. In many cases there are dwarf species but there are also dwarf varieties of large species. The following low-growing plants offer a wide selection.

Abronia umbellata—Sand Verbena
Ageratum houstonianum—Floss Flower, Dwarf
Anagallis linifolia—Pimpernel
Antirrhinum hybrids— Snapdragon, Dwarf
Begonia semperflorens—Wax Begonia
Bellis perennis—English Daisy
Brachycome iberidifolia—Swan River Daisy
Calendula officinalis—Pot Marigold, Dwarf
Celosia argentea cristata— Cockscomb, Dwarf
Cheiranthus cheiri— Wallflower, Dwarf
Coleus, Dwarf
Dianthus barbatus—Sweet William, Dwarf
Dianthus chinensis—China or Annual Pink, Dwarf
Eschscholzia californica—California Poppy, Dwarf
Felicia affinis
Heliophila leptophylla—Cape Stock
Iberis umbellata—Annual Candytuft
Linaria maroccana—Toadflax
Lobelia erinus—Edging Lobelia
Lobularia maritima—Sweet Alyssum
Mathiola bicornis—Night- or Evening-Scented Stock
Mathiola incana annua—Ten-Weeks Stock, Dwarf

Myosotis sylvatica—Annual Forget-Me-Not
Nemesia strumosa
Nemophila menziesi—Baby Blue Eyes
Nierembergia rivularis—Cup Flower
Nolana atriplicifolia—Chilean Bellflower
Petunia, Dwarf
Phacelia campanularia— California Bluebell
Phlox drummondi—Annual Phlox, Dwarf
Platystemon californicus—Cream Cup
Portulaca grandiflora—Rose Moss
Reseda odorata—Mignonette, Dwarf
Salvia splendens—Scarlet Sage, Dwarf
Sanvitalia procumbens— Creeping Zinnia
Tagetes erecta—African Marigold, Dwarf
Tagetes patula—French Marigold
Tagetes tenuifolia pumila— Dwarf Marigold
Torenia fournieri—Wishbone Flower
Tropaeolum hybrids— Nasturtium, Dwarf
Verbena hybrida—Garden Verbena, Dwarf
Viola cornuta—Viola
Viola tricolor hortensis—Pansy
Zinnia, Dwarf

Along the entrance walk at Longwood Gardens, grand beds are laid out in a formal manner reminiscent of the nineteenth century. The brilliant splashes of color are full of interest for visitors.

ANNUALS IN BEDS

Plants which are grouped together in a showy pattern, often a geometric one meant to be viewed from above, are referred to as bedding plants. In displays of this type, any spaces or holes would be immediately apparent. (This is not necessarily true of a border which is meant to be seen from in front, rather than above.) Bedding plants are almost always annuals because their bloom is so continuous and profuse.

Plants for summer bedding display are set out as soon as danger of frost is past. Tender plants used, and usually grown from cuttings, include geraniums (pelargoniums) in variety, heliotrope, lantana, cuphea and fuchsia (the last named for shady places). Annuals grown from seed for bedding purposes include ageratum, alyssum, *Begonia semperflorens,* California poppies, dahlias of the dwarf strains, dianthus, gaillardia, dwarf marigolds and phlox, single petunias, sanvitalia, torenia, and verbena. For foliage effects coleus, alternanthea, and dusty miller are frequently planted.

Planting beds were popular many years ago and are still used in some parks but they have little application in the contemporary garden. However, they might conceivably be useful for those who are interested in preserving an old-fashioned garden, perhaps as part of a historical landmark.

8

Annuals for Problem Gardens

Young couples on the go—whether in service, doing graduate work or subject to transfer by their companies—want inexpensive, quick effects—a one-year garden. This can best be accomplished with annuals.

Annuals are also a good way to acquire gardening experience since they are the least expensive and easiest to grow. The culture of most annuals is simple enough, so that it takes little practice to grow them well. They are, after all, the weeds of the world, which need little pampering. A maximum amount of sun (in most cases), an occasional feeding with liquid fertilizer, watering during dry weather and staking of some of the taller kinds, are the basic requirements.

One of the quickest annuals to flower, only three weeks from seed, is the many-colored, single or double portulaca. Even in a dry and hot summer, this low annual can be counted on to thrive, asking only for a sunny spot in well-drained soil, not too rich. The only trouble with portulaca is that flowers open only when the sun is shining.

Nicotiana is another quick-growing annual, attaining some three feet in height. The flowers of older kinds opened only at night and closed during the bright sun of the day. Now, however, there are new strains that remain open during the day, such as Daylight and the Sensation hybrids. Calliopsis (annual coreopsis), in yellow, gold and mahogany, also matures rapidly.

Nigella (love-in-a-mist) has a dainty, feathery, sky-blue flower and looks well planted in masses. Shirley poppies sown in June will give weeks of gay blossoms. Calendulas are better sown late (in June) for strong, healthy plants that bloom until the last killing frost. They flower best when nights grow cooler. Marigolds and small-flowered zinnias supply the garden, as well as the home, with profuse color.

UNTIL PERMANENT PLANTINGS TAKE OVER

On the new place, annuals quickly help cover up the raw edges and offer privacy and beauty for your home. Until you can afford them and while you are working toward more permanent plantings, use annuals as temporary occupants. Many annuals will thrive on sunny new lots in mediocre soil.

Marigolds serve as a good filler until evergreens fill in enough to make a hedge beneath the wire fence. The fence itself is effectively softened with annual vines.

FOUNDATION PLANTING

That first year in a new house annuals are indispensable for quickly covering the foundation and giving the house a cheery, lived-in look. For a pleasing foundation planting, choose annuals that complement the color and texture of the house and the surrounding landscape. Any planting will be far more effective if large blocks of harmonious colors are used. When the annuals are killed by frost, take them out and replace with permanent plants.

Temporary Hedge. Where height is needed, fast results may be had with hollyhock, sunflower, datura, love-lies-bleeding (*Amaranthus caudatus*), prince's feather (*Polygonum orientale*), tree mallow, or summer cypress.

For lower hedges 3 to 4 feet tall use tall marigolds, cleome, the tall cosmos or giant celosias. For lower-growing hedges 1½ to 3 feet in height, try some of the dense-growing annuals like garden balsam, Bonfire or Splendens Tall type of old scarlet sage, strawflowers, four o'clocks, lantana, or Mexican fire plant. The ornamental grasses may also be used as temporary hedges.

TO FILL IN BARE SPOTS

In the Bulb Beds. Use annuals to fill the bare spots in spring beds when bulbs are through blooming and the foliage dries and withers. Most annuals are shallow rooted so they do not rob the bulbs of food. They also leave the ground free for working with the bulbs in spring and fall.

Self-sown or fall-planted annuals with finely divided foliage serve the purpose well. They grow up quickly, do not cut off all the light, yet provide enough cover. Especially good is larkspur planted in the fall. Shirley poppies come up fast in June. Calendulas cover the sprawling foliage before it yellows, and California poppies are also useful.

Replacing Perennials. Plant annuals to hide spots where perennial foliage of Oriental poppies, doronicum and bleeding-heart disappears during the summer and to supply color when June perennials have finished flowering. This is when annuals must supply the principal color in the summer border. Interplant annual poppies, gaillardia, marigolds, sweet alyssum, zinnias and calendulas with gladiolus, monarda and other summer-blooming perennials that are able to withstand the heat.

After Flowers of Shrubs Fade. If the shrub border lacks color after the shrub blossoms have faded, choose vigorous annuals that carry their

Pink alyssum makes a good filler plant around pink geraniums and establishes a harmonious color scheme. The alyssum eliminates weeds and soil splash on geranium blooms.

bloom high enough to be seen. Plant them in large clumps. Cleome, tall cosmos, foxglove, hollyhock, larkspur, nicotiana and salpiglossis are good for this purpose. Occasionally a shrub or perennial may die. Annuals are easily slipped into the vacancies until permanent substitutions are available.

FOR HOT, DRY PLACES AND SANDY SOIL

If you have a country place or a large lot you may encounter a difficult, hot, dry area with poor soil or a corner that is hard to water. Many annuals will do well in such situations. Portulaca and the annual poppy make ideal ground covers for such areas. Others that will do well include:

Abronia umbellata—Sand Verbena
Amaranthus—Amaranth
Argemone grandiflora—
     Prickly Poppy
Celosia argentea—Cockscomb
Centaurea cyanus—Bachelor's Button
Cleome spinosa—Spider Flower
Coreopsis tinctoria—Calliopsis
Dimorphotheca aurantiaca—
     African Daisy
Emilia sagittata—Tassel Flower
Eschscholzia californica—
     California Poppy
Euphorbia marginata—
     Snow-on-the-Mountain
Gaillardia pulchella—Blanket Flower
Godetia grandiflora—Satin Flower
Gourds, Ornamental

Gypsophila elegans—Baby's Breath
Helianthus annuus—Sunflower
Ipomoea purpurea—Morning-Glory
Kochia scoparia—Summer Cypress
Limonium sinuatum—Statice
Mesembryanthemum crystallinum—
     Ice Plant
Mirabilis jalapa—Four O'Clock
Nolana atriplicifolia—
     Chilean Bellflower
Perilla crispa—Beefsteak Plant
Phlox drummondi—Annual Phlox
Rudbeckia hirta selections—
     Gloriosa Daisy
Salvia splendens—Scarlet Sage
Sanvitalia procumbens—
     Creeping Zinnia
Tropaeolum hybrids—Nasturtium

FOR MOIST, COOL PLACES

For a planting near a pool or brook where the soil is moist and cool choose annuals that enjoy a moist, cool condition around their roots. The following will do well:

Alonsoa—Mask Flower (sun)
Anchusa capensis—Summer Forget-
     Me-Not (sun or light shade)
Asperula orientalis—Woodruff (partially shaded)
Calendula officinalis—Pot Marigold
     (sun or light shade)
Dianthus caryophyllus—
     Annual Carnation (sun)
Dianthus chinensis—
     Annual Pink (sun)
Iberis umbellata—Annual Candytuft
     (sun or light shade)
Kochia scoparia—Summer Cypress
     (sun)
Lathyrus odoratus—Sweet Pea (sun)

Myosotis sylvatica—Annual Forget-
     Me-Not (sun or light shade)
Nemesia strumosa—Nemesia (sun)
Nemophila menziesi—Baby Blue Eyes
     (sun)
Nicotiana alata—Flowering Tobacco
     (sun or light shade)
Oenothera drummondi—Evening
     Primrose (sun or light shade)
Polygonum orientale—Prince's
     Feather (sun or light shade)
Torenia fournieri—Wishbone Flower
     (partial shade)
Trachymene caerulea—Blue Lace
     Flower (sun)

FOR PART TO HEAVY SHADE

One of the best flowering annuals for shade is impatiens, also called patience plant and patient Lucy. *Vinca rosea* (Madagascar periwinkle) will grow where other plants give up and coleus is one of the best in

Patient Lucy, one of the most satisfactory shade-loving annuals, creates a hedgelike effect, with a border of *Begonia semperflorens*.

the foliage group. *Begonia semperflorens* (wax begonia) does well in shady areas. The little gem, torenia, is a good performer in partial shade. Use it or the low, dainty lobelia or pansies as edgers in shaded areas.

Although most annuals are not shade lovers some can be grown in light or part to heavy shade. Collinsias do well in shade covering gravelly soil, but cannot take intense summer heat. Garden balsam, myosotis (forget-me-not), foxglove, godetia, lobelia, monkey flower (*Mimulus* hybrids), nicotiana, woodruff (*Asperula orientalis*), baby blue eyes (*Nemophila*), and Virginia stock (*Malcomia*) will all grow in part to heavy shade.

FOR LIGHT SHADE

Annuals that will do quite well in light shade include:

Anchusa capensis—
  Summer Forget-Me-Not
Begonia semperflorens—Wax Begonia
Bellis perennis—English Daisy
Calendula officinalis—Pot Marigold
Centaurea americana—Basket Flower
  or Star Thistle
Centaurea cyanus—Bachelor's Button
Chrysanthemum parthenium—
  Feverfew
Clarkia elegans—
  Rocky Mountain Garland
Cleome spinosa—Spider Flower
Cynoglossum amabile—
  Chinese Forget-Me-Not

Eschscholzia californica—
  California Poppy
Euphorbia marginata—
  Snow-on-the-Mountain
Ipomoea purpurea—Morning-Glory
Lobelia erinus—Edging Lobelia
Lobularia maritima—Sweet Alyssum
Lunaria annua—Honesty
Lupinus hybrids—Annual Lupine
Mirabilis jalapa—Four O'Clock
Oenothera drummondi—
  Evening Primrose
Petunia
Schizanthus wisetonensis—
  Poor Man's Orchid

GROUND COVERS

Low-growing annuals make ideal ground covers between newly planted shrubs and trees that have not yet become well established or attained full size. In large gardens just scatter the seed of annuals that are easily grown. A ground cover of pink sweet alyssum around pink floribunda roses gives stunning results.

For repetition of the same color scheme on a nearby slope beside the driveway, rely on sprawling and squatty annuals such as black-eyed Susan vine, yellow creeping zinnia (*Sanvitalia*), baby blue eyes (*Nemophila*), annual pinks, portulaca in salmon, yellow and white and petunias and verbenas in blue, pink and white. A bold mass of lemon and

Portulaca makes a good ground cover in a hot, sunny location. Verbenas and petunias are other good annuals in such a garden.

gold African marigolds introduced toward the top of the slope gives importance to this mass planting of annuals which act as ground covers.

For covering sunny, sandy, dry banks or slopes nothing can equal portulaca. *Vinca rosea*, California poppy and the Iceland poppy will do well. Try collinsia for shade or forget-me-nots in shade where there is plenty of moisture.

ROCK OR WALL GARDENS

Although many annuals are too spreading in growth to adapt to the small rock garden, several, mostly creeping or mat-forming in habit, are very useful. Those making a limited growth and not overpowering the other plants will give quick effects for little money expended. Some of the smaller annuals as ageratum, petunias and snapdragons will add color during the summer but must be kept well watered during dry spells.

Rock and wall garden possibilities include:

Abronia umbellata—Sand Verbena
Adonis annua—Pheasant's Eye
Ageratum houstonianum
Alonsoa—Mask Flower
Anagallis linifolia—Pimpernel
Androsace lactiflora—Rock Jasmine
Antirrhinum hybrids—
   Snapdragon, Dwarf
Asperula orientalis—Woodruff
Bellis perennis—English Daisy
Brachycome iberidifolia—
   Swan River Daisy
Calandrinia grandiflora—
   Rock Purslane
Cuphea platycentra—
   Cigar or Firecracker Plant
Dianthus caryophyllus—
   Annual Carnation
Dianthus chinensis—Annual Pink
Dimorphotheca aurantiaca—
   African Daisy
Emilia sagittata—Tassel Flower
Erysimum murale—Fairy Wallflower
Eschscholzia californica—
   California Poppy
Felicia bergeriana—Kingfisher Daisy
Gazania longiscapa—African Daisy
Gilia capitata—Blue or Globe Gilia
Godetia grandiflora—
   Satin Flower, Dwarf
Gypsophila elegans—Baby's Breath
Heliophila leptophylla—Cape Stock
Helipterum manglesi—
   Swan River Everlasting
Iberis umbellata—Candytuft
Layia elegans—Tidy Tips
Limnanthes douglasi—Marsh Flower
Limonium sinuatum—Sea Lavender
Linum grandiflorum—Annual Flax

Lobelia erinus—Edging Lobelia
Lobularia maritima—Sweet Alyssum
Lychnis coeli-rosa—Rose of Heaven
Malcomia maritima—Virginia Stock
Mentzelia lindleyi—Blazing Star
Mesembryanthemum crystallinum—
   Ice Plant
Myosotis sylvatica—Forget-Me-Not
Nemesia strumosa
Nemophila menziesi—Baby Blue Eyes
Nierembergia rivularis—White Cup
Nolana atriplicifolia—
   Chilean bellflower
Oenothera drummondi—
   Evening Primrose
Papaver alpinum—Alpine Poppy
Papaver nudicaule—Iceland Poppy
Phacelia campanularia—
   California Bluebell
Phlox drummondi—Annual Phlox
Platystemon californicus—Cream Cup
Portulaca grandiflora—Rose Moss
Primula polyantha—Polyanthus
Sanvitalia procumbens—
   Creeping Zinnia
Saponaria calabrica—Soapwort
Tagetes erecta—
   African Marigold, Dwarf
Tagetes patula—
   French Marigold, Dwarf
Tagetes tenuifolia pumila
Thunbergia alata—
   Black-Eyed Susan Vine
Torenia fournieri—Wishbone Flower
Ursinia anethoides
Verbena hybrida—Garden Verbena
Vinca rosea—Madagascar Periwinkle
Viola cornuta—Viola

FOR FRAGRANCE

Fragrance in flowers has always been a joy to gardeners. Mignonette, for its delicious aroma, and the clove-scented dianthus or pinks have

A rough wall is softened by a planting of tall marigolds and gloriosa daisies
Zinnias are also used at the top. Good plants for a hot, sunny location.

Zinnias, tall marigolds, and *Salvia farinacea* are the central plants, with dwarf marigolds and sweet alyssum as edgers. Note large groupings and well-placed drifts.

long been grown and cherished for this reason. Some flowers which seem odorless during the heat of the day, like the moonflower, stock and nicotiana, have an appealing evening perfume and the white-flowered kinds are more luminous at twilight. Heliotrope, the sweet pea, evening primrose, nasturtium and woodruff are scented favorites. Blazing star, ageratum, candytuft, sweet alyssum, sweet rocket, sweet sultan, sweet william, the pansy, petunia, scabiosa, snapdragon and some of the verbenas are others which have faint, delicate fragrance. A note of caution on this subject—the calendula and marigold have odors which are objectionable to some.

FOR FOLIAGE

Some annuals are grown primarily for their foliage value. Summer cypress (*Kochia scoparia*) is one of the neatest and showiest of the shrub-like, foliage annuals, frequently called burning bush because of its burning red autumn foliage. The castor-bean plant is handsome with colorful, large, lobed leaves and of value to the new home owner who needs a temporary shrub-like plant, either as a specimen or as a dense background or screen.

Foliage plants like amaranthus, argemone and the Mexican fire plant are large and coarse and best used as a substitute for shrubbery in the back of a large border or as a temporary hedge. Their foliage is prized by arrangers.

The well-known snow-on-the-mountain, with its gray-green leaves margined with white, and dusty miller are effective in the garden as a foil for brighter flowers. The beefsteak plant with its red-purple leaves and the many varieties of coleus are useful as bedding plants or in the mixed border and for cutting, because of their highly decorative foliage.

Finely cut leaves of cypress vine and decorative cup-and-saucer vine, with compound leaves and climbing tendrils, are much in demand by flower arrangers. Properly placed, the graceful foliage of the ornamental grasses and rainbow corn are striking in the garden and indoors.

SEASIDE GARDENS

Most seaside gardens depend mainly on annuals for their color. For some reason, fragrances are more pungent and colors are brighter, or at least they always seem so, when the same annuals are near the sea. Annuals supply color with a minimum of effort and expense just when

Sweet alyssum plants make a fine edging for a seaside garden. Between them are well-grown ageratum (perhaps placed somewhat too formally for a seaside garden) and some double petunias for variety. In the middle row, tall salvia carries its scarlet flowers, while marigolds grow next to the fence, which breaks the wind from the water. Dahlias (in the foreground) and salvias are highly susceptible to salt damage, and are effective in seaside gardens only if there are no summer storms off the water and if the plants are well-staked and hosed after every onshore wind.

needed, at the height of the beach season. Requiring only a basketful of soil for their shallow roots and periodic feeding and watering, they bloom from June till frost. With late fall milder than inland, annuals are frequently blooming profusely near the sea when their inland relatives have been killed by the frosts. With frosts annuals die, so no year-round care is required for them.

As far as is possible, plan the garden away from the wind and salt spray. Summer storms near the water, which carry salt, can be very damaging unless the plants are immediately hosed. Choose plants that will withstand the drying sun, sandy soil and strong winds of the coast. Some kind of windbreak, perhaps a wall or fence, will give protection. Sheltered areas near the house can give the look of a secret garden—the perfect contrast for the vastness of the sea.

Choose the most vigorous, drought-resistant annuals such as the heat-loving petunias, marigolds and zinnias. Petunias are among the best annuals for the shore garden, especially compact, *multiflora* varieties. Low-growing sweet alyssum is a fine edging, as is ageratum. Marigolds add a bright touch, but the tall kinds must be staked. Placing annuals closer together than is normal helps plants support each other in windy locations. Annual phlox and self-sowing nicotiana usually do well. In fact, try any annual if it does not require shade, dampness or a cool temperature.

When planting a seaside garden:

1. Place 4 inches of loam on top of the sand. Most annuals have shallow roots.
2. Sow seed when soil is workable.
3. If seedlings become overcrowded, thin or transplant some.
4. A dark mulch will cut down on the reflection of light soils as well as help keep the soil moist.
5. Fertilize and water more than normally to compensate for the drying winds. Quick acting, water-soluble fertilizers are best for annuals. A quick food is profitable in midsummer, after the first blooming, when the growth starts to slow.

IN THE MOUNTAINS

In mountain areas, good soil preparation to supply the necessary humus and fertilizer is important. Wind may also be a problem. In addition, due to the shorter growing season in many mountain regions and the severe winter temperatures, annuals slow to develop, as well as biennials and perennials, must be started early in cold frames or purchased as young plants, and grown as annuals.

In most such regions the air is moister and cooler than in the drier and hotter temperatures of the greater portion of the United States. See list of recommended annuals *For Moist, Cool Places.*

CHILDREN'S GARDENS

Gardening can be a breathlessly exciting experience for a small child and open a door to the many wonders of nature and a lifelong interest. Including children in the garden makes the home grounds more meaningful and gives the family a splendid opportunity to work together on a pleasant, outdoor project. Properly encouraged, children enjoy gardening, and few other leisure time activities produce so many benefits. Start with a very simple, primary project.

Don't give young children the tedious, uninteresting jobs of weeding, a day long job of raking leaves or mowing and expect them to be enthusiastic. Provide simple, exciting gardening experiences suited to their ages. The child from 4 to 7 is fascinated with planting seeds and watching them grow. As a child advances in age and experience, more difficult and exacting tasks may be undertaken. In the beginning supply conditions that are practically failure-proof. Annuals are best suited to the young child's garden because they mature quickly and when through producing they die, so they require no year-round care.

The child's garden should be its very own, perhaps marked with its name or in some way designated as something quite special.

The site of the child's garden plot should be small, perhaps 4 x 4 ft.— something he can manage. Give it an ideal location with sufficient sun, good soil and a convenient water supply. Some protection from other children and pets is important. In other words avoid unnecessary disappointments to retain the child's interest and enthusiasm.

Parental assistance is important in soil preparation, garden layout and weeding but the child should feel he is doing most of the work.

Suggest only simple, quick-growing, foolproof plants with seeds that are large, cheap and easily handled, where success is practically assured. Encourage children to plant and care for such annuals as the scarlet-runner-bean vine, sunflowers, nasturtiums and zinnias. Most children are delighted to plant a few quick growing vegetables such as radishes, lettuce and onion sets along with their annuals. At first avoid small-seeded, slow germinating plants as petunias or carrots. If the child wants petunias buy young plants from a professional grower.

Nothing will discourage a young gardener quicker than crop failure. Success is essential to continued interest. It has been said "Children grow in gardens and they grow with gardens. The emphasis can be on the garden or on the children, but equal stress on each usually produces the best all-around results."

Zinnias and dahlias on a hill.

9

Annual Vines and Climbers

Although annual vines are frequently used to conceal unsightly objects, or as fillers until more permanent plantings grow large enough, some gardeners prefer annual vines to the permanent evergreen hedges and tangle of woody perennial vines. They enjoy the absence of pruning and painting problems as well as the varied decorative effects which annual vines make possible.

These colorful accent plants vary in height from trailers like *Thunbergia alata,* black-eyed Susan (3 to 5 feet), to climbers like the morning-glory (15 feet). Some, like the sweet pea, are grown for their flowers, others like the hyacinth bean for interesting seed pods, and still others like the gourds for their interesting fruit.

Nothing gives quicker returns for an investment then these versatile vines. Planted from seed and maturing quickly, they cover large areas in 6 to 8 weeks. They add beauty to the landscape and may be used in a variety of ways—to cover rough banks and old tree stumps, over porches, along fences or tumbling over stone walls. A simple trellis or lattice softened with a vine can glorify the entrance to a cottage. They form a thick growth of foliage, which provides concealment, privacy, and shade.

Since their stems are too weak to support their tops, climbers must have a support of some kind. Some climbers twine their stems around a support and are thus reasonably safe from strong winds and other disruptive factors. Some like the cup-and-saucer vine (or the familiar grape vine) are graspers and cling to supports by means of petioles attached to the leaves. These vines can grow on supports comparatively small in diameter. String and wire are often used on lamp posts, clothes posts, tree stumps, bird house poles, and porches to start them climbing.

One reason annual vines are not grown more in the North is that some take so long to bloom they should be started indoors to give satisfactory results. Even morning-glories are not well under way until fall, if sown in the open, whereas, started indoors, they will bloom much sooner. Certainly in northernmost gardens, several of the vines should be started inside to amount to anything over a long period of time. Try a vine from the dozen or so listed below.

Heavenly blue morning-glories offer an abundance of one of the purest colors known to horticulture. Easily grown, but often rather late to come into flower, morning-glories can be used thickly to conceal unattractive structures or sparingly to embellish attractive ones.

A fence supplies the structural background for morning-glories and other annuals. Potted geraniums add accent color.

Calonyction aculeatum (Moonflower) will form a high patio screen or cover a marginal background trellis. It is excellent near a place used in the evening, delightfully fragrant, with white flowers that open at sundown. It requires little care if planted in light, well-drained soil, and is capable of twining or climbing more than 30 ft. Soak seed 24 hrs. before sowing and start early in pots. Use with *Ipomoea* (Morning-Glory) which goes to sleep before the moonflower opens.

Cardiospermum halicacabum (Balloon Vine) is a rapid grower to 10 ft., with small greenish-white but numerous flowers. Its inflated fruits like miniature balloons are quite decorative. Sow seeds where they are to grow.

Cobaea scandens (Cathedral Bells or Cup-and-Saucer Vine) must have an early start indoors. Set out in May. Its large purplish-blue or white bell-shaped flowers, in saucer-like bracts, are borne on long stems in late summer. When the blossoms drop, attractive seed pods form in the heart of the chartreuse bracts. As the cooler nights arrive, the compound leaves turn a rich purple-green. If given a start with string or wire until the strong tendrils take hold the vine will climb on stone or stucco. It grows best in sun and has no enemies.

Dolichos lablab (Hyacinth Bean) is a fast-growing bean with broad, flat, wine-purple, pealike pods and large heart-shaped leaves. It has showy purple, violet or white flowers. Excellent for the picket fence around a property.

Echinocystis lobata (Wild Cucumber) is a native climber with lobed leaves and profuse white flowers, but once used in a garden it is hard to get rid of.

Gourds (Ornamental) like a long period of hot, sunny weather to bring their fruit to perfect maturity. They are likely to be troubled with insects. Their large, coarse leaves are good for screening purposes. When mature, fruits should be harvested and dried gradually in an airy place. Can be made into darning balls, bowls, jugs, bird houses or used for Thanksgiving decorations.

Humulus japonicus (Japanese Hop Vine) is a lightning-fast grower that can travel 20 ft. in 5 or 6 weeks. It bears greenish-purple flowers in scaly clusters, thrives on heat and drought and insects do not like it. Give it a flexible wire fencing support rather than wood, as it strains upward hard enough to pull out its roots. Will tolerate partial shade. Useful only for foliage.

Ipomoea (Morning-Glory) is perhaps the most popular of the annual flowering vines. Growing to 15 feet in height, its heart-shaped leaves and profusion of funnel-shaped flowers make it an attractive decoration along the fence, for trellises or beside the kitchen door. Although Heavenly Blue is a favorite, Pearly Gates is an excellent white, Candy Pink a choice pure pink, Red Dawn a rose-red with flowers 5 in. across, and Cherrio has bright scarlet-red flowers that remain open almost all day.

Momordica balsamina (Balsam Apple) climbs luxuriantly and is popular mainly for its weird, warty fruits which burst open to display scarlet seeds.

Phaseolus coccineus (Scarlet Runner Bean) generally is regarded as the most spectacular of all red-flowered vines. A heavy bloomer all summer it needs full sun and plenty of water. *P. c. albus,* with white flowers, has much the same habit.

Quamoclit pennata (Cypress Vine) has fine, fernlike foliage which leaves the woodwork of the trellis or fence exposed to view. Its small, starlike, scarlet flowers are open only in the early morning and again after sundown. *Alba* is a white form. Cypress Vine will tolerate partial shade. *Q. sloteri* (Cardinal Climber) is a popular species with its deeply cut palm-like foliage, considerably more robust. Its 2-inch blossoms resemble small morning-glories, opening at dawn and fading at sunset. *Q. coccinea* (Star Ipomoea) is showy and quick growing with crimson flowers and a yellow throat. Grows to 10 feet.

Thunbergia alata (Clock Vine or Black-Eyed Susan Vine) has glowing orange-yellow flowers with a black eye from midsummer until frost, a long blooming season. A low-growing creeper, it is useful in hanging baskets and porch boxes. Start in March and plant out in a fairly rich soil. Will tolerate partial shade.

Tropaeolum (Nasturtium) is enjoying popular revival and answers the need for a bright color for the medium height screen and wall planter, so widely used with ranch homes and patios. Although it may climb 8 to 9 ft. it is apt to do better drifting downward, producing a livelier display of exotic colors ranging from cream through orange, scarlet and purple. *T. majus* is the most widely grown. *T. peltophorum* (*T. lobbianum*) produces the largest flowers with the most intense colors, has hairy leaves and long-spurred orange and red blooms. The Golden Gleam strains are semi-double. A related strain *T. peregrinum* (Canary-Bird Vine) is of real value for those with shade problems for it tolerates partial shade. A native of Peru, its round leaves are light green and deeply cut into five lobes. Its fringed yellow flowers are not very showy but they do not need to be. Ordinary garden soil is good for all types. Go light on manure which produces leaf growth at the expense of blooms. They must have ample water during hot, dry weather. Watch for aphids on the young growth, buds and undersides of leaves. Spray with malathion, rotenone or pyrethrum to control these plant lice.

10

Annuals for Cutting

A cutting garden usually relies exclusively on annuals which can supply huge quantities of flowers. In the typical cutting garden, the plants are set out in rows with no thought given to their decorative quality outdoors. Since annuals live for only one season anyway, they can be cut as needed with no concern for the appearance or needs of the plant itself.

The garden intended only for cut material can be planted out of sight anywhere on the property, even in a strip only a few inches wide. Plants will do best with plenty of sun, some protection from winds and, ideally, far enough from the roots of large trees and shrubs so they do not have to compete for food and water. However, if the best site for your cutting garden is just outside a shrub border ringing the secluded part of the garden, dig the bed deep enough to cut off the interfering roots.

THE DECORATIVE CUTTING GARDEN

As land becomes scarcer and gardens smaller, it is sometimes difficult to find a hidden area which offers the right cultural conditions for annuals. There is no reason why the annual cutting garden cannot be as decorative as the flower border, provided that some care is taken when flowers are removed. With judicious cutting, the form and color in the plant supplying the blossoms need not be destroyed. Of course, annuals bloom more than ever when flowers are cut.

248

Close to the house, where they may be easily cut and their color and fragrance enjoyed, such annuals as snapdragons, marigolds and petunias mingle informally. The clipped edging (*Teucrium*) provides a unifying touch, as does the paving.

ANNUALS BEST FOR CUTTING

The two qualities a flower must have to recommend it for cutting purposes are long enough stems and good keeping qualities. Other than this, grow anything you want. Select colors that match the exact hue of containers, that repeat the floral pattern of wallpaper, that will bring fragrance to a bedside bouquet in the guest room. It's a fascinating hobby for women to think of flowers in relation to their decorative needs, but it's only fair to warn you that men don't always sympathize with such scheming. That is, until they hear guests exclaiming—and exclaim they do—over the *perfectly* divine way the flowers match the garden pinks painted on the china.

The flower-show exhibitor has another set of requirements. She may want asters and salvia perhaps, in a matching blue tone, with asters supplying the round forms and salvia furnishing spiky contrast. Or she may plant zinnias in a gradation of bloom sizes, and in pinks, roses, and reds. Or perhaps she will want unusual forms to catch the judge's eyes at a flower show.

The cutting garden is an ideal spot for trying out new and unfamiliar varieties. Perhaps you are uncertain of their color or habit. Grow here the annuals with non-glamorous habits, as salpiglossis, excellent for bouquets. Or try those annuals that flower for only a short period, like baby's breath, leaving the plant unattractive until the second crop. It is also a good place to have in reserve plants that can be lifted and transplanted to bare spots in the garden when more color is needed.

Round Forms. In annuals good for cutting:

Arctotis stoechadifolia—African Daisy
Calendula officinalis—Pot Marigold
Callistephus chinensis—Annual or
    China Aster
Centaurea cyanus—Bachelor's Button
Chrysanthemum carinatum—
    Painted Daisy
Chrysanthemum coronarium—
    Crown Daisy
Chrysanthemum segetum—
    Corn Marigold
Coreopsis tinctoria—Calliopsis
Cosmos
Dahlia mercki—Bedding or
    Dwarf Dahlia
Dianthus caryophyllus—
    Annual Carnation
Dianthus chinensis—Annual Pink
Dimorphotheca aurantiaca—

    African Daisy
Gaillardia pulchella—Annual
    Blanket Flower
Papaver alpinum—Alpine Poppy
Papaver nudicaule—Iceland Poppy
Papaver rhoeas—Shirley Poppy
Rudbeckia bicolor—Annual
    Coneflower
Rudbeckia hirta selections—
    Gloriosa Daisy
Scabiosa atropurpurea—
    Pincushion Flower
Tagetes—Marigold (all kinds)
Tithonia rotundifolia—
    Mexican Sunflower
Trachymene caerulea—Blue
    Lace Flower
Viola tricolor hortensis—Pansy
Zinnia

Annuals for Height. Spike forms or long-stemmed flowers usually make up the skeleton or structural design of a flower arrangement. For such purposes select from the following:

Antirrhinum hybrids—
    Snapdragon, Tall
Aquilegia hybrids—Columbine
Campanula medium—Canterbury
    Bells
Celosia argentea plumosa—
    Plumed Cockscomb
Cleome spinosa—Spider Flower
Cynoglossum amabile—Chinese
    Forget-Me-Not
Delphinium ajacis—Annual Larkspur
Digitalis purpurea—Foxglove
Emilia sagittata—Tassel Flower
Grasses, Ornamental
Helianthus annuus—Sunflower
Helichrysum bracteatum—
    Strawflower
Heliotropium arborescens—
    Common Heliotrope
Lupinus hybrids—Lupine

Machaeranthera tanacetifolia—
    Tahoka Daisy
Mathiola incana annua—
    Ten-Weeks Stock
Molucella laevis—Bells of Ireland
Myosotis sylvatica—Annual
    Forget-Me-Not
Nicotiana alata—Flowering Tobacco
Penstemon gloxinioides—
    Beard Tongue
Petunia (on long stems)
Phlox drummondi—Annual Phlox
    (on long stems)
Salpiglossis sinuata—Painted Tongue
Salvia farinacea—Mountain Sage
Salvia patens—Blue Sage
Salvia splendens—Scarlet Sage, Tall
Verbena hortensis—Garden Verbena
    (on long stems)

Fillers. The annuals listed below will serve as good fillers in any bouquet:

Anagallis linifolia—Pimpernel
Anchusa capensis—Summer
    Forget-Me-Not
Gypsophila elegans—Annual
    Baby's Breath
Limonium sinuatum—Statice

Lobularia maritima—Annual
    Sweet Alyssum
Lychnis coeli-rosa—Rose of Heaven
Nemesia strumosa
Nemophila menziesi—Baby Blue Eyes
Nierembergia rivularis—Cup Flower

For Miniatures. Use individual florets of multiple blooms like alyssum and verbena, or select some of the following for your flower arrangement:

Ageratum houstonianum
Cynoglossum amabile—Chinese
    Forget-Me-Not
Heliotropium arborescens—
    Common Heliotrope
Iberis umbellata—Annual Candytuft
Limonium sinuatum—Statice
Linaria maroccana—Toadflax
Lobelia erinus—Edging Lobelia
Lobularia maritima—Annual
    Sweet Alyssum

Mathiola incana annua—Ten-Weeks
    Stock
Reseda odorata—Mignonette
Scabiosa atropurpurea—Pincushion
    Flower
Trachymene caerulea—Blue
    Lace Flower
Verbena hortensis—Garden Verbena
Viola cornuta—Viola
Viola tricolor hortensis—Pansy

Dainty, Airy Annuals for Mixed Bouquets:

Ammobium alatum—
Winged Everlasting
Arctotis stoechadifolia—
Blue-Eyed Daisy
Browallia speciosa
*Catananche caerulea—*Cupid's Dart
Chrysanthemum parthenium—
Feverfew
*Clarkia elegans—*Rocky
Mountain Garland
*Cynoglossum amabile—*Chinese
Forget-Me-Not
*Dianthus chinensis—*Annual Pink
Dimorphotheca aurantiaca—
African Daisy
*Gomphrena globosa—*Globe
Amaranth
*Gypsophila elegans—*Annual
Baby's Breath
Helichrysum bracteatum—
Strawflower
Heliotropium arborescens—
Common Heliotrope

*Helipterum manglesi—*Swan
River Everlasting
*Limonium sinuatum—*Sea Lavender
Machaeranthera tanacetifolia—
Tahoka Daisy
*Myosotis sylvatica—*Annual
Forget-Me-Not
*Nicotiana alata—*Flowering Tobacco
*Nierembergia rivularis—*Cup Flower
*Nigella damascena—*Love-in-a-Mist
*Phacelia campanularia—*California
Bluebell
*Reseda odorata—*Mignonette
*Salpiglossis sinuata—*Painted Tongue
*Schizanthus wisetonensis—*Poor
Man's Orchid
*Tagetes—*Marigold (small)
*Torenia fournieri—*Wishbone Flower
*Trachymene caerulea—*Blue
Lace Flower
*Viola tricolor hortensis—*Pansy
*Xanthisma texanum—*Star of Texas
*Xeranthemum annuum—*Immortelle
Zinnia (small)

HELP CUT FLOWERS LAST

1. Pick flowers in the early morning or in the cool of the evening, when they are filled with water.

2. Use a sharp knife when cutting, making a long, slanting cut. Slit larger, heavier stems vertically about 1 inch from the base. Cut stems as long as possible and shorten as necessary when making the arrangement.

3. Flowers keep best if cut at just the right stage in their development. In general, cut flowers when they are sufficiently mature, at least half open, so they can finish opening in water. Buds should be advanced enough to show their petal color. Flowers cut past their prime do not last long. Spikes, like snapdragons and Canterbury bells, if cut when half in flower, will finish opening in water and last a week or more.

4. However, for more interesting compositions you will pick flowers in various stages of development including buds, flowers partly open, and a few in full bloom. Leaves can be an important part of an arrangement. Pick some along with the flowers to which they belong.

5. Carry a pail of water into the garden and place each stem in water as cut. Let flowers stand in deep water for several hours or better still overnight to condition them properly.

6. All equipment should be spotlessly clean to keep down bacterial count of the water. Any decayed material or foul water will clog the tiny water tubes in the stem and decrease the water intake. Strip everything below the water line in all cut flower arrangements, and remove any faded blossoms.

7. It is necessary to sear the stems of flowers such as the annual poppy, Canterbury bell, the euphorbias, heliotrope and hollyhock. This may be done with a flame or boiling water. It should be done as soon as cut, before conditioning the flowers in water. Whenever the stem is shortened it should again be seared or sealed shut.

8. Flowers need good air circulation so arrange them loosely enough for air to reach them.

9. Many trade-named chemicals are sold for keeping cut flowers. In most cases their purpose is to check bacterial growth and retard the decay of stems and foliage. Always use as directed on the package.

Quality flowers, properly conditioned, should last well. Cut stems as necessary, keeping the stem ends well covered with clean fresh water. There should be good fresh air, no droughts or currents of hot air, and no direct sunlight. A cool, humid atmosphere is a big asset. Place the arrangement in a cool place for the night. To change water and not dislodge the arrangement siphon the stale water out with a bulb syringe and replace with fresh water.

SOME DRY WELL

When you no longer have fresh flowers, dried bouquets, well designed for a specific space, can add beauty and interest to any room. Do not keep the arrangement around too long, however, no matter how lovely. After a few weeks tuck it away for a time or take it apart and save the materials for another year.

Not all flowers dry well but those that do should be gathered at just the right time, usually just as they mature, at their height of perfection. If too mature they will shatter. Experiment. Pick when absolutely dry. For variety and contrast use buds as well as almost-open flowers. You will find darker shades tend to come out darker while a pale, nondescript color is often improved. Some flowers dry better than others. Dry about twice as much material as you want, to allow for breakage.

A dried arrangement, made by Colonial Williamsburg's flower arranger Edna Pennell, contains blue and white larkspur, blue salvia, baby's breath, strawflowers, honesty and pearly everlasting.

In general allow one week for material to dry, then store in closed boxes in a closet away from humidity. After drying, large clustered flowers may be separated into individual florets or small clusters and used in miniature or small bouquets.

Our grandmothers used strawflowers and everlastings, drying them as they did their herbs, but we know today many other annuals can be preserved in their natural color and form by drying them in sand or borax and white cornmeal, silica-gel, or other material. Silica-gel (Flower-Dri) is a chemical compound of coarse and fine granules. The coarse grains are colored blue but lose this hue when the compound has absorbed its capacity of moisture. Package directions instruct the user to embed the flower in the material, seal the container with tape, and leave it alone for a week. After several usings the chemical will have absorbed its capacity of moisture and must be dried out in the oven before it is ready for reuse.

This is a fascinating and rewarding hobby. Use the method best suited to the flowers you grow and wish to dry.

Place Flower Heads Up. Place stems in a container, flower heads erect. Leave until dry. This method is often used successfully for annuals such as the ornamental grasses which are also hung upside down to dry.

Hang Upside Down. This method is used for many annuals and is one of the easiest ways to dry plant material. Tie the stems together with a string and hang heads down in a dry place as our grandmothers did with herbs. In general, strip the foliage. Any large flower or one that might shatter easily should be hung one to a string. To curve stems, soak stems one-half hour in warm water. Dry tied to a hanger.

Some annuals well suited to this method of drying include:

Ageratum houstonianum (place
  stems in water for 24 hrs.)
Althaea rosea—Hollyhock
Ammobium alatum—
  Winged Everlasting
Catananche caerulea—Cupid's Dart
Celosia (erect method 3 days, then
  hang upside down)
Centaurea cyanus—Bachelor's Button
Centaurea imperialis—Sweet Sultan
Delphinium ajacis—Annual Larkspur
  (cut in bud, let foliage remain)
Gilia capitata
Gomphrena globosa—Globe amaranth
Gypsophila elegans—Annual
  Baby's Breath

Helichrysum bracteatum—
  Strawflower
Helipterum manglesi—Swan
  River Everlasting
Ipomoea purpurea—Morning-Glory
  Seed Pods
Limonium sinuatum—Sea
  Lavender, Statice
Polygonum orientale—Prince's
  Feather
Scabiosa atropurpurea—
  Pincushion Flower
Tagetes—Marigold, Double
Xeranthemum annum—Immortelle

Sand or Borax and White Cornmeal. This method maintains the shape and color of annual flowers like the dahlia, marigold, pansy, zinnia, blue lace flower, and Mexican sunflower. Fill a pan or box with 1 part powdered borax and 6 parts white cornmeal to a depth of three or four inches. Place flowers, heads down, on this. Cover by gently pouring mix over flower heads and stems. Store in a dark, dry place. Remove mix by carefully brushing each bloom with a soft brush, then store in covered boxes.

Do not leave flowers too long, as petals may discolor. Remove one flower after a couple of days and check. Keep doing this until you feel they are properly dried. Keep a record of the time required for another year. The lighter textured types require only two or three days, the tougher textured flowers take longer; in the borax-cornmeal mix (box open) allow 4 to 5 days in a warm spot. The top of a furnace is excellent. In silica-gel, box tightly covered, drying takes a week; hanging also requires at least a week. You may leave flowers hanging until ready for use.

One part beach sand to 6 parts cornmeal makes a good mix for drying leaves. Ocean beach sand is salty so must be washed and takes a long time to dry. Leaves done this way preserve their natural form and are less flat than those pressed.

Silica-gel (Flower-Dri). A friend who has been making lovely dried arrangements for several years likes silica-gel for dark-petaled flowers since it is difficult to completely brush off all the white cornmeal from dark petals. A gentle shaking will completely remove all the silica-gel. Dark-petaled pansies, and snapdragons are much better done in silica-gel. For light-petaled flowers borax and cornmeal is less expensive. The use of a shallow tin box containing the silica-gel makes it necessary to cut the stems and replace them with wires. Also one must be more careful about following the step-by-step directions. For reuse, dry silica-gel in an open pan in a 250° F. oven for one-half hour since it does pick up moisture from the air. When cool it is ready to use again. It is not necessary to heat the borax and cornmeal which do not take up moisture from the air and can be used over and over again.

Use sand or borax with white cornmeal, or use silica-gel, for the following:

Antirrhinum hybrids—
    Snapdragon, Spikes
Calendula officinalis—Pot Marigold

Callirhoe pedata—Poppy Mallow
Campanula medium—Canterbury
    Bells

Centaurea cyanus—Bachelor's Button
Chrysanthemum carinatum—
    Painted Daisy
Chrysanthemum coronarium—
    Crown Daisy
Chrysanthemum segetum—
    Corn Marigold
Coleus foliage
Cosmos
Dahlia mercki—Bedding or
    Dwarf Dahlia
Dianthus caryophyllus—
    Annual Carnation
Dianthus chinensis—Annual Pink
Digitalis purpurea—Foxglove
Dimorphotheca aurantiaca—
    African Daisy
Euphorbia marginata—
    Snow-on-the Mountain
    (foliage and flowers)
Helianthus annuus—Sunflower

Iberis umbellata—Annual Candytuft
Impatiens balsamina—Garden Balsam
Lupinus hybrids—Lupine
Mathiola incana annua—
    Ten-Weeks Stock
Oenothera drummondi—
    Evening Primrose
Salvia farinacea—Blue Salvia, Spikes
Salvia patens—Blue Sage, Spikes
Salvia splendens—Scarlet
    Sage, Spikes
Tagetes—Marigold, Single
Tithonia rotundifolia—
    Mexican Sunflower
Trachymene caerulea—Blue
    Lace Flower
Viola cornuta—Viola
Viola tricolor hortensis—Pansy
Xanthisma texanum—Star of Texas
Zinnia, type with curled petals

Leaves. There are several leaves of annuals that offer substance and solidity, so often lacking in poorly designed dried arrangements. Some of the bold dramatic kinds are highly effective in designs for contemporary settings.

Many of them can simply be stood erect in a jar or hung upside down to dry. Some, as geranium leaves, you may want to press. To dry and press leaves pick them when green or at the height of their autumn color, or select them in their various stages of color. To press place on several thicknesses of newspaper, which is absorbent. Weigh down with bricks or heavy books. Choose a warm, dry place. Place each leaf by itself so it will not touch another and stick together. Once a week turn each leaf and when thoroughly dry, in about three weeks, store carefully until needed. For *drying leaves,* consider some of the following annuals:

Amaranthus—Amaranth
Argemone grandiflora—Prickly Poppy
Cobaea scandens—Cup-and-Saucer
    Vine
Coleus
Emilia sagittata—Tassel Flower
Euphorbia heterophylla—
    Annual Poinsettia
Euphorbia marginata—
    Snow-on-the-Mountain

Grasses, Ornamental
Helianthus annuus—Sunflower
Kochia scoparia—Summer Cypress
Perilla crispa—Beeksteak Plant
Ricinus communis—Castor
    Bean Plant
Senecio cineraria—Dusty Miller
Silybum marianum—Lady's Thistle

Seed Pods or Seed Heads. Many of the seed pods are interesting and will dry naturally. Either stand them upright in a container, hang them heads down or store in a covered box. If you want seed pods, try letting some of the annuals listed below go to seed. The seed pods will keep better and retain better color if they are dipped in a clear shellac or sprayed with clear plastic after they are thoroughly dried. "Plant Shine" has the same effect and is easy to use. It does not give an artificial look, just highlights the foliage or seed pods.

Althaea rosea—Hollyhock,
   Seed Heads
Cleome spinosa—Spider Flower
Cobaea scandens—Cup-and-Saucer
   Vine
Coreopsis tinctoria—Calliopsis
Datura metel—Angel's Trumpet
Dianthus
Dolichos lablab—Hyacinth Bean
Echinocystis lobata—Wild Cucumber
   (pick when dry)
Gourds (let mature on vine)
Grasses, Ornamental
Gypsophila elegans—Annual
   Baby's Breath

Lunaria annua—Honesty
   (let dry on plant)
Lupinus hybrids—Lupine
Oenothera drummondi—
   Evening Primrose
Papaver alpinum—Alpine Poppy
   (bend stems into curves)
Papaver nudicaule—Iceland Poppy
Papaver rhoeas—Shirley Poppy
Physalis alkekengi—Chinese Lantern
Ricinus communis—Castor Bean
   Plant (seeds poisonous)
Rudbeckia bicolor—
   Annual Coneflower

11

Annuals as House Plants

Many of the annuals grown outdoors in the summer are equally good indoors, but they must be renewed annually for satisfactory results. Usually the space available for growing plants indoors will restrict their size and height, so it is advisable to look into the dwarf types. It is also important to buy seeds of the winter-flowering varieties or those seeds best suited for pot culture.

If you have plenty of sunny windows why not try a few? You can be successful, without benefit of a greenhouse, if you can fill the following requirements:

1. Annuals need direct sunlight to do well, particularly during the short winter days. If you do not have a fluorescent-light arrangement, a sun-heated pit or a cold greenhouse, you must have a sunny glassed-in porch or windows with a southern exposure.

2. Most annuals that do well as house plants thrive best at a day temperature of 65° F., 55° F. at night.

3. They do not like dry air. Pans of water placed on or behind radiators will help.

4. It is no trouble to keep plants properly fed and watered but they also need weekly baths. Place them in a laundry tub or sink and spray the foliage with a fine mist of water.

5. At the same time look for aphids and mealy bugs on the underside of the leaves. If detected soon after their appearance, they are easily controlled. Use a house plant aerosol spray containing malathion.

From Seed. Sow seeds of impatiens, lantana, browallia, and forget-me-not (*Myosotis scorpioides*) in the spring or early summer and let the seedlings grow into healthy, sturdy plants in the garden during the summer. Do not let these plants bloom outdoors. Pinch out the flower buds as they form until the plants are brought into the house in the fall for winter flowering. As the young seedlings begin to grow, pinch out the terminal shoot or tip, to promote bushiness.

The seeds of some flowers like the nasturtium, winter-blooming varieties of sweet alyssum and the French marigold are best sown in August and September for winter flowers. Through December, January and February sow seeds of the black-eyed Susan, morning-glory, cup-and-saucer vine, and similar flowers that do well as house plants.

Florists grow such annuals as candytuft, calendulas, snapdragons, stock, etc. which you may care to try if you can supply sufficient light and the coolness required. They are, however, much harder to grow indoors.

It my be advisable because of the time saved, to buy young plants of begonias, coleus and geraniums rather than grow them from seed. It is difficult to get some of the annuals to bloom freely during the short, midwinter days. Artificial lighting is a big help, of course. A cold frame will prove helpful in getting seedlings started. You naturally will not grow nearly as many seeds for house plants as for the summer garden. Remember, pinching back is very important with house plants to get dwarf, stocky specimens.

From Cuttings. Make cuttings of geraniums, heliotrope, impatiens and lantana early in the summer for indoor winter flowers. This is one of the most satisfactory methods of propagation. In September take cuttings of coleus, hyacinth bean, fuchsia and nasturtium. Make the cuttings from the new growth which is sufficiently firm so that it will snap when bent but hang by a bit of tissue. Make the cut just below a joint and straight across the stem with a sharp knife, just long enough to carry three sets of leaves, about 3 to 5 inches. Remove the lower leaves before inserting the cutting in a rooting medium. Dip base of cutting in Rootone or a similar root-inducing hormone powder and insert almost up to the first set of leaves in a moist rooting medium, well aerated and drained. A mixture of equal parts of coarse sand and vermiculite works very well. Firm the medium down around the cutting with the fingers.

A single cutting may be inserted into a handful of sphagnum moss which has been soaked and then squeezed, so it is moist but not dripping. Place in the center of an 8-inch square of polyethylene- or vinyl-type plastic. Gather plastic up around the ball of moss. Tie snugly but not tightly with the leafy tip of the cutting protruding from the plastic package. Place anywhere that light and temperature are suitable (70°-75° F.) and steady. Roots will form without additional water. When properly rooted, take cutting out and plant it.

For several cuttings use a 6- or 8-inch bulb pan (a shallow flower pot). Plug the hole with a cork. Fill half full with sand. Then take a 2- or 3-inch porous clay pot, plug the drain hole with a cork and place in the center of the bulb pan. Fill the bulb pan to ½-inch of the top with rooting medium. Keep the small pot filled with water. Seepage through the clay pot will supply sufficient moisture for the rooting medium. Keep cuttings in partial shade and protected from bright light. When the roots are ½ to 1 inch long, cuttings can be transplanted to pots.

Pot Up Plants from Garden. In the fall you can pot up China asters, calendulas, dwarf marigolds, lobelias, sweet alyssum, nicotiana, nierembergia and petunias which will flower indoors for some time. You will have better success with smaller plants than with the very large ones. Don't expect them to last long, just enjoy their blooms while they do. Try some seedlings of the wax begonia from the flower border. They breed nearly true and you may be successful in continuing some nice young plants.

12

Container Gardens
with Annuals

Colorful annuals growing in pots, tubs, boxes, hanging baskets, planters and other containers will decorate and brighten the patio, terrace or porch and add great warmth and cheer to the surroundings. Even in a backyard of concrete and gravel, a sense of nature can be introduced and an outdoor living area developed.

Container-grown plants require more care than plants growing in the open ground. Their roots are confined to a smaller soil area, from which they must draw nutrients, and the soil will naturally dry out faster, so it is necessary to cultivate and water more frequently and regularly. And because these plants in containers are more conspicuous, always on display, they will need meticulous housekeeping. Faded flowers or discolored foliage must be removed daily and the plants must be kept at their best.

FOR PATIO OR TERRACE

No patio is complete without the glamour of a few dramatic, colorful pot plants placed in strategic places for pictorial effects, but avoid over-decorating. The terrace or patio is an outdoor living room and should be kept simple and livable, an attractive place to relax with family and friends. A fence on one side may give just the necessary privacy and also supply a background of vines and annuals.

262

Geraniums, petunias and single French marigold Dainty Marietta are used in these different-type containers at different levels, and so tie together the four planters. The nail kegs, painted the same color as the building, would have looked better cut in half.

The popular trend toward more outdoor living has encouraged home owners to maintain mobile gardens, with annuals freely used to produce special effects for special occasions. Portable plant boxes and flower tubs are equipped with casters to facilitate moving.

Clay pots in decorative baskets, wooden or concrete tubs, urns, and old kettles are some of the many containers that may be used. They should be in scale with the surroundings and large enough to really put on a show. Such containers will usually require larger and taller plants than the average-sized window box. It is possible to buy many types of pot-grown annuals from your florist if you do not care to grow them from seed. One seed catalog in 1965 had a page showing several attractive annuals being grown in wooden tubs. Included in the group were:

Ageratum, Blue Blazer—puffs of deep blue hide compact, 5 inch mounds of foliage; an F_1 hybrid.

Celosia, Flame of Fire Improved—sturdy 2 ft. plants with rich, deep-red pyramids of long-lasting decoration.

Coleus, Volcano—a bright red, at its best in the shade, and easily grown.

Marigold, Sunspot—first F_1 hybrid with odorless foliage; a rich, deep orange with 3½-inch flower spheres of loosely packed petals and 3½ ft. plants.

Petunia, Melody—a Garden Giant All-Double Petunia with 4-inch fringed flowers, candy-pink in color.

Petunia, Starfire—12-inch plants with 2½-inch flowers striped quite evenly, with sharply defined alternating areas of brilliant scarlet and bright white.

Zinnia, Daisy Mae—2-inch, daisy-like single flowers of intense yellow; 15-inch plants.

Observe the procedures given later in this chapter under *Window Boxes* and you will have no difficulties.

RAISED, PLANTER OR TERRACE-TYPE BEDS

Planter or terrace-type beds, raised slightly above ground or higher, are often a planned part of the modern landscape. Included in the foundation of the house or edging the terrace, and filled with plants, they relieve the monotony of paving. These beds make an ideal starting area and can be kept colorful all season. Annuals grown from seed or young plants purchased from the florist are inexpensive and little trouble to maintain. Raised planters lift annuals so they are nearer eye level and help simplify plant care. They provide more root room than other types of container gardening.

In the spring, enjoy flowering bulbs such as dwarf tulips, hyacinths or daffodils edged with pansies, followed by dwarf petunias and other annuals throughout the summer, if sunny enough. Among the most satisfactory shade-tolerant annuals are impatiens, browallia, *Vinca rosea,* and torenia. Needing only a few hours of sun to do quite well are such favorites as asters, alyssum, coleus, pansies, lobelia, and snapdragons. In the fall, if you wish, pull out the annuals and use chrysanthemums. The neatness and convenience of raised flower beds are real assets. For a recommended list see annuals *In Beds and Borders.*

FOR CITY GARDENS

Container gardening is particularly suited to city gardens. Young plants and tender ones bought from the local florist—for example, geraniums, petunias and lantanas—will provide summer-long color in a sunny location. Begonias, fuchsias, impatiens and coleus will tolerate considerable shade. Fancy-leaved caladiums may be counted on for brilliant color from May to October. Annual vines have their place, like that truest of blues, the Heavenly Blue morning-glory, but for exquisite evening pleasure grow some moon vines, even in pots, and at dusk sit and watch the huge, saucer-shaped, creamy-white discs unfurl and perfume the evening air.

Ingenious ways of achieving a desired effect, good planning, and carefully chosen plants for the space available can make the smallest or the shadiest of city gardens a source of interest, satisfaction and beauty.

ROOF GARDENS

A roof garden may be on top of a house, a garage or a porch. It should offer privacy and a good view, rest and relaxation, but there are other considerations. Will the roof take the additional weight? Most northern roofs built to take snow can take the weight of containers. The plant area can be stationary, or portable. Often an interesting corner can be planned using portable plant boxes. Portable boxes should be attractive, not too large to handle easily, and of sizes that may be grouped together or changed into different groupings, as desired. Annuals do not require over 8 inches for their roots, and shallow boxes will reduce the weight, which is desirable.

Because of their free exposures, the rate of evaporation will be high, so there should be convenient water outlets with hose connections and gravel areas with drainage for the water. Leaves, twigs, etc. must be picked up so they will not clog the drains.

An ornamental fence or some protection on the side exposed to the wind is almost a must, as well as some type of arrangement for sun protection, but one that will not obstruct the view or air. Ingenuity and originality are always assets but especially so in planning a roof garden.

Variegated vinca is one of the favorite hanging plants for window boxes, but other annuals should also be used for height and color.

WINDOW BOXES

Many city gardeners have only this one means of gardening. With careful planning, interesting combinations can be achieved. A white house offers little difficulty in planning a color scheme but it can act as a reflector, increasing the effects of both sun and shade. Yellow and orange marigolds with blue ageratum and lobelia against a white house with white sweet alyssum trailing over the edge of the box are effective as well as easy.

More care in using color is needed for a reddish brick wall. White and light colors show off to best advantage. Periwinkle (*Vinca rosea* and *V. rosea alba*) with its phlox-like flowers in pink and white and lush, dark green, glossy foliage is effective; petunias, verbenas and sweet alyssum may all be had in suitable light colors.

A wide range of annuals is available for every exposure and color need and different schemes can be used each year. Geraniums, petunias and wandering Jew are the ones most often combined, perhaps, but there are many other good combinations. Trailing forms are popular for the foreground, gracefully spilling over the sides to break the horizontal lines of the box. Creeping zinnia (*Sanvitalia procumbens*) is lovely, its somewhat trailing branches covered with attractive buff-gold, double zinnia-like flowers. Black-eyed Susan (*Thunbergia alata*) is a dainty vine, its attractive foliage forming dense mats set with dark-centered yellow, orange, buff or white flowers.

Of all the plants used for window box and container gardening, the petunia is least expendable. Easily grown from seed or purchased young plants, it is practically trouble-free, floriferous and quickly makes a colorful showing. Its flowering period is long, from May until frost, and it has a wide color range from pure white, pink, rose and red, through purples, lavender and blues, and even a pale yellow. The balcony type is much used for window boxes.

Ageratum, lobelia, sweet alyssum and dwarf French marigolds are excellent for edging boxes or planters. Some of the taller plants like cosmos, nicotiana and African marigolds would be out of scale in a small window box but are well suited to large planters or boxes. Verbenas, Cape marigold (*Dimorphotheca*), nierembergia, portulaca and California poppies like heat and can take the hot summers, but cool climate annuals like nemesias, pansies and stocks are best grown in containers only for spring and early summer use.

Consider Placement of Box. A box high up on a house should have trailing vines and large bright flowers, like geraniums, that can be seen from a distance. A box at street level may not need trailing plants and perhaps should have a tough small-flowered plant like lantana, which is less likely to be damaged. A basement box should be planted to look well from above, as impatiens does.

The Box. A window box for the plants must not be so large that it will be difficult to handle or too heavy to secure properly. Boxes resting on wide window ledges, the firm sides of front steps, or adequate porch railings can safely be larger than others. Lengths, of course, will be determined largely by the space to be decorated. A box 8 to 9 inches deep is ample for annuals, which do not have deep roots; a width of 8 to 12 inches across the top is about right.

On the whole, window boxes made of wood are the most satisfactory, provided a suitable wood is selected and the box is constructed with care. Cypress and redwood are resistant to decay and will last for years. Cedar is also excellent, while a good grade of white pine will give satisfactory results. The lumber used should be at least 1 inch thick to avoid warping and to provide insulation and stability. Metal boxes conduct heat and in the sun the soil gets too hot.

All boxes must be supplied with drainage holes, one-half inch holes every six inches. Place broken pieces of flower pot or a screening over the drainage holes to prevent clogging. If you make your own box use brass screws, which do not rust or pull out as nails do. Reinforce the corners with angle irons.

Treat the inside of the box with a preservative to keep the wood from rotting. Do not use creosote since it is poisonous to plants. After the preservative has been applied and dried, use two good coats of paint or stain on both inside and outside, to preserve the wood and for good appearance.

Unless you know how, to be safe, have a carpenter secure your boxes for you. Use bolts or lag screws and treat them to prevent rusting. Leave some space (an inch or more) between the box and the house for air circulation. If the boxes are to rest on a solid surface raise them on cleats, bricks or blocks of wood, so the drainage holes will not become clogged, and for circulation of air. Also any excess water will then easily evaporate.

Soil. Fill the box with a good soil mixture. A good all-purpose mixture consists of two parts good garden loam, one part sand and one part peat moss or similar humus material with a complete fertilizer (used in quantities according to directions on the label). This provides a loose, porous soil mixture, that drains easily, yet holds moisture, so it will not dry out too rapidly. This same soil can be used year after year if reconditioned each spring. Do this one week before planting. Remove the top inch of soil and replace it with peat moss, stirring through the soil thoroughly, down to the bottom. Break up any hard lumps, then add fertilizer according to the directions on the package.

A liquid fertilizer or a dry one mixed with water is safest. Remember too much fertilizer may injure plants. Follow directions on label. Generally ½ gallon or 2 quarts of made-up solution of fertilizer and water is sufficient for one application for a 30-inch box.

A 1-inch layer of drainage material such as broken pieces of flower pots, broken bricks, pebbles or cinders on the bottom of the box, will prove helpful. A curved piece of broken flower pot arched over each drainage hole will permit passage of water and air and keep the loam from washing through the holes. A thoroughly moistened sheet of sphagnum moss on the bottom of the box will also prevent the soil from sifting into the drainage holes.

When to Plant. For a spring box, buy started bulbs from the florist or transplant them from a garden bed, in early April, when they are 2 or 3 inches high. Edge short-stemmed daffodils and early tulips with pansies as soon as they appear; add English daisies and forget-me-nots in early May. *Vinca rosea* and ivy can trail over the box, with the spring plants, and then be left to continue to spill over the box when the spring bulbs are replaced with annuals.

Seedlings of summer plants should be put in the last week in May. With adequate care the summer plants should last from May until frost. Grow some from seed or buy young seedlings from a florist or garden center.

Annuals that may be grown from seed include alyssum, marigolds, nasturtium and dwarf zinnias. These take nine to ten weeks to flower from seed and may be sown at the end of April.

In the fall, if summer plants become straggly, fill the gaps with pots of short chrysanthemums. Coleus, small begonias, salvia and dwarf asters may also be used.

Placing of Plants. Most annuals growing in containers have been transplanted from flats, bands or peat pots. Exceptions may be sweet alyssum, linaria, nasturtium and Virginia stock, generally sown where they are to grow in the open ground or in containers. They are often sown as ground covers at the base of container-grown trees, shrubs or bulbs.

Set plants out in groups using the taller ones toward the rear, center, or on both sides, medium heights in an intermediate position, and the trailing or low kinds around the edges. Depending upon the type of plant, and the effect you want, place them 5 to 8 inches apart, sweet alyssum 5 inches, petunias 8 inches. Plan two or three rows of plants, staggering the rows. Allow room for growth. A 30 by 8-inch box will take 3 tall, 2 medium and 3 trailing plants, depending upon the size of plants. For mass effects plant more closely than you would in the ground. Some, like butterfly flower, need plenty of room in order to do their best.

In transplanting, disturb the soil around the roots as little as possible.

Care or Maintenance. Water window boxes daily if the soil feels dry. Fertilize every two weeks with an application of complete fertilizer in readily available liquid form starting a month after planting and continue until flowers start to bloom. Discontinue when plants are in full flower. Pull out any grass or weeds that may come up. Scratch around plants to break up the hard crust that forms on the top of the soil. If it seems to crust over unduly, cover with a light layer of moist peat moss.

Pinch back young plants to encourage bushiness and side buds. Pansies, petunias, phlox, coleus and impatiens will all produce more compact, bushy plants if pinched back. For continuous bloom pick off dead or fading flowers.

Syringe foliage with a fine spray once a week to remove dust and soot. If you see insects, wash with soapy water (not a detergent) and rinse with clear water 3 or 4 hours later. Or use an all-purpose spray carefully following directions on label.

SELECT PLANTS ACCORDING TO EXPOSURE

Sun-Loving Plants. These plants are generally more showy and offer a large selection. If they do not receive sun all day long they will still do well if they get sun all afternoon.

Ageratum—4-8 inches
Alyssum—3-4 inches
*Geraniums—8-12 inches
Ivy Geraniums—Trailer
Heliotrope—10 inches
*Lantana—8-15 inches
*Lobelia—4-6 inches
Marigold—4-8 inches

Nasturtium—8-18 inches
*Petunia—12-24 inches
Phlox, Annual—6-8 inches
Portulaca
*Trailers—English Ivy, *Vinca major*
Verbena—8-10 inches
Zinnia—8-12 inches

*plants most easily grown

For Morning Sun. If the window box gets the morning sun or several hours of sun each day you can grow many attractive flowers which do well in moderate light.

Ageratum—4-8 inches
Alyssum—3-4 inches
Begonias, Bedding—8-15 inches
Ferns
Browallia—9-18 inches
Foliage Plants—•Coleus, Caladium
•Fuchsia—9-18 inches
•Geranium—8-12 inches
Heliotrope—10 inches
House Plants—Many
Impatiens—8-15 inches

Lantana—8-15 inches
Lobelia—4-6 inches
Marigold—4-8 inches
Morning-Glory—Climber
Nicotiana—9-15 inches
Nierembergia—2-6 inches
Thunbergia—Trailer
Torenia—9-12 inches
•Trailers—English Ivy and
   Vinca Major

   •plants most easily grown

For Shade. Locations receiving little or no sun are by no means hopeless. A foliage box with plants of different types and sizes of leaves can be handsome, lacy ferns, large-leaved philodendrons and small-leaved vinca for example. Coleus and the caladium, with their variegated foliage, will add color. Bedding begonias and impatiens will flower in full shade, but in full shade impatiens bears its flowers on top and grows tall so should be used in a basement planter to be seen from above. Fuchsias bloom off and on but tend to be leggy. Foliage plants or begonias planted in front of fuchsias and impatiens will hide the long stems. For large bright colors in a foliage box sink geraniums in their pots where needed and replace them when they stop flowering. If you have a sunny spot somewhere else, rotate the plants to revive those that show a lack of sun.

In shaded areas, plants are likely to grow tall and thin. Use bushy foliage plants and begonias to give body and substance to the planting. In shade use a little more fertilizer and be careful not to overwater.

•Bedding Begonias—8-12 inches
Browallia—9-18 inches
Caladium
•Coleus
•Ferns
Fuchsia—9-18 inches
•House Plants—Philodendron, etc.

Impatiens—8-15 inches
Thunbergia—Trailer
Torenia—9-12 inches
•Trailers—Vinca, Ivy,
   Wandering Jew
Tuberous Begonia—10-12 inches

   •plants most easily grown

BEACON HILL WINDOW BOX PROJECT

A contest for city dwellers which combines the fun of gardening with the pleasure of making Beacon Hill more beautiful is sponsored jointly by the Beacon Hill Garden Club and the Beacon Hill Civic Association of Boston, Mass. In 1958 when the contest first started 350 boxes representing 150 entries were judged. Five years later the number of boxes and entries had more than doubled and there were many boxes in evidence in this famed section of Boston, not entered in the contest, but undoubtedly inspired by it.

Boxes are not only placed on window ledges but on porches, balconies, front steps, rooftops, fire escapes and walls, wherever they can add a decorative note.

There were many problems at first. The most appropriate box proved to be one that measures 30 inches long, 8 inches wide at the top, 7 inches wide at the base and 7 inches deep. During the first few years the wooden boxes were made and distributed to participants by volunteer groups like scouts and campfire girls. Today the boxes are made by the Morgan Memorial and sell for $2.25 each. In the beginning, green, white and black paint were recommended but today black is the standard color because it is more in keeping with the nineteenth century architecture of the handsome brick houses.

The first year, free soil was placed in a central spot and boy scouts delivered it in pails, three pails to a box to those who needed it. Now the soil is placed in several convenient places on the Hill and each participant gets his or her own. Large shopping bags have proven to be more practical than pails for this purpose.

Judging takes place from July 15 to August 5, when boxes are generally at their best. Prizes are awarded for the best individual box, the best two or more boxes on a single building and for the best street, a group effort by neighbors. There are two awards in the children's division. Business places on the Hill are also encouraged to decorate with boxes filled with flowers; containers filled with geraniums, petunias, chrysanthemums and other flowering plants attract clients and admiration.

A group of volunteers will help set up boxes for those unable to do so. When owners go on vacation they arrange for neighbors or friends to do the watering. Instructions for the care of the boxes are given on one of the application sheets. Free mimeographed literature suggesting a wide variety of plants is distributed annually to participants.

The Chairman of the project reports, "Not only has this contest done much to improve the appearance of Beacon Hill, but people with window boxes are automatically more interested in keeping up the appearance of their property. They wash windows, sweep up sidewalks, and paint doors and entranceways. More than that, it has taught us to be better neighbors, and if ever gardening has a common denominator, certainly it is exemplified in this window-box project on Beacon Hill in the heart of old Boston."

HANGING POTS AND BASKETS

Hanging planters are often used at an entrance or for porch decoration, generally to be enjoyed at standing eye-level. Baskets can be hung from poles, lampposts, arbors, walls or from low eaves of the house, any place where a spot of color will be enjoyed. If hung above eye-level, they should be planted for the graceful beauty of plants trailing over their sides, with a large vivid splash of color in the center. Baskets may be purchased, already planted, from the florist or garden center or you may plan and plant your own.

Soils in hanging baskets should be water retentive as well as rich in nourishment. One of the best materials for wire baskets is sphagnum moss, which is first soaked in a weak fertilizer solution. It may take two or three days to saturate the moss if it is very dry, but it is important to wet every particle. After it has been soaked, mix it with two-thirds

Ivy geraniums are good hanging-basket plants, blooming well when fertilized regularly and watered often. Ivies cannot be treated as casually as the bedding types, if superior plants are wanted. Many poor shades of pink and magenta ivy geraniums are sold, so it pays to search until clean pinks or bright reds are located.

One of the most dramatic uses of annuals in America is the hanging of nasturtiums for a few weeks each year from the third-floor balconies above the interior court at the Isabella Stewart Gardner Museum, Boston. The court is covered with a glass roof, so the nasturtiums are protected from weather. Pink shadings which flush the white walls seem to be reflections of the brilliant nasturtiums so that on a sunny day, Fenway Court glows with color.

good rich garden loam. To each bushel add one cupful of bonemeal and one handful of dehydrated cow manure, which is easily available and clean.

Line the wire baskets with moss (copper is more expensive but will not rust). At the base of the wire frame insert a deep saucer, so that the saucer's base shows at the bottom through the wire, to catch excess water and prevent dripping. The moss will hold the soil in place and also provides a drainage layer. Fill the moss-lined basket with soil.

For immediate effects select large plants ready to bloom and edge with smaller growing kinds as wax begonias and some of the edging trailers like ivy or vinca. When planted, place basket in a bucket of water until the top surface is moist. Then hang up to dry. After two weeks and thereafter, once a week, dip the basket in a fertilizer solution. Daily watering will be necessary and in very hot, dry weather some baskets may require watering twice a day. Roots of plants like the fuchsia and tuberous begonia should never be allowed to dry out.

If plants are constantly exposed to the sun and wind it is helpful to place the potted plant in a basket and surround it with peat moss which can be easily kept moist.

Plants For Hanging Baskets:

Anagallis arvensis caerulea—
    Poor-Man's Weatherglass
Browallia speciosa
Campanula isophylla—Ligurian
    Bellflower
Cobaea scandens—Cup-and-Saucer
    Vine
Coleus—Trailing Queen
Coleus—Upright, for center
Convolvulus tricolor—Dwarf
    Morning-Glory
Cuphea platycentra—Mexican Cigar
    Plant
Dimorphotheca aurantiaca—African
    Daisy
Erect house plants, useful for center
    Begonia
    Cordyline
    Dracaena
    Ferns
    Fuchsia, Upright
    Pelargonium hortorum—
        Geranium, Zonal type
Felicia bergeriana—Kingfisher Daisy
Fuchsia—Trailers
Lantana

Lobelia erinus—Edging Lobelia
Lobularia maritima—Sweet Alyssum
Nierembergia rivularis—Cup Flower
Pelargonium pelatum—Geranium,
    Ivy-Leaved
Petunia—Balcony Types
Phlox drummondi—Annual Phlox
Portulaca grandiflora—Rose Moss
Schizanthus wisentonensis—Poor
    Man's Orchid
Tagetes patula—French Marigold,
    Dwarf
Thunbergia alata—Black-Eyed Susan
    Vine
Trailers to spill over the sides
    Cymbalaria muralis—Kenilworth
        Ivy
    Hedera helix—English Ivy
    Saxifraga sarmentosa—Strawberry
        Geranium or Begonia
    Tradescantia fluminensis—
        Wandering Jew, Inch Plant
    Tropaeolum hybrids—Nasturtium,
        Dwarf
    Vinca major—Periwinkle

RETAIL SOURCES FOR SEEDS

Burgess Seed and Plant Co., Galesburg, Michigan 49053

Burnett Brothers, 92 Chambers St., New York, New York 10007

W. Atlee Burpee Co., Philadelphia, Pennsylvania; Clinton, Iowa; Riverside, California

J. Howard French, 1215 West Baltimore Pike, Lima, Pennsylvania

Gill Brothers Seed Co., Montavilla Station, Portland, Oregon 97216

Joseph Harris Co., 3670 Buffalo Rd., Rochester, New York 14624

Charles C. Hart Seed Co., Wethersfield 9, Connecticut

H. G. Hastings Co., Box 4088, Atlanta, Georgia 30302

Herbst Brothers Seedsmen (Agents for T. Sakata and Co.) 678 Broadway, New York, New York 10012

D. Landreth Seed Co. (a division of Robert Buist Co.) 6 So. Front St., Philadelphia 5, Pennsylvania

George W. Park Seed Co., Greenwood, South Carolina

Pearce Seed Co., Morrestown, New Jersey 08057

Sutton and Sons, Reading, England

Thompson and Morgan, Ipswich, England

This is by no means a complete list but it includes firms with which we are familiar. Visit your local garden centers, florists and nurserymen to see what they have to offer. Thompson and Morgan list a good many of the rare varieties not available through the usual sources.

PHOTO CREDITS

The numbers listed refer to the pages on which the photographs appear.

All-American Selections: 20, 25, 39, 48, 82, 96, 103, 105, 126, 136, 137

American Association of Nurserymen: 238

Ball Co., George J.: 104, 229, 233

Bodger Seeds, Ltd.: 18, 19, 21-23, 26, 27, 30, 32, 35, 40, 41, 43, 44, 46-50, 52-55, 57, 59, 61, 63-70, 72, 74-77, 79, 80, 84, 86, 89, 92-97, 99, 101, 107, 110-113, 115, 116, 118-120, 125-128, 130, 132-135

Burpee Co., W. Atlee: 31, 34, 37, 51, 98, 106, 109, 111, 115, 119, 123, 124, 131

Ferry-Morse Seed Co.: 45, 62, 84, 87

Gardner Museum, Isabella Stewart: 274

Genereux, Paul E.: Plate III, George Taloumis, Salem, Mass., owner; Plate IV, Plate VI, 100, 222, 231, 235, 236, 241, 244, 249, 266, 273

Grensted, E. A.: 92, 98

Griffin, Arthur: Plate II
Groffman, Nelson: Plate I, Plate V, 263
Hampfler, G.: 224, Longwood Gardens
Kagey, Charles G.: 254, Colonial Williamsburg
Massachusetts Horticultural Society: 75, Bob Taylor photo; 266.
McFarland Co., J. Horace: 23, 24, 27, 29, 36, 86, 95, 114
Pan-American Seeds, Inc.: 104, 105
Park Seed Co., George W.: 36, 83
Sanford: Plate VII (cover illustration)
Taloumis, George: 213, 219, 243
Vondell: Plate VIII

INDEX

Page numbers in *italic* type signify principal references.

284

Philodendron, 271
Phlox, *107-108*, 184, 193, 196, 198, 200, 201, 202, 203, 205, 215, 225, 239, 270, Plate IV
blue, 212
Phosphate, 191, 202
Phosphoric acid, 156
Phosphorus, 186
Photoperiodism, 180
Physalis, *108*
Pimpernel, 22, 108
Pincushion flower, 108, *118-119*
Pinching back, 192-193, 260, 270
Pink, 41, *52-54*, 108, 196, 232, 234
Planning
the border, 218
the garden, 196
Plant breeders, 143
Plant Shine, 258
Planting, 155-157, illus. 156
in bulb beds, 157, 228
in fall, 157-158, 195, 228, 260
foundation, 228
optimum time for, 172
seedlings, 200
in spring, 158, 164, 166, 205
started plants, 174
in winter, 158, 260
Plantings, successive, 155
Platystemon, *108-109*
Poinsettia, *59-60*
Poisonous annuals, 149-150
Polyanthus, 109, *110-111*
Polyethylene tent, 182
Polygonum, *109*, 228
Polyploids, 146-147
Poor man's orchid, 109, *120*
Poor man's weatherglass, 22
Poppy, 13, 110, 142, 185, 189, 193, 196, 199, 200, 201, 202, 203, 204, 205, 214, 225, 228, 229, 253
Alpine, *99-100*
California, 34, *59*, 72, 228, 233, 267
corn, *100*
Iceland, *99-100*, 233
Mexican, 27, 91
Mexican tulip, *72*, 91
oriental, 228
prickly, 27, 110
Shirley, *11*, 100, 227, 228
wind, *89*, 134
Poppy mallow, *34*, 86, 110
Portulaca, 13, *110*, 201, 203, 226, 229, 232, 233, 267, illus., 233
Pot marigold, *33*, 85, 110
Pot plants, 12, *259-261*, Plate III
Potash, 156
Potassium, 186
Potato family, 150
Potting, 204, 205, 261

Pots, 167, 174, 182, 204, 206
hanging, 273-275
for started plants, 172
Power cultivator, 155
Pricking-out, 168, illus. 169
Prickly poppy, 27, 110
Primrose, 190
evening, 60
hybrid, 110-111
Primula, *110-111*
Prince's feather, 22, 109, 111, 228
Propagating, 173, 260
Propagating House Plants, 175
Purple everlasting, *135*
Purple groundsel, *121*
Purple mullein, *131*
Purple ragwort, 112, *121*
Purslane, 29, 33, 114, 120
Pyrethrum, 189, 247

Quacking grass, *65*
Quamoclit, *111-112*, 246
Quick-flowering annuals, 12, 13, 226

Rabbit's-tail grass, *66*
Radishes, 240
Ragwort, purple, 112, *121*
Rainbow corn, *66*, 112, 237
Rainbow plant, *21*
Rattle brome, *66*
Records, garden, 172, 196, 198
Red light rays, 177-178
Red Spider mite, 190, 191
Rehmannia, *112*
Reseda, *113*
Rhodanthe, *69-70*
Ricinus, 113-114, 150
Rocket larkspur, *51-52*
Rocket, sweet, *70*
Rock gardens, 13, 191, 202, 233-234
Rock jasmine, *23*, 114
Rock purslane, 33, 114
Rocky Mountain garland, *43*, 114
Roof garden, 265
Root-bound seedlings, 172
Rooting, 176, 177, 205
cuttings, 166, 183, 204, 260-261
medium, 175, 176, 182, 260
Roots, 12, 157, 164, 168, 171, 172, 174, 182, 186, 228
Rose moss, *110*, 114
Rose of heaven, *84-85*, 114
Roses, 82, 232, Plate V
Rotenone, 189, 247, 260
Round forms, for cutting, 250-251
Rows, sowing in, 160
Rudbeckia, *114, 115*, 189
Rust, 192, 199, 201, 203